The Portland Super Shopper

THE
PORTLAND
SUPER
SHOPPER

David and Carolyn Gabbe

Forward by
Terry Hofferber Moore & Connie Hofferber Jones

ELLIOTT & FAIRWEATHER, Inc.
Mercer Island, Washington

The listings and information in *The Portland Super Shopper* were current at the time of the final editing, but are subject to change at any time. No gratuities of any kind have been solicited or accepted from listed firms.

First Printing, September, 1991
Cover art and book design by Mike Jaynes
Typography and production by Lasergraphics

Elliott & Fairweather
Post Office Box 1524
Mercer Island, Washington 98040–1524 U.S.A.

Current titles from Elliott & Fairweather:
The Greater Seattle Super Shopper
The Portland Guidebook
The Vancouver Super Shopper
Rise & Shine Vancouver
Vancouver Out to Lunch
Discover Seattle With Kids

Printed in the United States of America
Distributed in Canada by Raincoast Books Ltd.

FORWARD

Welcome back to The Portland Super Shopper

A lot has changed for us since we brought you an early look at bargain hunting in the Portland metro area. We've gotten married, have families, moved, come back, and started new projects. But we've never lost our zest for saving money or our delight in sleuthing real bargains.

Things have also changed for *The Portland Super Shopper*. Another publishing company, Elliott and Fairweather, is carrying on the super shopper tradition and David and Carolyn Gabbe are authoring this guide to great bargain buying. With this edition of *The Portland Super Shopper*, we are truly happy to hand over the baton to a new team.

You've changed, too. For one thing, you probably use a computer now and *The Portland Super Shopper* will help you save on software and computer supplies. It also delves into the world of outlet malls and warehouse sales, two things that didn't exist in the Portland area when we completed our research.

So, remembering that nothing in life is so sure as change, and that change is what keeps us all interesting and vital, enjoy your new *Portland Super Shopper* and all the ways it can help *you* change your life!

Terry Hofferber Moore
Connie Hofferber Jones
August 1991

INTRODUCTION

While mention of the Portland area may conjure up visions of roses and river fronts for many, for true bargain hunters it's a dream of dollars saved! Where do you begin when every appliance you own goes on the blink at the same time? The *Portland Super Shopper* will lead you to the Kida Company and other price paradises. Suppose you're hosting a party during the Rose Festival; you'll want to be sure to head for the unique Hoody's Outlet Store or maybe Reaser's Thrift Shop. Have a hungry gang of Cub Scouts to feed? You'll be glad you read here about Grandma's Foods Factory Outlet or the colorful Moore's Mill. You can economize on all you need for everyday or special occasions by using this handy guide.

A few tips help:

- Use the *Portland Super Shopper* and your telephone to make comparisons and be sure your item is in stock.

- Have the courage to negotiate for a lower price or a cash discount.

- Don't judge a store by its appearance—often prices are kept low by cutting in housekeeping or services.

- Use catalogs and Sunday Supplements by mass merchandisers, such as those in *The Oregonian*, to search for good values.

- Watch for newspaper advertisements and ask clerks about periodic sales.

- Plan your shopping early in the year to take advantage of the fact that most retailers adhere to the following yearly timetable in scheduling sales and promotions:

   January: Coats, jewelry, lingerie, cosmetics, electronics, and luggage

   February: Furniture, kitchen appliances, and hosiery

   March: Washing machines and dryers, silver, china, and glassware

   April: Jewelry, lingerie, sleepwear, and air conditioners

   May: Home furnishings, housewares, and luggage

   June: Furniture, lingerie, and sleepwear

   July: Garden and patio supplies, and swimwear

   August: Garden furniture and fashion accessories

   September: Back-to-school items

   October: Coats

   November: Furniture and coats

   December: A wide variety of merchandise on sale before and after Christmas

Other great sale times include presidents' birthdays, Easter, Memorial Day, Mother's Day, Father's Day, Independence Day, Labor Day, and Thanksgiving. Also watch for end-of-season sales (usually January, April, June, and November), where you'll find super-low prices on inventory being cleared out to make room for next season's merchandise.

- There is no state law that says stores must take merchandise back unless goods sold as first-quality do not perform as advertised or a flaw is discovered after purchasing an item. Every business sets its own return policy, which should be clearly visible somewhere in the store or printed on the sales receipt. If you don't see a sign, ask.
- Check all warranties, guarantees, and delivery charges before making your purchase.

Definitions of Terms Used Throughout This Book

- Close-outs, overruns, and discontinued styles are first-quality merchandise that factories sell at big discounts to whomever offers the best deal. These are sometimes goods that were returned by retail stores because the products weren't shipped on time or didn't sell.
- Private-label merchandise is manufactured specially for a store. Specialty clothing chains use private-label merchandise to project a distinctive fashion image and offer their customers styles that are not available elsewhere. It's difficult to comparison shop when you're dealing with private-label goods. Private labeling allows retailers to cut out the middlemen, so prices may naturally be lower. Or, the products may be copies of more expensive items that sell for less because the manufacturer used a different material or altered the style slightly to cut costs.
- Samples are prototypes used by sales reps when showing a line to prospective retail buyers. They're usually one-of-a-kind items.
- Irregulars or Seconds are flawed merchandise that should be marked "as is," which means the item cannot be returned.

Drastically reduced prices often indicate something is wrong with the item. Check carefully for flaws. Sometimes the defects are barely noticeable or can be easily repaired.

And Remember

- As we go to press, we're aware that some businesses will have moved, closed, changed their hours, or changed their names by the time you read this book. Call before you head out on a cross-town shopping adventure.
- Prices quoted are to serve as guidelines and may fluctuate with economic and seasonal changes.
- If you shop in one of the stores we've listed and find it disappointing, please let us know. If, on the other hand, you think a certain store is bargain-hunter's

heaven, tell your friends. We want these stores to stay in business!

- If we've failed to list your favorite bargain spot and you are willing to share it with us, drop us a line. We're continually updating our files to make the next edition bigger and better.

Table of Contents

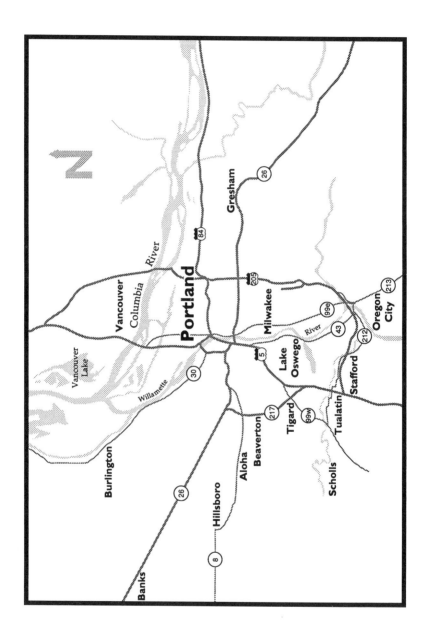

Clothing

Smart shoppers need not pay full retail again! Although the cost of apparel continues to rise at a fast clip, you can still buy more for less and get current-style, high-quality merchandise by shopping the many resources listed in this section.

Factory & Manufacturer's Outlets

For those of you whose pulses quicken at the sight of a bargain, there's nothing quite like bypassing the malls and making a beeline for the factory outlets. Buying direct from the factory outlet can mean a savings of up to 50% off regular retail—even more if you stumble in on a sale.

Factory outlets can be bare-bones operations located next to their manufacturing facilities, or off somewhere in separate warehouses, or even in new, glitzy outlet malls. While some outlets won't take credit cards, don't have individual dressing rooms, or don't offer cash refunds, others operate more like retail stores, offering top-notch service and liberal return policies.

Many a terrific bargain awaits you in factory outlets, but be a cautious shopper, especially where all sales are final and you're dealing with "as-is" factory seconds. Cautions aside, go forward and be adventurous—and leave no bargains untouched!

Barbara Johnson Clothing Outlet
Tualatin: 18005 S.W. Lower Boones Ferry Rd. ☎ 620–1777
Hours: Tues 12–8, Wed–Fri 10–6, Sat 10–5

Fashion-conscious women will find all the right things to dress well for less at this outlet at prices just 15% above wholesale. Designer labels abound! Racks of sweaters by *Susan Bristol, Garland, Lauren Hansen*, and *Skyr* are priced from $20–$50. While skirts, pants, and jacket ensembles by *Loubella* go for under $90, *Carol Anderson* dresses in colors from soft to sensationally hot run $24 to $65. Racks of golf clothes, warm-ups, gowns, robes, lingerie, and underwear—all major name brands—are to be had.

Checks, Credit cards

Champion Factory Outlet
Salem: 2385 Lancaster Dr. N.E. ☎ 370–9237
Hours: Mon–Sat 9:30–6, Sun 12–5
This outlet carries quality, discounted closeout and irregular sportswear direct from the Champion factory. You'll also find misprint sweatshirts and school returns at great savings. Warm-up sets, usually $23.99, were priced at $11.99; fleece tops normally $13.99 at $8.99; and polo shirts at $5.99 (regularly $8.99). These are but a few of the bargains found on rack after rack of sportswear in this outlet. In addition, pennants with professional team logos, which sell for $2.99 elsewhere are priced at $1.99.

Checks, Credit cards

Columbia Knit Factory Outlet Store
Milwaukie: 5200 S.E. Harney Dr. ☎ 777–7385
Hours: Mon–Fri 9–5
This Portland-based manufacturer of top-quality cotton knits offers rugby shirts for kids and adults and other apparel in a splashy rainbow of colors at true factory-store prices. Rugbies can be had for 50% or more off retail, while cotton sweaters, kids' and men's shirts, and women's dresses, cardigans, and skirts are 20%–70% off. A lot of Columbia's knits are made as private-label goods for catalog houses and retailers. Overruns and seconds usually end up at the outlet store where they are priced to move—and move they do! Watch for their advertised sales and call to inquire about unadvertised in-store specials.

Checks, Credit cards

Columbia Sportswear Factory Outlet
Lake Oswego: 3 Monroe Parkway *(Town Square at Mountain Park)* ☎ 636–6593
Portland: 8128 S.E. 13th ☎ 238–0118
Hours: Lake Oswego Mon–Fri 10–9, Sat 9–5, Sun 12–5; Portland Mon–Fri 9–6, Sat 9–5, Sun 12–5
This nationally known, Portland-based (family-owned, too!) sportswear manufacturer sells unique vests, parkas, outdoor clothing, ski wear, and hats. The outlets carry closeouts, overstocks, and irregulars, but you'll need a magnifying glass to spot flaws. Prices on their stock are generally 30%–40% below retail. Their popular bugaboo parka, which retails elsewhere for around $120, is priced at $77 for irregulars. Ultrex waterproof pants, which retail for around $90, are priced here at $58, also for irregulars. Columbia Sportswear also carries some things from other companies, such as *Wigwam* socks, *Hi-Tech* shoes, sweaters, duffel bags, and long underwear at prices below suggested retail.

Checks, Credit cards

Cracker Barrel Outlet Store

Lake Oswego: 3 Monroe Parkway *(Town Square at Mountain Park)*
☎ 697–2931
Hours: Mon–Fri 10–9, Sat 9–6, Sun 12–5

Cracker Barrel offers the famous Norm Thompson selection of gifts and clothing at exceptional savings every day. You'll find Norm Thompson's catalog close-outs, samples, end-of-season, and some seconds, all priced to move quickly. Fashions, footwear, sleepwear, and fine foods are priced at up to 50% off the original. Get on their mailing list for advance notice of periodic sales.

Checks, Credit cards

Dehen Factory Outlet

Portland: 404 N.W. 10th ☎ 796–0725
Hours: Mon–Fri 10–5, Sat 10–4

For about 50% off retail, you can pick up high-quality, 100% cotton rugby shirts, T-shirts, sweaters, and more for adults and kids. Although most merchandise are overruns, there are bargain boxes of seconds at even bigger savings. Because they do contract work for schools and ski resorts, you just might find sweatshirts with the Vail or Snowbird logo or school shirts from Ohio U and others. Dehen's has sales throughout the year, but the BIG one happens right after Thanksgiving, when rugbys are two for $30, sweaters around $12, and items in bargain boxes $5 each or two for $8. They take returns, but for in-store credit only.

Checks, Credit cards

Duffel Sportswear Outlet

Beaverton: 1870 N.W. 173rd Ave. ☎ 629–8777
Hours: Tues–Sat 10–4:30

Serious recreational athletes who want to look good as well as feel good shop Duffel's. Their fashion-conscious lines of active sportswear come in wild colors and patterns and stripes. Duffel's offers top-quality overruns, cancelled orders, and merchandise that are always a season behind (but no seconds) at prices around 24% to 40% off suggested retail. We found *Ralph Lauren* polo socks, usually $15 to $20, priced at $10, and New Zealand split shorts priced at $12 instead of the usual $19.50. Running tights were 40% off and Duffel supplex suits were around 25% off. Duffel's also carries sweatshirts, biking shorts, and sweaters—all in vivid colors and designs.

Checks, Credit cards

Fitwear Factory Outlet
Aloha: 3544-B S.W. 209th ☎ 649–5581
Hours: Mon–Fri 8–5

The whole family will find sportswear at savings of up to 50% on Spandex shorts and sweats. All stock are closeouts and overruns, and sells for $2 to $30. Their "special-cut" sweatshirts for bodybuilders (you'll find sizes to fit 300 pounders!) regularly retail for $20, but are priced at $10 here. You can find their products in pro-shops and gyms—but not at their attractive factory outlet prices.

Checks

Kandel Knitting Mills
Portland: 814 N. Hayden Meadows Dr. ☎ 288–6975
Hours: Annual Sale

Each year for only two days in December (usually in the first two weeks of the month) Kandel's opens its doors for a gigantic factory sale of overruns, seconds, and samples featuring cotton knits at true factory-outlet prices. One hundred percent preshrunk heavyweight cotton rugby shirts (seconds) for adults and kids go for $12 apiece, while lettermen's sweaters run $5 to $15. In addition, you'll find some incredible bargains in 100% cotton shaker-knit sweater bodies in wool, poly, or acrylic. Watch for their ads several weeks before the sale announcing dates, merchandise, and prices.

Checks, Credit cards

Kutters, Inc.
Portland: 104 S.W. 2nd ☎ 228–4858
Hours: Mon–Fri 10–6, Sat & Sun 10–5

Famous for their $12 dress shirts, Kutters also carries a wide selection of blouses, sweaters, jeans accessories, and coats for both males and females at great savings. Most of these items are overruns or close-outs. On the day we checked, there was a leather purse for $28 (recently seen selling for $74 at one of the large department stores). Other purses start at $8. Wondering where the name "Kutters" came from? No, it's not the owner's name. In the early days, they always cut the labels out of the garments they sold—hence the name Kutters. (They leave a lot of labels in nowadays.)

Checks, Credit cards

Pendleton Woolen Mills
Washougal: #2 17th St. ☎ (206)835–2131
Hours: Mon–Fri 8–4

Although a bit out of the way for some Portlanders, a visit to this factory outlet is a must for dyed-in-the-wool bargain shoppers. (Take I-205 into Washington; head east on Hwy 14 to Washougal.) This outlet sells Pendleton wool by the yard, overruns, and seconds that are carefully marked. You'll find prices of 40% to 50% off regular retail (and up to 75% off selected items) for men's and women's sweaters, men's wool shirts and robes, women's suits, coats, jackets, hats, and blankets—all carrying the quality Pendleton label. This half-hour drive is worth it!

Checks

Pykettes Factory Outlets

Clackamas: 11211 S.E. 82nd Ave. *(Ross Center)* ☎ 654–1439
Salem: 2245 Lancaster Dr. N.E. *(Village East)* ☎ 364–7751
Hours: Mon–Fri 10–8, Sat 10–6, Sun 12–5

Pykettes carries first-quality women's casual wear, as well as men's jackets, shirts, and jeans—all at discounted prices. They have a wide selection of large-size apparel for both men and women. During their seasonal clearance sales, selected items are red-tagged at discounts of 20% or more. During the winter clearance sale, we found many good buys, including blazers that usually sold for $50 priced at $24, and a variety of men's and women's winter separates at $12 apiece.

Checks, Credit cards

Sommerfield Sportswear Factory Outlet

Portland: 2245 S.E. Powell Blvd. ☎ 231–5139
Hours: Mon–Fri 9–5, Sat 10–1

If you didn't make the team but want to look like you did, you're in luck here. This outlet is part of a manufacturing operation that makes uniforms and jackets and offers 100% cotton rugby shirts, football, and basketball uniforms, and running suits—all at wholesale prices. These are quality samples and overruns, so you won't find flaws. The rugby shirts run around $20, while heavy satin jackets that retail regularly from $60 to $65 are priced at $30.

Checks

Off-Price Stores

Smart shoppers who know quality, style, and designer names, and who want the best—at a discounted price—shop off-price stores. While these stores may vary in size and decor, they all have one thing in common—quality merchandise at 20% to 70% off retail.

Some high-volume off-price stores manufacture their own lines; others use their quantity buying power and deal directly with the manufacturer to guarantee low prices. Many supplement their inventory with manufacturers' overruns, discontinued styles, and close-outs. However, some off-price stores rely on middlemen to do their buying, and may not be able to pass on such substantial discounts. So it pays to comparison shop among the off-pricers to get the best price.

Return policies vary between off-pricers and may be stricter than those of full-price stores, so be sure to check before buying.

Burlington Coat Factory

Beaverton: 8775 S.W. Cascade Ave. *(Cascade Plaza)* ☎ 646–9900
Hours: Mon–Sat 10–9, Sun 11–6

The whole family can shop economically at this store, which is part of a nationwide chain of off-price department stores. Perhaps best known for its large selection of quality outerwear, Burlington offers an outstanding selection of career and casual apparel and shoes for men and women, including well-stocked departments for juniors, young men, and children—all at around 20% off major department store prices. For even bigger savings, watch for their frequent markdowns, special promotions, and seasonal sales such as the big January coat sale.

Checks, Credit cards

Cassie's

Clackamas: 8660 S.E. Sunnyside Rd. *(Clackamas Promenade)* ☎ 653–1322
West Linn: 22000 Willamette Dr. *(West Linn Shopping Center)* ☎ 656–7141
Hours: Mon–Fri 10–8, Sat 10–6, Sun 12–5

Cassie's carries personal wardrobes at discount prices. Women will find career and casual apparel, designer wear included, from 25% to 50% off retail. Cassie shops manufacturers in New York and Los Angeles for quality good buys. She returns with famous-label apparel as well as unique gift items, scarves, handbags, and jewelry. In addition to frequent in-store specials, watch for Cassie's seasonal sales for further discounts.

Checks, Credit cards

Clothestime

Beaverton: 3831 S.W. 117th *(Canyon Place)* ☎ 643–5383
Gresham: 620 N.W. Eastman Pkwy *(Gresham Town Fair)* ☎ 667–3741
Portland: 11211 S.E. 82nd Ave. *(Ross Center)* ☎ 659–7064
Salem: 2295 Lancaster N.E. ☎ 371–6814
Hours: Mon–Fri 10–9, Sat 10–8, Sun 12–6

This large nationwide chain (over 350 stores) of off-pricers offers sportswear and contemporary fashion for junior and misses (up to size 13/14). Much of their inventory is specially manufactured, although you will find such labels as *Judy Knapp, Kitty Hawk, Guess, Limited Express,* and *Condor* at prices below those for the same brands in major department stores. Check out the clearance racks for some incredible bargains.

Checks, Credit cards

The Coat Rack

Beaverton: 8775 S.W. Cascade Ave. ☎ 646–6361
Hours: Mon–Fri 9–9, Sat 9–7, Sun 10–6

This shop carries coats, coats, and more coats in contemporary, stylish fashion for men and women at prices up to 40% off suggested retail. As you'd expect in Oregon, the biggest sellers at The Coat Rack are raincoats. You'll also find wool, leather, and cotton coats for women, overcoats and parkas for men, and suits for both men and women. They have sales at the close of each season, and if you're on the mailing list, you'll get first shot at them. If you really want big savings, come to their annual Fourth of July weekend sidewalk sale.

Checks, Credit cards

C.Y.'s House of Samples

Portland: 6800 N.E. Killingsworth ☎ 287–5770
Hours: Mon–Fri 10–8, Sat 10–6, Sun 12–5

C.Y.'s is home (a very big home at that!) to the biggest stock of sample merchandise found in the Northwest. Men, women, and kids of all ages will find quality casual, dressy, and sports clothing, designer labels included, at prices 40% to 60% below retail. They get in new merchandise every day, and current styles, as well as last season's, can be found. Selected items are further discounted, which helps make this store a house of bargains as well as samples.

Checks, Credit cards

Dress Barn

Beaverton: 3831 S.W. 117th Ave. *(Canyon Place)* ☎ 643–5892
Clackamas: 8926 S.E. Sunnyside Rd. *(Clackamas Promendade)* ☎ 654–1849
Hours: Mon–Fri 10–8, Sat 10–6, Sun 12–5

The Dress Barn caters primarily to career women, although they stock some casual wear as well. Attractive, fashionable suits, dresses, and coordinates can be found here at 20% to 50% off department store prices. They carry a wide selection of name brands, including *Jones of New York, Bill Blass, Leslie Fay, Sasson, Cherokee, Jonathan Martin*, and *Jordache*. Their merchandise is not buy-backs or seconds, but top-quality new apparel. Check out their clearance racks, where merchandise is discounted 50% or more. In February and August, they hold their semi-annual suit sales where all suits, already low-priced at $79 to $129, are discounted an additional $10 to $20. Blouses are 20% off when purchased along with a suit. They also hold a fashion show during these sales.

Checks, Credit cards

Dress for Less
Gresham: 16126 S.E. Stark *(Village Square)* ☎ 253–8005
Portland: 7776 S.W. Capitol Hwy *(Multnomah Village)* ☎ 244–6403
Hours: Gresham, Mon–Fri 10–8, Sat 10–6, Sun 12–5; Portland, Mon–Sat
10–6
Ladies and juniors will discover that Dress for Less stocks lots of dresses—
party, formal, prom, fancy, beaded, sequined, career, and casual—at
discount prices. The Multnomah Village store carries sizes 4–16, while at
Village Square, you'll find sizes 4–46. They also carry sweaters, jewelry,
blouses, pants, and beaded bags. We found lots of samples (mostly one-of-
a-kind) in sizes 8, 10, and 12 that were priced 50% off regular retail. Four
racks of dresses, some originally retailing for $100, were priced from $5 to
$30. Name brands are tucked in with the rest of the merchandise.

Checks, Credit cards

Final Choice
Beaverton: 3275 S.W. Cedar Hills Blvd. *(Beaverton Mall)* ☎ 643–0561
Oregon City: I-205 at McLouglin Blvd. *(Oregon City Shopping Center)*
☎ 655–1413
Portland: 10014 S.E. Washington (Mall 205) ☎ 255–1146
Salem: 831 Lancaster Dr. N.E. *(Lancaster Mall)* ☎ 371–6414
Hours: Generally, Mon–Fri 10–9, Sat 10–6, Sun 11–5
Final Choice delivers low prices on trendy fashions in junior and missy sizes.
A print dress with embroidered collar originally priced at $96 was marked
at $57.99; a gorgeous sequined sweater was down from $24.99 to $11.99.
We found a large selection of glittering fashion jewelry (could you believe
"diamond" bracelets for only $4.99?) and such accessories as barrettes (in
strawberry, pineapple, and grape) for $2.99, plus wallets, handbags, gloves,
and hairpieces.

Checks, Credit cards

The Leatherworks
Portland: 2908 S.E. Belmont ☎ 232–3280
Hours: Mon–Sat 12–6
Leatherworks claims that their prices are the lowest in the country. They
offer quality leatherwear at 20% to 30% off retail. Their in-store inventory
is limited, but shoppers can order from a huge selection of leather products
out of the store's catalogs with delivery in as soon as a few days or up to
several weeks, depending on where the goods are shipped from. These
catalog sales are the secret to the store's low prices.

Checks, Credit cards

Le Tanner's

Portland: 526 S.W. Yamhill ☎ 223–9040
Hours: Mon–Sat 10:30–6

This shop directly imports leather apparel and passes along the savings. All jackets, coats, and pants for men and women are at least 10% off retail, and stock is marked down 20% at seasonal clearance sales. They offer suede as well as rough, soft, and treated leathers. All merchandise is guaranteed.

Checks, Credit cards

Marshall's

Beaverton: 3849 S.W. 117th Ave. *(Canyon Place)* ☎ 646–2554
Hours: Mon–Fri 9:30–9:30, Sat 9–8, Sun 11–6

This off-price chain store is a place where the whole family can shop economically. They carry a wide selection of clothing for just about everybody, plus fashion jewelry, belts, handbags, shoes, and other accessories at discounted prices. You'll find a potpourri of designer labels, the less expensive ones interspersed with the higher quality names. Women will find stylish suits, as well as contemporary casuals, petite to large sizes. Men can choose from large stocks of dress shirts, pants, and casual wear, while the children's departments are amply stocked for toddlers to teens. For even bigger savings, watch for their specially tagged clearance items.

Checks, Credit cards

Modern Woman

Beaverton: 3831 S.W. 117th Ave. *(Canyon Place)* ☎ 643–6868
Clackamas: 8922 S.E. Sunnyside Rd. *(Clackamas Promenade)* ☎ 653–1368
Hours: Mon–Fri 10–9, Sat 10–6, Sun 11–5

This large off-price chain carries current, first-quality fashions for the large-size woman. You'll find fashionable clothing in sizes 16W–24W, plus a wide assortment of accessories. Designer labels, as well as their own specially made merchandise, can be found in abundance. Watch for their seasonal sales, where you can save an additional 25% off such items as blouses, pants, dresses, skirts, and blazers.

Checks, Credit cards

Nordstrom Rack

Clackamas: 8930 S.E. Sunnyside Rd. *(Clackamas Promenade)* ☎ 654–5415
Portland: 401 S.W. Morrison ☎ 299—1815
Hours: Clackamas, Mon–Thurs 9:30–8, Fri 9:30–9, Sat 9:30–7, Sun 11–6; Portland, Mon–Fri 10–9, Sat 10–7, Sun 11–6

The Rack has its devotees (or should we say addicts?) who regularly shop here and pick up top-quality career and casual apparel at unbelievable savings. The Clackamas store is spacious and much more spread out than the smaller downtown location, where racks cozy up to one another. But one thing's for sure—you'll find terrific buys at either location. At a red-tag sale, when some items are an additional 50% off, we found a lavender kid's sweater priced under $3, women's socks at 50 cents, a Nordstrom label women's polo shirt under $6, a men's wool vest under $5, and wool and denim separates at great prices. Some of their merchandise is purchased off-price and the savings passed along to you. Watch for their periodic red-tag sales where an additional 50% is knocked off their already-low prices. Occasionally an "as is" rack will pop up and you'll definitely find rock bottom prices on them.

Checks, Credit cards

Ross Dress For Less
Beaverton: 3495 S.W. Cedar Hills Blvd. ☎ 646–7900
Gresham: 300 N.W. Eastman Pky. *(Gresham Town Fair)* ☎ 666–4102
Portland: 11211 S.E. 82nd *(Ross Center)* ☎ 654–5732
Salem: 2325 Lancaster Dr. N.E. *(Village East)* ☎ 363–1951
Vancouver: 4708 N.E. Thurston Way ☎ (206)363–1951
Hours: Mon–Sat 9:30–9, Sun 11–7

Although this popular off-price chain concentrates on the basics rather than on trendy apparel, we recommend taking your time to go through the racks and pick out those designer labels tucked away with the regular stock. Overall, prices here are on the low side and selection is wide for women's junior, petite, and large-size career and casual clothing, hosiery, and lingerie; underwear for the whole family; and accessories—belts, scarves, jewelry, and handbags. Ross also carries a large stock of men's sportcoats, knit sweaters, slacks, belts, and ties, and they have a hip young men's department. To round things out, don't forget to check out the shoe department that caters to the entire family.

Checks, Credit cards

Smart Size
Beaverton: 3225 S.W. Cedar Hills Blvd. *(Beaverton Mall)* ☎ 643–5829
Portland: 1615 N.E. 21st ☎ 249–7047
4110 S.E. 82nd (Eastport Plaza) ☎ 775–0782
Hours: Generally, Mon–Fri 10–9, Sat 10–6, Sun 11–5

At Smart Size, the full-figured woman will find a wide selection of career and casual wear such as blazers, pants, skirts, sweatsuits, knit shirts, stirrup pants, and knit pants in sizes 32W–52W. This off-price chain focuses on basic and casual styles for all occasions. Some terrific bargains can be found during their frequent sales. The day we checked, sweaters, blouses, and coats were 50% off. Don't miss their clearance sections. When you use their in-store charge cards, you'll receive notice of future sales with your statements.

Checks, Credit cards

T.J. Maxx

Beaverton: 3805 S.W. 117th Ave. *(Canyon Place)* ☎ 641–1828
Portland: 11370 S.E. 82nd ☎ 653–7913
Vancouver: 8101 N.E. Parkway *(Vancouver Park Place)* ☎ (206)256–9606
Hours: Mon–Sat 9:30–9:30, Sun 12–6

With over 10,000 new fashions for the whole family arriving each week at every T.J. Maxx store, you'll have plenty to choose from! This store specializes in women's fashions in junior, misses and large sizes with lots of separates for career and casual wear. Designer labels pop up frequently, and you'll find brand name and designer fashions at 20% to 60% off department store prices. They also carry a good stock of casual menswear, as well as quality name brands in the children's departments. Each T.J. Maxx has giftware and domestic departments. With so much new merchandise constantly arriving, with each visit you'll think it's your first.

Checks, Credit cards

Your $10 Store

Beaverton: 11669 S.W. Beaverton-Hillsdale Hwy *(Beaverton Town Square)*
  ☎ 641–8087
Salem: 189 Liberty N.E. ☎ 588–2924
  4823 Commerical S.E. ☎ 588–2923
Hours: Mon–Sat 10–6, Sun 12–5

You'll find this shop small but the savings big on women's casual and sportswear, where everything is $10 (so there are no price tags on any apparel!). Watch for brand names to pop up in their stock of pants, cords, jeans, and shirts. This shop also carries earrings and necklaces for less than $10. Their sale-rack merchandise is $5.99.

Checks

Uniforms & Work Clothing

Whether you need coveralls for your weekend shop projects, work clothes for a job in the medical field, or industrial uniforms, you'll find a good selection at the outlets listed below.

Used work clothing, ranging from gently to roughly worn, is priced at a fraction of new prices.

American Industrial Outlet Store

Portland: 5225 S.E. 26th ☎ 233–5445
Hours: Mon–Fri 8–3:15

Gently to roughly worn coveralls, shirts, and pants can be found here at a fraction of their new costs. Coveralls go for $4.50, while shirts and pants are priced at $1.25. Also, used jackets, shop coats, and counter coats are good buys.

Checks

Career Uniforms and Shoes

Clackamas: 8982 Sunnyside Rd. *(Clackamas Promenade)* ☎ 654–7228
Hours: Mon–Fri 10–8, Sat 10–6, Sun 12–5

This shop sells new famous-brand uniforms for the medical field including lab coats, white tops, color tops, dresses and pants. Prices are competitive, but for really big savings, watch for periodic sales where they offer discounts of 20% to 50% off their regular uniform prices.

Checks, Credit cards

Coverall Uniform Supply Co.

Portland: 2522 N.E. M.L. King Blvd. *(Union)* ☎ 288–6881
Hours: Mon–Fri 8:30–4:45

Coverall carries a wide range of used "industrial uniforms" at 60% to 80% off new prices. Used shirts and pants are $2 each, coveralls $6, shop coats $3, and lined winter jackets $3.50. You'll find five styles of hats to choose from at prices in the $3 to $5 range. Ask about their weekly and bi-weekly rental service, which might prove more economical than purchasing.

Cash or company check

Women's Consignment & Resale Shops

Don't be squeamish about shopping at consignment and resale shops for previously owned clothes. Many of these shops have the look and feel of regular retail stores, and the quality and variety of their "gently worn" merchandise will please you. Of course, you won't be disappointed about the prices—they average one-third the original, with expensive items often going for less!

In addition to lots of used designer clothing, shoes, and accessories, many of these stores may carry a small assortment of new clothing and samples. Because sales are usually final, be sure to inspect each item before you buy.

Watch for some incredible deals on clothes that have been further discounted after 30 or 60 days. Just like the new clothing retail stores, consignment and resale shops have seasonal clearances, special promotions, and sales racks that often yield excellent buys.

Act II Exclusive Ladies Resale Boutique

Portland: 1139 S.W. Morrison ☎ 227–1477
Hours: Tues–Fri 10–5, Sat 10–4

Everything—but everything—you find in this shop reflects the owner's commitment to value and style. Act II absolutely crawls with designer labels such as *Liz Claiborne, Anne Klein, Escada, Bert Newman, Calvin Klein,* and

Evan Picone, all at about half the original prices. "Dress for success" and casual apparel (including accessories) are carefully selected, beautifully displayed, and available in a wide range of sizes.

Checks, Credit cards

Bonnie's Pre-Owned and Vintage Clothing
Portland: 4443 N.E. Fremont ☎ 281–4459
Hours: Mon–Fri 11–5:30, Sat 11–5

Bonnie's sells natural-fiber women's apparel for career and casual wear. The merchandise is top quality and includes many designer labels tucked in with classic ready-to-wear. The owner selectively shops estate sales and store liquidations to provide a wide variety of clothing (some for men such as jackets, sweaters, winter coats, and shirts). The stock is constantly changing and in sync with seasonal changes. When we checked, there was a 50% off sale on skirts. Bonnie's stock of vintage merchandise was down to a remaining few hats. Overall, you'll find her prices to be one-fourth to one-half what you'd pay in department or specialty stores.

Checks, Credit cards

Carousel Corner Resale
Portland: 9921 S.E. Stark ☎ 253–0430
Hours: Mon–Sat 10:30–5

Carousel Corner carries a wide selection of casual and career clothing for women sizes 4–44. Everything we saw was in excellent condition and nicely displayed. Although the shop has only about 1100 square feet, the merchandise is not crammed in together. Check the additional 50%-off sale racks for slow movers and the $1 racks. Some well-known labels at good prices frequently turn up. They offer a limited layaway plan and exchanges on returns.

Checks, Credit cards

CC Exchange
Portland: 506 N.W. 23rd ☎ 227–1477
Hours: Mon–Sat 11–5

You'll find a variety of gently worn women's apparel and accessories, including a potpourri of designer labels for career and casual wear. They sometimes acquire factory close-outs and new merchandise from retail store liquidations and knock as much as 50% to 70% off original prices. Look for terrific buys on their shoes, handbags, and jewelry.

Checks, Credit cards

The Clothes Closet
Lake Oswego: 252 S.W. B ☎ 636–5932
Hours: Mon–Sat 10–5:30

This shop has been around for 35 years. That says a lot about their service, low prices, and top-quality merchandise. You'll find a large selection of contemporary casual and career clothing for women of all ages. Experienced shoppers search out the designer labels from among racks of suits, blouses, dresses, and sportswear. There's a nice selection of lingerie including robes and nightgowns. Right before Christmas, they carry a large assortment of cocktail dresses and other smart apparel. Inventory is marked at around one-third the original price, and after three months, merchandise is marked down 50%. We found attractive suits marked down from the original price of $400 to $150.

Checks, Credit cards

The Clothes Hanger
Beaverton: 6636 S.W. Beaverton-Hillsdale Hwy ☎ 292–2251
Hours: Tues–Sat 10–5

The Clothes Hanger has been offering consistent quality for 28 years. You'll find a great selection of contemporary fashions, including seasonals, in sizes 2–44 for the working woman. They carry hundreds of designer labels. Wallets, belts, scarves, jewelry, shoes, and purses abound. Clothing and accessory prices start at 50% off the original retail, and after 90 days, are reduced a further 20% to 50%. Prices at The Clothes Hanger might be a bit higher than at many other consignment shops, but you'll be assured of getting only the highest quality merchandise. They have eight sales a year plus 50% off sales twice a year. Add your name to the mailing list to get first crack at all those sales.

Checks, Credit cards

Encore East
Gresham: 1000 N. Main ☎ 661–1087
Hours: Mon–Fri 10–6, Sat 10–5

Take a very picky owner and add repeat customers who pass on the word about this shop and know what you get? You get a consignment shop whose inventory turns over quite fast and whose sales have doubled in the past year. Encore East offers a great selection of high-quality "gently worn" apparel for women of all ages. There are several corner racks for career clothing, as well as new jewelry and watch displays. The "cruise clothes" racks contain summer clothes snatched up by those taking tropical cruises or trips. Nearby, we found racks of active winter and sports apparel (such as ski jackets, bibs, and jogging suits). Designer labels such as *Christian Dior, Calvin Klein,* and *Evan Picone* turn up frequently. We saw *Pendleton* suits reduced from $170 to $45.

Checks, Credit cards

Encore South

Milwaukie: 16074 S.E. McLouglin *(Holly Farm Mall)* ☎ 654–1553
Hours: Tues–Fri 10–6, Sat 10–5

This consignment shop looks much like a regular dress shop. They carry a wide range of merchandise—skirts, coats, jackets, dresses, blouses, sweaters, vests, lingerie, jogging outfits, skiwear, belts, new jewelry, even prom dresses (that many use as a wedding dress for the second or third time around). There's a good selection of clothing for professional women, as well as such "teen" labels as *Esprit, Generra,* and *Gap.* A shirt that would have been $45 to $50 at the *Gap* was $10. They have periodic sales such as Super Bowl Sunday when everything is marked down even further. You'll find sizes from 1–44.

Checks, Credit cards

Encore West

Portland: 13571 N.W. Cornell Rd. ☎ 626–8562
Hours: Mon–Fri 10–6, Sat 10–5

This shop sells a full range of contemporary clothing and accessories with the career woman in mind. Such labels as *Liz Claiborne, Ralph Lauren,* and *Esprit* go for a fraction of their original cost. We found a designer sweater that would have been $125 at Nordstrom priced at $25. About one-fourth of their merchandise was samples or retail store liquidation goods, so they've never been worn. All their jewelry is new. Slow movers are further discounted 50%, and every Saturday, selected items are reduced an additional 30%. Get on the mailing list for advance notice of the store's four annual sales.

Checks, Credit cards

Fashion Replay

Clackamas: 20406 S.E. Hwy. 212 ☎ 658–6604
Hours: Mon–Fri 10–6, Wed 10–7, Sat 10–5

This consignment shop carries a wide selection of new and used contemporary women's clothes and formals (in available sizes of 1–26). You'll find top-quality merchandise geared for career women and homemakers who want stylish clothes in fine shape at good prices. Their sweatshirts, jewelry, and handbags are new, and everything else the store accepts must be in excellent condition. Many items were once part of Nordstrom and Meier & Frank "collections" and one dress priced at $39.99 retailed at Nordstrom for around $145. Some quality new and used jewelry boxes were available.

Checks, Credit cards

Four Seasons Color Boutique

Portland: 222 N.E. 102nd ☎ 254–8289
Hours: Mon–Fri 10–5, Sat 10–5

This shop specializes in clothing for the young working woman (ages 25–40) in sizes 4–44. They also carry casual wear, some petites, maternity, jackets, jogging suits, skirts and sweaters. Some things are new with the original tags. Designer labels such as *Anne Klein, Liz Claiborne,* and *Calvin Klein* are sprinkled throughout. We spotted a two-piece wool skirt and top by *Joanie Char* that originally went for $200 marked $49.95. For some incredible buys, check out the racks of sweaters, suits, and slacks (in all sizes) as well as the half-price and dollar racks. Get on the mailing list for advance notice of their four annual sales. Year-round, you'll find tag sales. Blue tags—take an additional 15% off; gray tags—an additional 25% off; green and red tags fetch an additional 50% off.

Checks, Credit cards

Julie's Resale Shop

Portland: 6920 N.E. Sandy Blvd. ☎ 284–1336
Hours: Wed–Sat 10:30–5

At Julie's you'll find bargains on women's apparel of all kinds, including current-style career clothes, casual wear, designer brands, and a few '50s vintage dresses. There's a nice selection of lingerie—slips, robes, and even a basket of bras. We saw lots of accessories, including belts, scarves, jewelry, handbags, and shoes. We found a cotton chambray shirt originally priced at $50 marked down to $12. Check out the incredible bargains in the $1 and $2 baskets of T-shirts, slacks, skirts, and sweaters.

Checks, Credit cards

Kim's Resale

Beaverton: 12175 S.W. 2nd ☎ 644–1093
Hours: Tues–Thurs 10–6, Fri & Sat 10–5

This consignment shop, located in a little house, offers working women in their 20s and 30s trendy and fashionable clothes and accessories. We found good prices on business suits, jogging outfits, jackets, lingerie, and on the dozen or so wedding dresses. As soon as you enter the shop, check out the $1 clothes closet rack (tucked into a coat closet without doors) for some incredible buys. All jewelry is new and the owner specializes in unusual pieces. We spotted a wooden fish pin, a pin with a pig wearing sunglasses, world globe earrings, silver hearts, sterling loops, and more. We found earrings by *Cloisonne* that regularly retailed elsewhere for around $9 priced at $3.99. Watch for an additional 15% to 50% off on specially tagged merchandise.

Checks, Credit cards

New Life Resale Fashions

Hillsboro: 1615 S.E. Tualatin Valley Hwy. *(T V Mall)* ☎ 648–5279
Hours: Mon–Fri 10–6, Sat 10–5

One of the largest consignment shops around, New Life Resale Fashions has been in business for ten years. The store offers a huge selection of contemporary women's career and casual apparel plus a smaller amount of clothing for men, juniors, and moms-to-be. Brand names such as *Liz Claiborne, Adrienne Vittadini,* and *Pierre Cardin* adorn over 500 pieces at a fraction of the original cost (50% off if new, and 65% to 75% off if "gently worn"). Check out the "resort rack" during the winter that offers low-priced casual summer wear (ideal for those taking cruises or traveling to balmy Caribbean or Pacific resorts). Nearby on the "couture rack" we spied such upper-end designer labels as *Escada* and *Evan Picone* at well below original prices. Sweaters, originally priced at $300, were selling for $50 to $100. On Saturdays, look for inventory with special colored tags—you'll save an additional 20% on these items.

Checks, Credit cards

The Resale Cottage
Tualatin: 18003 S.W. Lower Boones Ferry Rd. ☎ 684–5051
Hours: Mon–Fri 10–5, Wed 10–6:30, Sat 10–4

Working women will find everything from career clothes to casual wear—lingerie, cocktail dresses, pants, jewelry, hats, shoes, and handbags. Labels such as *Liz Claiborne, Escada* and *Ellen Tracy* are priced from 65% to 75% off the original. Inventory gets marked down 20% after 30 days and 50% off after 60 days. This large shop has been around nearly ten years and prides itself on being a cozy, warm place to shop. The staff are friendly and helpful.

Checks, Credit cards

Rusty's Resale
Tigard: 12559 S.W. Main ☎ 620–3775
Hours: Mon–Fri 10–6, Sat 10–5

You'll find a nice selection of contemporary clothing in sizes 1–24 (nothing's over three years old) for the teen to 70-ish crowd, including large sizes, petites, maternity, and formals. In addition to blouses, skirts, dresses, coats and suits, Rusty's carries lingerie, cocktail dresses, shoes, scarves, and belts on consignment. The jewelry is new and some of the earrings priced at $1 were seen at other shops for $7. At least 15% of Rusty's inventory is new (the owner shops at store liquidations for merchandise); during the holidays, that increases to around 35%. They carry quite a few designer label items. Prices on blouses ranged from $4.99 to $25. Returns are by exchange only.

Checks, Credit cards

Sandra's Cedar Chest
Portland: 1012 S.W. King ☎ 227–7742
Hours: Tues–Sat 10–5, Wed & Thurs 10–6

Tucked away in the basement of an historic 100-year-old home, this consignment shop concentrates on upper end contemporary women's clothing. You'll also find maternity and petites. Labels such as *Anne Klein, Albert Nipon, Ralph Lauren,* and *Escada* are in abundance. Everything is clean, neat, and in top-notch condition—no missing buttons or spots on the clothes. A wool gabardine skirt in mint condition, which might have gone for $150 at Nordstrom, was under $30. Sandra's also carries new jewelry and handbags.

Checks, Credit cards

Savvy Plus
Portland: 3204 S.E. Hawthorne Blvd. ☎ 231–7116
Hours: Mon–Fri 11–6, Sat 11–5
This exclusive shop specializes in larger size (from 14–52) career and casual women's apparel. They cater to upscale clientele who look for top-quality clothing. Most of the apparel, made in the U.S. exclusively of natural fibers, sells in the $10 to $90 range. About a fourth of the jewelry is new, and some is crafted by local artisans. Look for specially tagged sale items and monthly markdowns. The store is very clean, the dressing rooms spacious, and the staff cheerful and quite helpful.

Checks, Credit cards

Sellwood Ladies Resale
Portland: 8079 S.E. 13th ☎ 236–6842
Hours: Mon–Sat 10–5
This small shop carries a good selection of women's contemporary career apparel as well as a bit of everything for teens to seniors. The owner is selective about what she'll carry, which will be obvious as you ferret out some bargains among such top-quality accessories as socks, gloves, boots, purses, shoes, and jewelry. Hats, many vintage, are in generous supply. One corner of the shop is devoted exclusively to vintage clothing. Designer labels turn up often, as do new garments that have been picked up from other retailers or as factory close-outs. Sales are periodic and you'll notice color-coded tags cutting the prices by 25% to 50%. Check out the half-off rack and the $1 table for terrific buys.

Checks, Credit cards

7th Avenue Boutique
Oregon City: 1001 Seventh Ave. ☎ 657–8099
Hours: Mon–Sat 10–6, Sun 12–5
This shop, under recent new ownership, carries everything from career clothes to sportswear, including suits, blazers, formals, bridal gowns, slacks, sweaters, and baby clothes. One-third of their inventory is new (picked up from liquidations and close-outs); the rest is composed of gently worn consignment merchandise. Brand names are mixed in with the rest of the

stock and you'll find the prices about one-third to one-half department store prices.

Checks, Credit cards

The Sewing Circle
Portland: 1034 S.W. Third ☎ 227–7985
Hours: Mon–Sat 11–6

Both men's and women's clothing can be found here, and the shop focuses on career wear. Tucked in with the regular merchandise you'll find vintage, black evening silks, and designer labels such as *Jones of New York, Liz Claiborne,* and *Adrienne Vittadini.* We found a blazer and skirt originally priced at $270 going for around $85. Jewelry ranged from $5 to $40 (including some quality men's cuff links), and great prices were seen on hats, shoes, purses, and scarves. Check out their color-tagged sale merchandise for even bigger savings.

Checks, Credit cards

The Silver Lining
Portland: 7044 S.E. Milwaukie ☎ 238–5578
Hours: Mon–Fri 11:30–6, Sat 11:30–5

The Silver Lining offers contemporary career apparel and casual clothing for women in the 30 to 60 age group. This shop is very much like a boutique, its apparel beautifully displayed and carefully selected. You'll find labels such as *Liz Claiborne, Evan Picone, Carol Little,* and *Laura Ashley* at 50% to 60% off the original. We noticed lots of new and used accessories, including belts, jewelry, hats, and shoes. Check out the sale rack apparel; after 60 days they're marked down 30%, and 50% to 75% after 90 days.

Checks, Credit cards

The Spare Room
Lake Oswego: 530 First St. ☎ 636–8170
Hours: Mon–Sat 11–6

This four-year-old shop sells top-quality, gently worn women's dress and casual wear with lots of designer labels. The stock is top-of-the line, the type you'd expect to find in a Nordstrom or Sak's. We overheard one enthusiastic shopper exclaim that the shop was so "cute and cuddly." With music playing in the background and candles softly glowing, we tend to agree. They also carry such collectibles as glassware and crystal pieces and craft items such as handmade soaps, wreaths, and silk earrings. Sales take place year-round and frequent markdowns are made to move the stock. Get on the mailing list for the bi-monthly newsletter for advance sale and merchandise information.

Checks, Credit cards

Twice Is Nice
Gresham: 853 E. Powell Blvd. ☎ 661–6507
Hours: Mon–Fri 10–5, Sat 10–5:30
This shop's been around for more than ten years, which attests to the owner's high standards for quality and selection. Twice Is Nice carries men's and women's contemporary career and casual wear. Men will find a nice selection of suits, tuxedos, shoes, and ties. Men's and women's designer clothes share rack space with ready-to-wear styles. You'll find many new jewelry pieces, as well as maternity wear and kids' things. Merchandise gets marked down 20% after 60 days and 50% after 90 days.

Checks, Credit cards

Visible Impact
Portland: 3541 S.E. Hawthorne Blvd. ☎ 232–9518
Hours: Mon–Fri 10–7, Sat 11–5
Visible Impact offers an interesting mix of women's career apparel with funky vintage items. We saw such things as beaded sweaters ($20 to $30); dresses from the '40s and '50s (around $24); leggings, leotards, boots, "coach bags," and kimonos; and contemporary work wear, designer dresses, formal wear, and jeans jackets ($18 to $25). Most things are in the "gently worn" category and inventory is constantly changing, with almost daily arrival of "new" merchandise. You'll find Visible Impact in the company of quite a few other trendy and funky shops that draw nice crowds on Hawthorne Blvd.

Checks, Credit cards

What Goes Around
Portland: 3206 S.E. Hawthorne Blvd. ☎ 232–1637
Hours: Mon–Sat 11–6, Sun 12–5
What Goes Around offers a potpourri of gently worn career and casual wear aimed at women 18–40. In addition to *Liz Claiborne* and *Esprit* labels, we saw a good selection of contemporary styles and of vintage formals, shoes, and purses. These formals (circa '50s) ranged from $18 to $60; on nearby racks jeans jackets were priced from $18 to $30 and pants at from $12 to $18. The owner offers funky things when she can find them, such as the purple suede "cutout" boots (from the '60s) selling for $20. Check out the sale rack where $5 will buy any two items and other terrific deals.

Checks, Credit cards

What's Upstairs
Portland: 736 N.W. 23rd ☎ 228–9143
Hours: Mon–Sat 11–5
Located in an old, gray, renovated house (upstairs—of course), this shop offers a full range of women's clothing and accessories in sizes 2–22,

including a room of sale merchandise that delivers incredible bargains. You'll find many well-known labels, such as *Adrian Arpel* and *Liz Claiborne*, at around one-third the original cost. We noted a jacket originally marked at $200 selling for $60, and "gently worn" jeans jackets by *Levi's, Bon Jour,* and *Calvin Klein* for around $20. Ask about their return policy.

Checks, Credit cards

Why Not Resale Shop
Portland: 8000 N.E. Glisan ☎ 253–5554
Hours: Mon 11–4, Tues–Fri 11–6, Sat 10–5
"Great labels and great prices" is the owner's motto, and you'll agree when you shop here and discover a wide selection of quality women's wear and accessories, especially the large stock of career wear. You'll find coats from $40 to $100, brand name suits from $50 to $100, and overall prices that are 60% to 70% below retail. Why Not has been around since 1969 and is a member of the greater Portland Association of Resale Shops. Watch for their seasonal and periodic sales.

Checks, Credit cards

Charity Resale Thrift Shops

Charity resale shops offer real bargains to money-conscious shoppers—especially those who recognize quality and brand-name labels. These thrift shops are usually packed with unique donated items. The good stuff goes quickly, so pick out a few favorite thrifts and shop the first few hours they're open each week.

Although clothing and accessories account for most of their volume, thrifts also offer housewares, appliances, books, furniture, toys, and assorted bric-a-brac at terrific savings.

When you shop the thrifts, be prepared to do plenty of rummaging. For many shoppers, half the fun is combing through racks of clothes and never knowing what surprises may pop up. But you can be assured of one thing: the money you spend comes right back to the community to benefit charitable purposes.

Assistance League of Portland Thrift Shop
Portland: 735 N.W. 23rd ☎ 227–7093
Hours: Mon–Sat 10–4
You'll be helping some good causes while saving money when you shop here. They offer clothing for the whole family, as well as toys, gifts, household items, and sports equipment. Designer-label apparel goes for $5 to $10, while camelhair coats, leather jackets, and men's suits can be found for under $25. The day we checked, an additional half-off sale was going on and some gorgeous sweaters were priced as low as $5.

Checks

The Bargain Tree

Portland: 838 S.W. 4th ☎ 227–7413
Hours: Mon–Fri 9:30–4:30, Sat 10–4

This well-run thrift shop is the most significant fund-raising source for the Junior League of Portland. They carry a wide selection of gently worn donated clothing and accessories for the whole family, including housewares, toys, and gift items. Designer labels pop up often and we saw some terrific-looking sportswear, suits, blazers (around $12 each for brand names), and dresses (a *St. John Knit* was $45). Be sure to shop their three annual "down-to-the-hanger" sales when everything goes and you'll get some incredible prices. During these week-long sales, prices are marked down an additional 50% to 75%, and on the last day (called "bag day"), you get to fill a 30-gallon plastic bag with apparel for $5.

Checks, Credit cards

Cedar Chest Resale

Hillsboro: 133 S. 3rd Ave. ☎ 648–4838
Hours: Mon–Sat 10–5

Cedar Chest Resale is a charity resale shop that operates on a consignment basis and donates its proceeds to senior programs, meals-on-wheels, and the "crisis fund"—all within the Washington County area. There's quite a mix here—from trendy women's clothing to cedar chests with 25-cent items and 50-cent racks where terrific buys can be found. We found $35 blouses marked at around $4 or $5 and a bedding ensemble, originally priced at $400, marked down to $80. Besides women's clothing, they carry a small stock of men's and kids' clothes, as well as pots and pans, books, and knickknacks. The shop is staffed by friendly, helpful volunteers.

Checks

Christie's Attic Thrift Shop

Portland: 7907 S.E. 13th ☎ 236–0222
Hours: Mon–Sun 9:30–5

The whole family can shop economically at Christie's Attic. They'll find a good selection of quality apparel (neatly displayed, too!) and accessories, including housewares, furniture, and bric-a-brac. The proceeds of this thrift benefit the Christie School at Marylhurst. Incidentally, much of the shop's inventory is donated by Lake Oswego residents. There are periodic sales, and during the last two weeks of each month, they hold a 25-cent sale on clearance items.

Checks

Council Thrift Shop

Portland: 1127 S.W. Morrison ☎ 227–6322
Hours: Mon–Sat 10–5

This shop, voted Portland's best thrift by the Downtowner, has also been called by some as the "Sak's Fifth Avenue of thrift shops." They carry a variety of gently used apparel and accessories for women, men, and children. In addition to beautifully displayed and carefully selected clothing, you'll find furniture, toys, books, and records. Designer labels are frequent finds, as are some incredible buys like a dress by *Adolfo* originally priced at $1,000 marked down to $65. Merchandise is brought in daily, and every week you'll find a sale where additional 25% to 50% markdowns are made. The day we checked, pants, sweaters, and skirts were on sale.

Checks, Credit cards

Discovery Shops
Gresham: 2017 N.E. Burnside *(Oregon Trail Shopping Center)* ☎ 669–0431
Portland: 1730 N.E. 40th ☎ 287–0053
   519 N.W. 21st Ave ☎ 274–9908
Tigard: 13975 S.W. Pacific Hwy ☎ 684–9060
Hours: Mon–Sat 10–4

Proceeds from these shops go to the American Cancer Society. The whole family will find new and barely used clothing, including contemporary designer and brand names, plus housewares, pottery, glassware, and knickknacks. Their volunteers are fashion conscious and very picky, keeping only about 24% of the items donated to them—the rest they donate to other thrifts or worthy causes. What this means, of course, is that you'll find top-quality merchandise at prices well below retail. In addition, some of the big retailers donate leftovers and clearance items to these shops. For even bigger savings, check out the color sale tags.

Checks, Credit cards

Nearly New Shop
Portland: 3508 S.E. Hawthorne Blvd. ☎ 235–8053
Hours: Mon–Sat 10–5

This thrift carries a large selection of nearly new men's and women's wear and accessories, including designer labels, name brands, and vintage wear. On the racks with other merchandise we found apparel by *Anne Klein, Liz Claiborne, Evan Picone*, and *Albert Nipon.* A gently worn *Pendleton* suit was priced under $15. They also carry housewares, knickknacks, books, records, tapes, and infant clothing. Watch for their periodic mark-down sales and always check out their 50-cent racks for terrific finds.

Checks

The Resale Shop
Beaverton: 8622 S.W. Hall Blvd. *(Progress Plaza)* ☎ 644–6364
Hours: Mon–Fri 10–4:45, Sat 12–4

The whole family can shop this 25-year-old charity shop, at the same benefiting St. Bartholomew Church. Career and casual wear, infant wear, light housewares, lingerie, and a good selection of accessories can be found here. This is a favorite haunt of the bank employees who work across the street, who drop in on their lunch hours to ferret out designer labels from among the gently worn clothing. Check out the bargain room, where you'll find prices marked down an additional 50%.

Checks

Second Edition Resale Shop

Portland: 12505 N.W. Cornell Rd. ☎ 644–6395
Hours: Tues–Thurs 10–5, Fri & Sat 10–4

All sales benefit the Cedar Mills Community Library, which is located next to the Second Edition. The whole family can shop economically here, as there's a wide selection of "gently worn" clothing as well as top-quality household items (such as dishes and linens). There are separate departments for women, men, and kids, and prices vary according to quality and brands. We found a cashmere sweater for $25, quite a few attractive men's suits for $20 or less, skirts for $5 to $7, wool sweaters from $4 to $7, and lots of shoes and accessories. Be sure to catch their annual September rummage sale (called "The Mess") that lures thousands of shoppers who sift through mountains of donations and find incredible bargains. The store is staffed by friendly and helpful volunteers.

Checks

William Temple House Thrift Shop

Portland: 2230 N.W. Glisan ☎ 222–3328
Hours: Mon–Sat 9:30–4

This thrift sells quality men's, women's, and children's clothing at low prices. We found blouses, skirts, and pants sale-priced at $1.50, while a mix of designer labels were at one-fourth to one-third original retail. They also carry such accessories as handbags, hats, and jewelry, plus kitchenware, furniture, towels, sheets, pillows, and quite a literary collection in the "library department." During their periodic sales, you'll save an additional 50%. Because sales are unadvertised, call to find out about them.

Credit cards

Menswear

While the shops in this section cater to the male bargain shopper, don't overlook the many women's consignment, resale, and charity resale shops that provide great bargains for men, too (and the kids as well).

Many men will find their complete business wardrobes at these consignment and off-price stores—with suits, shirts, and ties going for a fraction of their regular retail prices.

The major off-price chains—T.J. Maxx, Ross, and Marshall's—offer great prices on dress and casual wear, shoes and accessories. And don't forget to check out our sections on Factory Outlets, Sporting Goods, and Formal Wear for a variety of stores that carry off-price men's apparel.

Off-Price Stores

Estes
Portland: 2364 W. Burnside ☎ 227–0275
Hours: Mon–Fri 9–6, Sat 9–5

This shop custom tailors men's suits at prices well below the competition. The owner buys large quantities of the finest European fabrics and passes along the savings that come from volume buying. Besides price, this shop is unusual for the superior craftsmanship that goes into the flawlessly constructed garments made to the exact measurements and tastes of each customer. Custom-made suits made elsewhere (using the same fabrics as would Estes) run $1,400 to $1,500, while at Estes they're priced around $850.

Checks, Credit cards

Kuppenheimer Men's Clothiers
Beaverton: 10370 S.W. Beaverton-Hillsdale Hwy ☎ 641–5803
Milwaukie: 17186 S.E. McLouglin Blvd. ☎ 654–5131
Portland: 508 S.W. Taylor ☎ 228–3928
Hours: Mon–Sat 10–9, Sun 12–5

This nationwide chain offers businessmen and professionals quite a selection of suits, coats, slacks, shirts, and outerwear at factory-direct prices. Because they make everything they sell, they can keep the prices down and offer discounts of 30% to 40% off department-store prices. Watch for their big seasonal sales where prices are even better.

Checks, Credit cards

The Men's Wearhouse
Beaverton: 11915 S.W. Canyon Rd. ☎ 526–9414
Clackamas: 8876 S.E. Sunnyside Rd. *(Clackamas Promenade)* ☎ 653–7811
Portland: 851 S.W. 6th ☎ 274–0610
Salem: 401 Center St. N.E. *(Salem Centre)* ☎ 363–9551
Hours: Mon–Fri 10–9, Sat 9:30–6, Sun 12–6; Portland only, Mon–Fri 9:30–8, Sat 9:30–6, Sun 12–6

This national chain of off-price men's clothing stores offers an alternative to department and specialty stores. Along with their own on-premise tailoring service, you'll find price discounts of up to 40% for suits in styles that range from European cut to banker's classics to sporty designer-label tweeds. They also offer slacks, sweaters, shirts, ties (100% silk—three for $18), belts, and outerwear. We found a great selection of 100% wool suits for under $200. Watch for their "once a year" sale and save an additional 30% to 50% off their already low prices.

Checks, Credit cards

Tall & Big

Portland: 11211 S.E. 82nd Ave. *(Ross Center)* ☎ 653–9922
Hours: Mon–Wed 10–8, Thurs & Fri 10–9, Sat 10–6, Sun 12–5

This men's clothing mart carries extra-size dress and casual clothing for hard-to-fit men at prices 20% to 40% below those found in specialty and department stores. You'll find name-brand stock among their inventory of suits, coats, pants, shirts, belts, underwear, socks, and sweaters. Watch for their big sales held two or three times a year when they mark most stock 20% to 50% below their already-discounted everyday prices. Get on the mailing list for advance notice of these sales. Be sure to check out the clearance racks for some great buys such as 50% off jeans, outerwear, and miscellaneous items.

Checks, Credit cards

Resale Shops

Gentlemens Resale

Oregon City: 1115 Molalla Ave. ☎ 657–7570
Hours: Mon–Fri 10–6, Sat 10–5

Both men and women can shop here, but the store's primary focus is on top-quality men's career and casual wear. Look for business suits (from $29.95 to $89.95), tuxedos, jackets, slacks, sweaters, dress shirts, and jeans. Women will find contemporary career apparel and sportswear from well-known manufacturers, as well as accessories, jewelry, and some vintage merchandise. Prices on all their items are marked at 50% or more off department-store prices. The day we checked they got in a shipment of children's polo shirts with the *Lands' End* label—priced at $6 each. Watch for their periodic sales.

Checks

Sir Resale

Portland: 14331 S.E. Division ☎ 760–4880
Hours: Mon–Sat 10–6

Sir Resale sells quality men's dress and casual apparel including suits, coats, shirts, slacks, sweaters, and a sprinkling of hats and accessories. Designer labels turn up frequently. The owner is selective about what he'll carry, which results in a good selection of gently worn apparel. The day we checked there was a full wall of dress and casual shirts priced in the $1 to $5 range and a rack of leather jackets from $5 to $100. Be sure to get on their mailing list for advance notice of sales and incoming merchandise.

Checks

Maternity & Children's

Off-Price & Outlet Shops

One thing you can be sure of about children: the cost of their clothing will continue to escalate in the years to come. However, smart shoppers can increase the buying power of their clothing dollars by focusing on good quality clothing—especially important for play clothes and everyday infant wear.

Cotton and polyester blends are good choices because they wear and wash well. Wherever possible, buy clothes a size larger than necessary (of course, you'll have to hem pants)—your kids will grow into them in no time! If you have lots of kids to pass clothes between, buy uni-sex outfits—good for one and all. To save even more, avoid buying kids' clothes in season. Instead, watch for end-of-season clearances and buy for the next year.

Being pregnant doesn't mean you don't care about looking good. But the dilemma always seems to be whether you should spend all that money on new maternity clothes for only nine months. Maternity clothes that can be worn after the baby's born won't end up in the back of your closet. Jumpers can be the mainstay of your maternity wardrobe because they can be easily dressed up or down.

In addition, sporty men's sweatpants and jogging shorts, low pumps and sandals, pullover sweaters, and shawls and capes can continue to be worn long after baby's arrival.

Once again, don't overlook the major off-price chains—Ross, Marshall's, and T.J. Maxx—for great buys on maternity and kids' wear.

By following these tips as you shop, you're bound to come out the winner in the battle with high retail prices.

Dan Howard's Maternity Factory

Beaverton: 4005 S.W. 117th Ave. *(Canyon Place)* ☎ 643–1444
Hours: Mon–Wed 10–6, Thurs 10–9, Fri & Sat 10–6, Sun 12–5

Because this nationwide chain designs and manufactures much of the merchandise they sell (although they do carry other well-known lines), they can offer factory direct prices of up to 25% to 50% off. You'll find an extensive selection of maternity fashions for leisure or career wear in sizes 4–24. Get on their mailing list to find out in advance about sales and promotional events.

Checks, Credit cards

Hanna Andersson Outlet Store

Lake Oswego: 9 Monroe Parkway *(Town Square at Mountain Park)*
☎ 697–1953
Hours: Mon–Fri 10–6, Sat 10–5, Sun 12–5

This outlet store offers stylish, top-quality, all-cotton Swedish children's clothing, including dresses, jumpsuits, coats, hats, and mittens at prices 20% to 50% off retail. Most of their clothing—brightly colored, 100% cotton, washable, and durable—is made in Sweden. Hanna Andersson also operates a regular retail and mail-order business at 327 N.W. 10th in Portland and sends discontinued and unsold seasonal merchandise to its outlet store, where prices are slashed. Get on their mailing list to find out in advance about seasonal "blow-out" sales, when they discount merchandise up to 70%. Although children's clothing is their main focus, they also carry a limited stock of women's clothing—underwear, night gowns, socks, sweaters, and Swedish clogs.

Checks, Credit cards

Kids Mart

Beaverton: 4005 S.W. 117th Ave. *(Canyon Place)* ☎ 646–5991
Clackamas: 8946 S.E. Sunnyside Rd. *(Clackamas Promenade)* ☎ 652–9043
Gresham: 610 N.W. Eastman Pkwy. *(Gresham Towne Center)* ☎ 669–0252
Hillsboro: 2323 S.E. Tualatin Valley Hwy. *(Sunset Esplanade)* ☎ 640–6907
Vancouver: 8101 N.E. Parkway Dr. ☎ 253–2388
Hours: Mon–Fri 10–9, Sat 10–6, Sun 12–5

Kids Mart, the nation's largest chain of children's clothing stores, offers name-brand clothing (as well as clothes made especially for them) at everyday low prices. Pre-teens go for the trendy cotton knits and denim, while the hard-core bargain shoppers head for the clearance rack where incredible buys can be made. There are absolutely no problems with returns or exchanges. Get on their mailing list for advance notice of periodic sales.

Checks, Credit cards

Mothercare

Portland: 12000 S.E. 82nd Ave *(Clackamas Town Center)* ☎ 659–8247
Hours: Mon–Fri 10–9, Sat 10–6, Sun 11–5

There are 200 Mothercare shops throughout England and 30 in the U.S., but only one in the Pacific Northwest. They offer quality maternity clothing, layette, newborns to toddler (4T) for boys and girls, and most at discount prices. We found maternity dresses priced from $12 to $22 and, with spring in the air, clearance prices of 40% off winter clothes. They had a good selection of discount-priced dresses, shirts, pants, swimsuits, cover-ups, and bras for moms-to-be, and all carrying Mothercare's own special design and label.

Checks, Credit cards

Consignment & Resale Shops

Consignment and resale stores have been popping up like mushrooms to meet the increasing demand for good-quality recycled kids' and maternity clothing. Most of these stores are selective about the condition of the clothes they accept. They offer bargain shoppers—particularly those with lots of youngsters—an attractive way around the high cost of clothing.

Especially good buys can be found on such things as dress clothes and dress shoes, snowsuits, coats, and layettes—items that will be almost-good-as-new because they never really get worn that much.

In addition to clothing, you'll find children's furniture, carseats, toys, strollers, high chairs, and more at substantial savings. Another nice thing about these shops: they're great places to resell your own kids' clothing—a real advantage when you consider how fast kids outgrow things.

Baby and Me

Portland: 12595-B N.W. Cornell Rd. ☎ 646–2021
Hours: Mon–Fri 10–5:30, Sat 10–5

Lots of gently worn clothing for boys and girls from infants through size 12 fill Baby and Me. You'll also find maternity wear, books, games, toys, and a continually changing stock of baby furniture at 35% to 45% off original prices. *Buster Brown* and *Healthtex* seconds, as well as hand-crafted clothing at good prices, are tucked in with the rest of the stock. After 60 days, merchandise is marked down 25%. Watch for their seasonal sales for even bigger savings.

Checks, Credit cards

Gingerbread Express

Portland: 4410 N.W. Tillamook ☎ 284–2908
Hours: Mon–Sat 10–5

This shop carries a large selection of "pre-owned" children's clothes (sizes 0–14) and baby equipment—strollers, cribs, car seats, changing tables, carriers, bassinets, walkers, swings, and toys—at 50% or more off original prices. They have lots of new 100% cotton clothes, including name brands, at 30% off. Check out the winter and spring clearance sales as well as the bargain racks, where items are reduced an additional 50%. You'll also find a large stock of tights, hats, shoes, quilts, and leggings.

Checks, Credit cards

Kiddie Shack

Portland: 3737 S.E. Gladstone ☎ 775–4511
Hours: Mon–Fri 1–6, Sat 10–6

This small shop carries clothing for boys and girls in newborn to size 4T and a limited amount of baby furniture and toys. We saw several strollers and walkers at $12 apiece. New outfits (priced 30% off retail) are tucked in with the rest of the inventory. Used clothing goes for around 80% off original retail. New shoes (sizes 0–8) are about 10% off suggested retail. Watch for their big clearance sales in January and August. Merchandise in the store more than 60 days gets put on the dollar rack.

Checks

The Kids Closet
Portland: 12227 S.E. Stark ☎ 254–0610
Hours: Mon–Sat 10–5:30

Lots of clothing, mostly new, for infants through size 14 fill The Kids Closet. Their new clothing includes several brand names and sells for 20% or more off regular retail prices. A good selection of new and used baby furniture can be found, as well as new strollers and walkers for one-third to one-half off retail. Fashionable girls' blouses, usually $12.95 elsewhere, are priced at $4.95. The shop's best seller, *Baby's Choice* disposable diapers, runs $40 a case in the markets, but sells here for $25; folks come from miles around to scoop them up. Watch for their periodic sales, especially their biggest one that takes place after Christmas.

Checks, Credit cards

Kids Collection
Milwaukie: 10613 S.E. Main ☎ 654–7556
Hours: Tues–Sat 10–5

Clothing for newborns to size 14 and junior sizes 1–13 plus shoes, baby furniture, books, games, toys, and quilts fill this store. Many new items pop up, as well as such labels as *Esprit, Oshkosh, Guess,* and *Healthtex*—all at discounted prices. We found a nice child's coat, usually priced at $60, marked down to $20, and infant sleepers that ranged from $2.95 to $4.50. Check out the $1 and $3 racks for incredible bargains. The day we checked the shop was conducting a winter sale, where many items were further discounted 30% to 50%.

Checks

Kids Count Two
Gresham: 64 N.E. Division ☎ 667–3416
Hours: Mon–Fri 9–6, Sat 10–5

The owner is very picky about what she takes, and many items look almost new. You'll find a great selection of neatly displayed children's clothing from newborn to size 14 and junior sizes 1, 3, and 5 at up to 75% off retail. Dresses, usually $25, are priced from $7.95 to $9.95, and T-shirts under $2. In addition, the store carries never-worn sample merchandise in size 3 months, 12 months, 2, 4, and 10 at 40% off original prices. Shoes, baby furniture, books, games, and toys are good buys. Check out the bargain corner, where slow-moving merchandise is sent—but not for long.

Checks, Credit cards

Kids Exchange

Oregon City: 1678 S. Beavercreek Rd. ☎ 657–8052
Hours: Mon–Fri 10–6, Sat 10–5, Sun 12–5

For eight years, Kids Exchange has been offering gently worn clothing for infants to size 14 at prices 65% to 75% off original retail. Brand names pop up occasionally, as do incredible buys, especially on the $1 rack. After 90 days, merchandise gets marked down 50% and then soon thereafter sent over to the $1 rack for a quick exit.

Checks, Credit cards

Kids Only

Portland: 3249 S.E. Division ☎ 236–0060
Hours: Mon–Sat 9–6

At Kids Only you'll find a variety of quality, hardly worn children's clothing at low prices. The owners are picky about what they accept, which results in a good selection of gently used kids' wear. Although most of their stock is used, the day we checked the shop had just gotten in two dozen new *Dehen* sweaters marked at $6 each. They also carry shoes, strollers, baby furniture, and some toys.

Checks, Credit cards

Mulberry Bush

Tualatin: 19279 S.W. Martinazzi Ave. *(Martinazzi Square)* ☎ 691–1119
Hours: Mon–Sat 10–6

This store has the look and feel of a boutique. With its attractive displays and stylish merchandise, it's a real treat to shop. Clothing ranges from infants through size 7 for boys and girls. You'll find a large selection of new maternity and children's overstocks and samples, usually at 25% to 50% off department-store prices. Well-known labels, including *Oshkosh* and *Healthtex*, are mixed in with the rest of the inventory. The Mulberry Bush also carries a small amount of previously owned baby furniture and new plush toys at reduced prices. Watch for their periodic sales.

Checks, Credit cards

Second Generation

Portland: 4029 S.E. Hawthorne Blvd. ☎ 233–8130
Hours: Mon–Sat 10–5:30

This shop offers a full selection of both quality resale and new maternity and children's clothing, most in natural fibers. New clothing is moderately priced, while all used items are marked down to one-third or less of original prices. Their maternity selection, probably the largest in Portland, incudes tops, pants, dresses, nightgowns, and several styles of 100% cotton nursing bras. The children's clothing, many of which are 100% cotton items, are from newborn through size 6X, and can be found at up to 40% off during the shop's periodic sales. Pregnancy and child-care books, natural toiletries, *Nikky* wool and cotton diaper covers, and gifts for children and new moms round out the inventory.

Checks, Credit cards

Spanky's

Vancouver: 812 Main ☎ (206)693–5115
Hours: Mon–Sat 10–5:30

Spanky's has gently worn children's clothing from newborns to girls' size 14 and up to boys' size XXL, as well as baby gifts, maternity wear, and women's casual and career wear. *Guess* jeans for girls sell for $10 to $12; those for boys go for $6 to $8. Brand names turn up frequently, and women's two-piece dress-for-success suits are good buys. After 90 days, inventory is marked down an additional 50%.

Checks, Credit cards

The Toy Box

Hillsboro: 123 N.E. Third ☎ 648–0107
Hours: Mon–Fri 10–5, Sat 10–4

As you'd expect by its name, this shop carries a large inventory of toys and games (in addition to new and used children's clothing and footwear). You'll also find baby furniture—car seats, strollers, changing tables, and cribs—at prices from 50% to 70% off the originals. In addition to its periodic sales, The Toy Box marks down inventory 30% after 30 days. A nice feature here is that you can drop the kids off at the in-store play area while you ferret out those bargains.

Checks, Credit cards

Trudy's Kinderstube

Portland: 3570 S.W. Troy *(Multnomah Village)* ☎ 244–8368
Hours: Mon–Fri 9–5:30, Sat 9:30–5

At Trudy's "cozy children's room" (that's what Kinderstube means in German), you'll find carefully selected children's clothing from infants to size 14, all nicely displayed and perfectly reconditioned. Trudy washes, line dries, and irons all clothing—and being a fine seamstress, she does any mending herself. In addition, Trudy makes sweatpants in sizes 2–6X that sell for $7.95 to $10.95. These handmade creations are stitched with French seams and non-roll elastic waists and are snapped up nearly as soon as they're finished. From her quaint Multnomah Village shop, Trudy's been offering top-quality clothing at low prices for over ten years.

Checks

We Love Kids
Milwaukie: 11200 S.E. Fuller Rd. ☎ 775–9946
Hours: Mon–Sat 10–6

We Love Kids carries clothing from newborn to size 12 for boys and girls. Such labels as *Oshkosh, Healthtex, Cherokee, Levi's*, and *Disney* appear regularly, as does a small amount of new clothing. You'll also find new and used toys and an occasional piece of furniture, which goes very quickly. On average, you can expect to pay around $3 to $4 for their gently worn children's clothing.

Checks

Wee Three
Beaverton: 4825 S.W. Hall Blvd. ☎ 644–5953
Hours: Mon–Fri 9–5, Sat 10–5

Gently worn children's clothing and footwear, including labels as *Healthtex, Levi's, Carters*, and *Oshkosh*, can be found here at 50% or more off department-store prices. All clothing is sorted, sized, and neatly displayed in this bright, cheery shop (located in a little old house on Hall). After 30 days, inventory is marked down 20% (color-coded tags). There's a playroom for the kids while the grown-ups shop.

Checks, Credit cards

Shoes & Accessories

In addition to shopping those stores in this section, be sure to check out such off-price chains as T.J. Maxx, Ross, Marshall's, and Burlington Coat Factory, which offer reasonably priced shoes and accessories for the whole family. Fashion jewelry, purses, bags, belts, scarves, ties, hats, hosiery, and wallets are always discounted 30% or more off retail.

Smart bargain accessory buyers can save a lot of money in consignment shops, where accessories are usually inexpensive and plentiful. Of course, you may have to dig into bins and racks in search of that perfect bargain scarf or tie. At such bargain prices, however, you may just want accessories for every outfit!

The lowest-priced discount footwear chains in the Portland area are Volume Shoe Source and Picway, which specialize in basic styles, synthetic materials, and great prices on name-brand athletic shoes. Be sure to check out the stores in our Sporting Goods section for more great buys on athletic shoes.

Al's Shoes

Portland: 5811 S.E. 82nd ☎ 771–2130
Hours: Mon–Fri 10–8, Sat 10–6

This local family-owned store offers friendly, helpful service and discounts of 10% to 15% or more on all their footwear, which includes such lines as *Timberline, Hush Puppies, Streetcars, Converse,* and *New Balance.* Al's carries a large stock of casual and dressy shoes, boots, and active sports-footwear—all at discounted prices and in a wide range of styles and sizes. Watch for their periodic sales and check out the bargain shelves, where odd sizes are marked way down. The staff will make you feel like you're back in the '50s in your small-town neighborhood shoe store.

Checks, Credit cards

B & R Sportshoes

Portland: 2940 N.E. Alberta ☎ 281–5819
Hours: Mon–Fri 10–7, Sat 10–6, Sun 12–5

B & R Sportshoes carries men's, women's, and children's shoes for walking, running, tennis, basketball, soccer, aerobics, and casual wear from such manufacturers as *Nike, Saucony, Adidas, L.A. Gear, Avia, Converse,* and *Starter.* All their shoes are regularly discounted 15% off suggested retail, and four times a year they hold big "two for one" shoe sales. In addition, they carry a small amount of sportswear, including starter jackets and "crinkle" warm-ups that usually retail for around $95 but run under $50 here.

Checks, Credit cards

Big Bang

Clackamas: 8960 S.E. Sunnyside Rd. *(Clackamas Promenade)* ☎ 653–2630
Portland: 616 S.W. Park ☎ 653–2630
Hours: Clackamas, Mon–Sat 11–7, Sun 12–5; Portland, Mon–Sat 11–7

If you'd like to accessorize your outfits with creative and unusual fashion jewelry (especially at prices generally from $2 to $10), Big Bang is the place for you. There are lots of earring hoops, but why not try something more adventuresome to hang from your ears, such as goldfish, tiny globes, peace symbols, or miniature skeletons at $2 each. How about some handmade Indian bangles for 50 cents apiece, large-stoned cocktail rings for $10, or cat's eyes vintage-style sunglasses, also for $10? Lots of vintage clothing and bargain racks of wool sweaters, shirts, and jackets for $5, as well as men's classic bowties ($6) and tie clips ($4) round out the inventory. Stop by their warehouse downtown above their second floor, where you'll find jewelry, clothing, hairpieces, and tons of other accessories starting at 50 cents. Some truly incredible bargains await you up there.

Checks, Credit cards

The Chinook Outfitters
Lake Oswego: 149 A Ave. ☎ 635–4566
Hours: Mon–Fri 10–5

This company has its shoes, hiking boots, and outdoor footwear made in the Orient and sells the seconds and samples at low wholesale prices in this small location attached to the company administrative office. Most of the inventory just happens to be for men with size 8 feet (because that's the sample size that looks the "cutest" when showing to corporate customers). Gore-Tex hiking boots that run from $70 to $120 in the department stores go for $40 to $80 here. All-leather boat shoes are priced at $25 or two for $40. A nice selection of sport bags, nylon gym bags, and belts rounds out the stock.

Checks

Cowtown Boots Factory Store
Beaverton: 4130 S.W. 117th Ave. ☎ 646–0609
Hours: Mon–Sat 10–6

Cow punchers and city slickers (including juniors and seniors) shop here for good buys on top quality handmade boots. Because everything in this boot store is made especially for them, they're able to offer factory-direct prices— prices so low you can probably pick up a couple of pairs for the price you'd pay for just one pair elsewhere. Handmade, all-leather Ropers were sale priced at $49.95, while a pair of elegant, long-lasting Sharkskin boots was $79.95. Styles range from your basic workboots to popular dressboots in snake or genuine Teju lizard hides. Watch for their year-end sale where they knock off around 20% on most merchandise.

Checks, Credit cards

Danner Factory Outlet
Portland: 12722 N.E. Airport Way ☎ 251–1111
Hours: Mon–Sat 9–5

This outlet, inside the Danner Shoe Manufacturing Company, carries boots and shoes for every kind of outdoorsman, including a small selection of women's footwear. These are factory seconds, meaning that there's a nick in the leather or a stitch is crooked, but chances are you'll have to search hard to find the defect. All footwear is tagged to indicate what kind of cosmetic boo-boo was made. But there's no defect in the prices of these top-quality factory seconds. We found Gore-Tex-lined hiking boots ranging from $65 to $90 compared with $100 to $160 elsewhere. There are no sales promotions on their everyday low-priced seconds, but every Thanksgiving you'll find 20% off the regular retail for their many first-quality boots that they display at the factory outlet store.

Checks, Credit cards

Details By Patricia

Portland: 1238 N.W. Glisan St. (97209) ☎ 222–0115
Hours: Periodic sales

This company manufactures fashionable women's belts in leather and fabrics that retail for $30 to $85 in department stores and specialty shops all over the U.S. Several times a year they convert the showroom at their manufacturing site into an outlet and hold some incredible sales on samples and last season's belts. At a recent sale wrapper belts that retailed for $30 were priced at $5, and a huge stock of "high-end" leather belts were $5 to $30. To get on the mailing list and receive advance notice of upcoming sales, drop them a postcard. Sometimes they'll run an ad in *Downtowner* or *Willamette Week* announcing a sale.

Checks, Credit cards

Jaylee's Handbag Factory Outlet

Portland: 8030 S.E. Harold ☎ 777–2269
Hours: Mon–Fri 8:30–5:30

Jaylee's offers a wide selection of quality handbags, sport bags, and garment bags in synthetic leather, canvas, and tapestry at below-wholesale prices. We found handbags for $5 to $15, and synthetic leather garment bags for $6. These bags are overruns, discontinued colors, or quality factory seconds (minor blemishes, crooked stitches).

Checks, Credit cards

Nike Factory Outlet

Portland: 3044 N.E. M.L. King Blvd. *(Union)* ☎ 281–5901
Hours: Mon–Fri 10–7, Sat 10–6, Sun 11–5

No way does this outlet resemble the futuristic, flashy Nike store downtown, but you will find shoes, shorts, socks, bags, sweats, and T-shirts at 25% to 50% off retail. They stock last-season's merchandise as well as discontinued and irregular merchandise that will please the whole family. Any defects in the shoes are cosmetic and would not affect their performance. We found men's *Nike Air Advantage* tennis shoes at $49.95 ($75 elsewhere), plus a huge stock of T-shirts starting at $2.95.

Checks, Credit cards

McGee's Blinds & Awnings

Portland: 3525 S.E. Hawthorne Blvd. ☎ 235–6591
Hours: Mon–Fri 8–4:30

What does a canvas awning manufacturer do with scraps and leftovers too small to use? Why of course they make tote bags! These rugged, handy, 15" canvas striped bags (which might resemble your neighbor's awning) sell for $8 apiece, about half of what similar bags would cost. They last forever and are capable of holding some pretty heavy weights. They also make use of materials that would otherwise be thrown out.

Checks, Credit cards

Nordstrom Shoe Rack

Clackamas: 8930 S.E. Sunnyside Rd. *(Clackamas Promenade)* ☎ 654–5415
Portland: 401 S.W. Morrison ☎ 299–1815
Hours: Clackamas, Mon–Thurs 9:30–8, Fri 9:30–9, Sat 9:30–7, Sun 11–6; Portland, Mon–Fri 10–9, Sat 10–7, Sun 11–6

This is probably the best place around to get incredible buys on a wide selection of quality, fashionable shoes and boots (even hard-to-find women's shoes to size 12). Pretty much whatever you'll find at their regular retail level will be reflected here at the rack, both as to styles and range of sizes. Watch for their periodic sales, especially the one after Christmas, when you'll find dress shoes and boots at rock-bottom prices.

Checks, Credit cards

Picway Shoes

Gresham: 302 N.W. Eastman Pkwy. *(Gresham Town Fair)* ☎ 661–1706
Hillsboro: 2231 S.E. Tualatin Valley Hwy. *(Sunset Esplanade)* ☎ 640–6270
Portland: 12154 S.E. Division St. *(Division Center)* ☎ 760–9394
    7901 S.E. Powell *(Powell St. Station)* ☎ 771–0542
    619 S.W. Alder ☎ 223–7831
    11384 S.E. 82nd Ave. *(Clackamas Square)* ☎ 654–7811
Salem: 703 Lancaster Dr. N.E. ☎ 370–9231
Vancouver: 8101 N.E. Parkway ☎ (206)256–2867
    7425 N.E. Highway 99 ☎ (206)693–2077
Hours: Generally, Mon–Sat 10–9, Sun 10–6

This chain offers discount footwear in a full range of sizes for the whole family. They carry dressy and casual footwear as well as name-brand athletic shoes such as *L.A. Gear* and *Reebok* at prices below department and specialty stores. Hard-to-find sizes, such as women's size 12, plus a good selection of non-leather shoes start at $13.99 to $16.99, and sales on selected footwear take place every couple of weeks. When we checked, they were running a $5 off sale on their non-major brands of athletic shoes.

Checks, Credit cards

Volume Shoe Source

Locations: Over 20 locations in the area. Check the Yellow Pages.
Hours: Generally, Mon–Fri 10–9, Sat 10–6, Sun 11–6

You don't have to buy in volume to pick up great low prices. They carry dressy and casual shoes for men (sizes 6 $\frac{1}{2}$–13), women (sizes 5–12), and kids' that range from $11.99 to around $50. Their own brand of athletic shoes, *Pro Wings*, runs around $12 to $20. You'll find a good selection of non–leather shoes (canvas or vinyl). When we checked, their women's dress shoes were marked $2 to $10 off regular prices. Watch for their sale ads in the newspapers or on TV.

Checks, Credit cards

Formal Wear, Bridal Attire & Vintage Clothes

Formal Wear & Bridal Attire

Fancy "duds," elegant evening wear, wedding dresses, and tuxedos can be expensive purchases when you consider how few times you'll wear these outfits. Renting makes good economic sense if you're only planning to wear these outfits once in a great while. While men have long been renting tuxes, women are discovering rental garments for formal occasions.

To be able to buy deluxe for few bucks, you'll have to hit the big sales at formal wear rental shops. You'll find second-hand tuxedos and wedding gowns, many in top-notch condition, discounted well below new retail prices.

Additional sources of formal and bridal wear may be found in the sections on Women's Consignment & Resale shops, Charity Resale Thrift Shops, and Menswear. Also, check out the newspaper classified ads under "clothing" for some terrific buys.

A-Bra Boutique

Portland: 2548 S.E. 122nd Ave. ☎ 760–3589
Hours: Mon–Thur 10–6, Fri 10–3

This shop carries strapless bras, wedding stockings, honeymoon lingerie, gloves, and hairpieces, as well as new gowns and formals. You'll find big savings on their used wedding gowns that range from $25 to $450 ($250 to $700 for new) and used veils that go for $40 to $85 (new veils run $50 to $120) and used formals for $20 to $130. Also available are used dresses and hats for the mother of the bride and flower girls.

Checks, Credit cards

An International World of Weddings

Aloha: 17943 S.W. Tualatin Valley Hwy. ☎ 649–9583
Portland: 4012 S.E. 82nd Ave. *(Eastport Plaza)* ☎ 774–4240
Hours: Aloha, Mon–Sat 10–6; Portland, Mon–Sat 10–9

We found hundreds of wedding gowns in all the latest designer fashions (in sizes 3–26½) renting for $110 to $300. Bridesmaid gowns in sizes 4–20 in satin, chiffon, taffeta, and lace over satin were available for rent in the $45 to $65 range. Mother-of-the-bride dresses rented for $55 to $125 (about one-third of what it would cost to buy them), flower girl dresses rented in the $45 to $50 range, and veils for $25 to $75. Watch for their ads or call to find out about their big sales, where rental dresses can be purchased at up to 70% off.

Checks, Credit cards

Belle & Bow Tie Tux
Portland: 4306 N.E. Hancock ☎ 284–5969
Hours: Mon–Sat 10–7, Sun 12–5
Of all their locations, only the Hollywood store rents wedding gowns. We counted 15 gowns in styles that were about one to two years old and renting in the $100 to $200 range.

Checks, Credit cards

Black Tie Formal Wear
Beaverton: 11917 S.W. Canyon Rd. ☎ 626–2418
Clackamas: 9757 S.E. Sunnyside Rd. ☎ 659–1538
Hours: Mon–Fri 10–9, Sat 10–6, Sun 12–5
Black Tie rents and sells, so whether you're hearing wedding bells, planning a gala bash, or looking for a great-looking Halloween costume, you'll find all your tux and accessory needs at low prices at Black Tie. New, all-wool tuxedos start at $199, while used designer-label tuxes can be picked up for half that. We found used shirts for $12.50, shoes for $10, and ties and cummerbunds for around $7.50 a set. If they don't have your size in the store, they can get it in three days from their warehouse. For even bigger savings, shop their annual mid-October warehouse sale held in their Clackamas store. You'll find some incredible buys on used items, such as shirts for $1, pants and coats for $5 apiece, and ties and cummerbunds at 50 cents each. Towards the end of the warehouse sale, all unsold merchandise is practically given away.

Checks, Credit cards

The Bridal Arts Building
Vancouver: 10017–A N.E. Sixth Ave. ☎ (206)574–7758
Hours: Mon–Sat 10–6, Sun 12–5
They advertise that you'll find "All your wedding needs under one roof," which seems to be the case when you discover a photographer, florist, cakemaker, caterer, and gown and accessory shop all in this building. Both the current and previous season's wedding gowns in sizes 6–20 rent for $100 to $300. The inventory is large, with three to six gowns in each size. New gowns from last season (never rented or worn) run from $200 to $500, while season–old rental gowns are priced under $75.

Checks, Credit cards

Cromwell Formal Wear

Portland: 711 S.W. 14th ☎ 226–4356
Hours: Mon & Fri 10–8, Tues–Thurs 10–6, Sat 10–5

You'll find used tuxes being sold only at Cromwell's downtown location. Used coats and pants go for $115 to $135 a set, with shoes priced from $5 to $15. These basic style tuxes are also available in children's sizes for about the same prices. Although you'll find used tuxes being sold year-round, the biggest selection is in late September and early October.

Checks, Credit cards

Gingiss Formalwear

Beaverton: 11751 S.W. Beaverton-Hillsdale Hwy. *(Beaverton Town Square)* ☎ 643–7022
Portland: 12000 S.E. 82nd Ave. *(Clackamas Town Center)* ☎ 653–7668
Vancouver: 5001 N.E. Thurston Way *(Vancouver Mall)* ☎ 256–6424
Hours: Mon–Fri 10–9, Sat 10–6, Sun 12–5

Although Gingiss sells used tuxes year-round, you'll find the biggest selection in the fall when they're restocking and making room for new tuxes by selling off the used. Used coats and pants go for $80 a set, shirts are $10, and shoes go for $20. New cummerbunds and bow ties are priced at $10 and up (used not available). If you call with your size, they'll gladly check their stock for you.

Checks, Credit cards

La Haie's

Hillsboro: 277 E. Main ☎ 648–2341
Hours: Mon–Fri 9–7, Sat 9–5:30, Sun 12–4

This men's shop sells used tuxes ($400 when new) at prices ranging from $80 to $180, depending on condition. Black cummerbunds and bow ties sell for $21 when new, and $15 if used. Used patent leather shoes go for $15 (new, $55), and used shirts at a fraction of the new prices. It's probably not a bad idea to buy shirts new instead of used, since most of the used shirts have yellowed and show heavy wear. You'll find the biggest selection of used tuxes in October, when the shop restocks and holds its close-out sale to move the old inventory.

Checks, Credit cards

Mr. Formal

Portland: 1205 S.E. Grand Ave. ☎ 232–1542
Hours: Annual sale

The whole year Mr. Formal rents and sells new tuxes. But only in the middle of October do they hold a huge "warehouse" sale at their Grand Ave. store (call for exact dates) and sell used and discontinued tuxes at great savings. At this sale they also mark down new tuxes and shoes. Used tux jackets (black) go for $85 to $95, while used pants are priced from $30 to $35 and shoes around $10. New tuxes that ordinarily sell for $325 are marked down to around $250 and new shoes are discounted 20% at the October sale.

Checks, Credit cards

Satin Doll
Portland: 8111 S.E. Flavel ☎ 774–0267
Hours: Mon–Wed 12–5, Thurs–Sat 12–6
Satin Doll sells a nice selection of new wedding gowns and attire They also have wedding gowns that you can rent for $75 to $275 and bridesmaid dresses that rent from $25 to $49. If your interest is in buying any of their previously rented gowns and dresses, the owner will be happy to negotiate sale prices with you.

Checks, Credit cards

Something Different Bridal and Formal Wear
Tigard: 12285 S.W. Main ☎ 620–1736
Hours: Mon–Thurs 11–7, Fri & Sat 11–5, Sun 12–4
You won't be leaving Something Different empty-handed. Wedding gowns rent for $150 to $500, and if you don't see anything you like in the shop, it's possible to choose a gown from one of the store's catalogs. (You will have to wait for the gown to reach the store, so order well in advance of the big day). There are a lot of stylish bridesmaid's dresses available to rent for $60 to $75, flower girl dresses (in sizes 4–12) run $40 to $55, and mother-of-the-bride dresses rent for $150. Look for some good buys at year's end when they sell their rental dresses.

Checks, Credit cards

Unique Bridal Fashions
Portland: 12233 S.E. Stark ☎ 252–3973
Hours: Tues, Wed, Fri 10–6, Thurs 10–7, Sat 10–4
Although you won't find any wedding gowns for rent here, you will find bridesmaids's dresses (sizes 4–44) renting at $45 and flower girl dresses (sizes 3–12) renting for $20 to $40. There's a large selection of different styles with at least one dress in each size.

Checks, Credit cards

Vintage Clothes

For you vintage clothing connoisseurs, the Portland area has a number of shops offering old period clothes. It may take a little digging to find just the right vintage clothes or accessories to develop your individual fashion style, but it's often worth it—and always fun!

In addition to those shops listed below, refer to the Women's Consignment & Resale Shops, Charity Resale Thrift Shops, and Menswear sections for additional sources of discount vintage threads.

Because each store's inventory is constantly changing, we have only listed the store names and given a brief description of what each carries.

Big Bang
Clackamas: 8960 S.E. Sunnyside Rd. *(Clackamas Promenade)* ☎ 653–2630
Hours: Mon–Sat 11–7, Sun 12–5
Women's.

Checks, Credit cards

Big Bang
Portland: 616 S.W. Park ☎ 274–1741
Hours: Mon–Sat 11–7 (Warehouse, Mon–Sat 12–5)
Men's, women's wedding attire.

Checks, Credit cards

Cal's Books & Wares
Portland: 732 S.W. First ☎ 222–5454
Hours: Mon–Fri 10–5:30, Sat 11–4
Women's.

Checks, Credit cards

Fashion Passion
Portland: 602 & 616 N.W. 23rd ☎ 223–4373
Hours: Tues–Sat 11:30–6, Sun 12–4
Men's, women's, rentals, and wedding attire.

Checks, Credit cards

Keep 'Em Flying
Portland: 510 N.W. 21st ☎ 221–0601
Hours: Mon–Sat 12–6, Sun 1–5
Men's and women's.

Checks, Credit cards

Nan's Glad Rags
Hillsboro: 1207 N.W. 231st ☎ 648–8463
Hours: Tues–Sat 10–5:30
Men's, women's, and rentals.

Checks, Credit cards

Ray's Ragtime

Portland: 1021 S.W. Morrison ☎ 226–2616
Hours: Mon–Sat 12–5

Men's, women's, and wedding dresses.

Checks, Credit cards

Reflections in Time

Portland: 1114 N.W. 21st ☎ 223–7880
Hours: Tues–Fri 11–6, Sat 12–5

Men's and women's.

Checks

Fine Jewelry

Whether you're looking for a good investment, an elegant gift, or something special for yourself, shop smart and you're bound to save big. Retail jewelry stores that offer low prices are usually located in smaller spaces far away from fancy mall locations. They buy direct, manufacture on the premises, and cut their overhead to the bone to pass on savings to their customers.

You'll find the best buys on quality gemstones and jewelry at wholesalers and brokers who sell to the public. Their showrooms may not be fancy and appointments are sometimes required, but you'll be delighted with the prices.

Only an expert can judge the value of a diamond, which will be based on four factors: color, clarity, cut, and carat weight (known as "the four Cs"). So before you buy any expensive jewelry, insist on an independent appraisal.

Another place to ferret out bargain-priced jewelry is at Best Products. Be sure to check out their low catalog prices when comparison shopping.

Affordable Jewelry

Portland: 304 S.W. Washington ☎ 227–4653
Hours: Mon–Fri 9–5

This small shop doesn't carry the large quantity of stock on its sales floor as the large jewelry stores do, but you'll be hard put to find bigger savings anywhere else. Whatever you want that is not on display can be ordered through catalogs and available in about a week. Their prices on loose stones and finished jewelry run anywhere from 50% to 65% off retail, and some items are even 90% off. Fourteen karat gold chains that sell for $25 per gram in other jewelry stores go for $11 per gram here. *Seiko* watches, in 14K gold nugget style with quartz movement, sell for around $2,000 to $2,500 elsewhere, but are priced at $600 here. Window shop the large jewelry stores, then give Affordable Jewelry a chance to save you a lot of money.

Checks, Credit cards

Alder Gold

Portland: 243 S.W. Alder ☎ 222–3492
Hours: Mon–Fri 7–5, Sat 8–1

Alder Gold sells loose diamonds, rubies, sapphires, and other precious stones, as well as a huge selection of finished jewelry at 25% to 75% off retail prices. For even bigger savings, you can buy precious stones loose and have them custom mounted, saving around 20% on the finished price of that same jewelry. They have a large stock of gold chains that they sell for $17 per gram (there are 31.1 grams in an ounce). They also sell used gold chain for $10 per gram. Gold and silver bullion, coins, *Rolex* watches, tennis bracelets, and estate jewelry are also available.

Checks, Credit cards

All That Glitters Loan & Jewelry Manufacturing

Portland: 515 S.W. 3rd ☎ 274–8702
Portland: 12200 S.E. Division ☎ 761–9699
Hours: Generally, Mon–Fri 9–6, Sat 11–5, Sun 1–5

The owner advertises, "We won't be undersold." You'll save 50% or more off their big inventory of wedding sets, diamonds, and precious gems. They specialize in custom design and manufacture of fine jewelry and pass along the incredible savings made possible when no middleman is involved. Their stock includes an exquisite selection of pre-owned European brand name gold watches (some with diamonds) that sell for $100 to $1,000. In addition to four expert goldsmiths on the premises, there's a gemologist available to answer any "stone" questions. Wander back to the pawn shop in the back of the store for more incredible buys.

Checks, Credit cards

Pacific Gold

Portland: 308 S.W. Alder ☎ 224–1650
Hours: Mon–Fri 7:30–5:30

This store offers discounts of around 65% off regular retail on loose precious stones, gold and silver jewelry, and watches. It sells gold chains for $12.50 per gram, while mainstream jewelers charge around $25 per gram. A diamond-enhanced strand of pearls priced at $10,000 here was seen elsewhere for three to four times that amount. The commissions they add to the prices of gold coins are 30% less than those charged by other coin dealers. *Seiko* 14K gold nugget watches priced at $700 here sell elsewhere for $2,000 to $2,500. Although Pacific Gold's keeps its inventory low to minimize overhead (and maximize savings passed on to the customer), they're able to order items carried by the larger jewelers.

Checks, Credit cards

Portland Gold Traders West

Beaverton: 4716 S.W. Scholls Ferry Rd. ☎ 292–4071
Hours: Mon–Sat 11–6

Portland Gold Traders offers new, pre-owned, and estate pieces at discounts of 50% or more. They have over 1,000 pieces to choose from, including rings, pendants, chains, bracelets, charms, and watches. A new 18K gold watch priced at $5,000 elsewhere carried a $1,650 price here, while gold chain prices were one-third or less of those found in major jewelry or department stores. You'll find big savings on their diamonds. Tell them the stone size, clarity, and color you want, and the owner will locate that diamond on the wholesale market, have it shipped to the store, and pass the savings along to you.

Checks

Prestige Investments

Portland: 901 S.W. Taylor ☎ 232–0020
Hours: By appointment only

Prestige is actually in the wholesale jewelry business, supplying many local stores with precious stones, watches, and finished jewelry. By appointment only, the firm offers to the general public its enormous stock of diamonds, pearls, rubies, sapphires, jade, emeralds, gold jewelry, and watches at prices 50% or more off retail prices. All of their precious stones are appraised by an independent gem lab according to strict Gem Institute of America Standards, so you can be assured of proper quality and grading.

Checks

The Shane Company

Tigard: 10124 Washington Square Rd. *(Washington Square Too)* ☎ 639–6505
Hours: Mon–Fri 10–9, Sat 10–6, Sun 11–6

The Shane Company guarantees the lowest prices around, and they'll refund the difference if you could've gotten a better price elsewhere. They carry the largest selection of wedding sets in Oregon, and you'll find their overall prices to be 20% to 50% lower than those at other jewelers. Choose from a large selection of loose gemstones (and the mounting can be done in the store the same day if you're in a rush). They also carry bracelets, pendants, necklaces, fashion rings, pearls, and other fine jewelry. Sales people are salaried, so you'll find them more friendly and helpful than pushy. The Shane Company guarantees all their merchandise and provides free certified appraisals with all jewelry purchases.

Checks, Credit cards

Food

Most people spend anywhere from $100 to $200 a week on groceries. This translates into big bucks each year—from $5,200 to $10,400. Careful shopping and a few diet changes could mean savings of several thousand dollars in a year!

By adhering to the following suggestions for trimming your food costs, you could reduce your food bills by 10% to 50%.

Check out the food ads and weekly grocery store supplements. Stock up on all the specials and "loss leaders" (terrifically good buys advertised just to get you into the store). Shop just once or twice a week and always take a list; this will save you time and help cut down on impulse buying.

Save money by taking advantage of merchandise coupons, store double coupons, and refund offers. Buy generic products and store brands, which are cheaper than nationally advertised products. Buy in bulk or the largest sizes available. If you can't freeze or store it all, get a few families together and share.

Buy in-season fruits and vegetables that are grown locally. They will taste better and be cheaper by not having been stored and trucked across the country. Try buying your produce from farmers or at farmers' markets. The savings will be substantial and the produce about as fresh as it gets.

Look for big discounts on such things as day-old bread, dented cans, torn labels, and bruised fruits and vegetables. These "seconds" are usually as nutritious as "firsts," and the prices will be much better. Always check your cash register receipts at the check-out for possible errors, especially on big purchases.

Perhaps the greatest savings can come about from basic changes in your eating habits. Avoid nutritionally empty snacks and high-priced convenience foods. Drink more water and make your own beverages and meals from scratch.

Food Warehouses

When you shop warehouse grocers, you'll find the whole range of foods—from fresh meat, produce, dairy, and baked goods to packaged, canned, and frozen items. Just like the local supermarket—except that you'll find things in five- or ten-pound containers. You might have to buy in case lots, although some warehouses will break up case lots and sell individual cans or packages.

In addition to food items, the typical warehouse grocer may carry bar supplies, paper products, cleansers, industrial supplies, kitchenware, cookware, and equipment.

Even when you buy in volume, it's best to comparison shop. A regular supermarket's loss leaders could just be the best prices around. And don't forget to shop Costco, where you'll find consistent low pricing on everything from soup to nuts.

The Bee Co.
Portland: 800 N. Killingsworth St. ☎ 283–3171
Hours: Mon–Sat 9:30–6

The Bee Company knocks 20% to 50% off retail prices of canned and packaged goods, frozen foods, deli products, beer, and wine, as well as pet foods, soaps, and detergents. You won't find milk, fresh meats, or fresh produce, but you will find a good selection of brand-name items from *Campbells, Oscar Meyer, Kellogg's, Purina, Betty Crocker, Folger's, Heinz,* etc. They're able to offer attractive discounts by buying close-outs, surplus, and goods damaged in shipping. Some great buys on the day we checked were: six-packs of imported Caribbean beer, regularly priced at $6, $1.99; 48-oz. bottles of vegetable oil, regularly $2.69 each, $1.49; Smucker's grape jelly in the 2-lb. jars, regularly retailing at $2.69, $1.19. Although they do carry the big #10 cans and 5-lb. jars (and some things can be found in case-lot size or in bulk), most items are sold in individual units. All products are separately priced, and new things come in daily. The store is located three blocks off the I-5 freeway.

Checks

Canned Foods Grocery Outlet
Beaverton: 3855 S.W. Murray ☎ 641–2970
Longview: 1946 Eighth Ave. ☎ (206)577–3663
Oregon City: 878 Molalla Ave. ☎ 655–7975
Salem: 299 D St. N.E. ☎ 581–1728
Vancouver: 5800 N.E. Fourth Plain ☎ (206)695–9257
Hours: Generally, Mon–Sat 9–6, Sun 11–5

With 68 locations in Oregon, Washington, California, Idaho, Utah, and Nevada, these outlets buy in quantity and pass along the savings to their customers. Each outlet is independently owned and operated. While there are no additional discounts on case-lot purchases, they do offer discounts of 25% to 40% off retail prices on all their merchandise. They deal with close-outs, surplus, factory seconds, and freight-damaged goods. All products are guaranteed and customers may return any merchandise with no questions asked. Although you won't find fresh produce, meats, or milk, each store carries a wide variety of canned, frozen, and packaged groceries from *Del*

Monte, Libby, Sara Lee, Kraft, Oscar Meyer, Smucker's, and others. Some great buys we noted were: *Del Monte* Vegetable Classics, with a regular retail price of $1.49 each, for $.49. *Ortega* Chile Salsa, regularly $2.99 for the 28-oz. jar, was $1.69; *Seven Seas* Italian Dressing in the 16-oz. bottle, with a regular price of $1.59, was $.89; *Top Shelf* dinners (10-oz. size) were $1.99 instead of $2.99.

Checks

Food For Less

Gresham: 2441 E. Powell Valley Blvd. ☎ 669–8520
McMinnville: 2410 N. Highway 99 ☎ 472–0494
Portland: 7979 S.E. Powell Blvd. ☎ 774–4665
Salem: 1517 Hawthorne N.E. ☎ 363–2477
Tualatin: 17942 S.W. McEwan Rd. ☎ 624–0537
Hours: Daily, 24 hours exept Christmas Day

These independently owned and operated grocery stores are committed to offering customers the lowest overall prices on everyday items sold by the major chain grocery operations. However, Food For Less concentrates on basic everyday items, not on specialty foods. While there are no mark-down sections and no discounts for case-lot purchases, we noted discounts on most items. *Nice 'N Soft* toilet tissue (12-pack), $2.99 to $3.79 at the majors, was only $1.99; *Top Ramen* noodles (3-oz. packs) were 10 cents each instead of 25 cents; *Best Foods* Mayonnaise (32-oz.), retailing for $1.69 to $2.38 elsewhere, was only $1.27; *Pampers* diapers (32 count), $9.99 to $10.99 at the major's, was $8.99. Big savings can be found on the "institutional" aisle, where large containers of fruits and vegetables may be found. Even bigger savings are available to customers who apply for the "ESP" (electronic savings program) club card. Card holders receive additional discounts of 5 to 50 cents off selected items.

Checks

Reser's Thrift Store

Beaverton: 15570 S.W. Jenkins Rd. ☎ 643–6431
Hours: Mon–Fri 11–6

This is a small outlet store (adjacent to the factory) carrying such food items as salads, meats, jerky, pepperoni and pizzas at prices up to 50% off retail. The food items are high quality, although some are close to the code date or are factory seconds (i.e., pizzas that aren't quite the right shape or pepperoni sticks that are not wrapped tightly). We noted great prices on pizzas that sold for about 50% off the price of comparable pizzas found at a large grocery store chain. Also, on the day we checked, they were selling 8-lb. cartons of salad for $1 per carton. The merchandise changes almost daily, so call ahead to see if they have what you're looking for.

Checks

United Grocers Cash & Carry
Aloha: 3950 S.W. 170th ☎ 649–4903
Clackamas: 15700 S.E. 82nd Dr. ☎ 655–6045
Gresham: 2521 N.W. Division ☎ 666–6868
Portland: 731 S.W. Stephens ☎ 232–7157
  6433 S.E. Lake Rd. ☎ 652–7357
  910 N. Hayden Meadows ☎ 289–1022
Salem: 1355 Salem Industrial Rd. N.E. ☎ 363–5731
Hours: Generally, daily 7–5

There are 33 Cash & Carry locations in Oregon, Washington, and California serving the grocery needs of businesses and nonprofit organizations. You'll find wholesale prices on packaged, canned, and frozen products, as well as on fresh meats, produce, and dairy. Purchases must be made in case or half-case lots except that #10 cans may be bought individually. Also, some produce may be purchased in small quantities, such as carrots in one- or five-pound bags. Although all prices are wholesale, keep in mind that a regular grocery chain could have an advertised special or loss-leader at a better price than the same item at Cash & Carry.

Checks

Bakery Goods

Buying day-old bakery goods, "seconds" (i.e., fresh but irregular or misshapen cookies), and even raw dough (bake the goodies yourself at home) can help ease the pressure on your food budget.

Most groceries with in-shop bakeries set aside a special place for day-old baked goods; local bakeries frequently do the same. Shop these sources early and you'll get the best pick of the day-old crop.

Bagel Land
Portland: 4118 N.E. Fremont ☎ 249–2848
Hours: Mon–Fri 7:30–6, Sat 8–5, Sun 8–1

You'll find great prices on day-old and fresh bagels here. A six-pack of day-old bagels goes for $1.15, while the same fresh goes for $1.95. You'll find plain, poppy seed, sesame seed, cinnamon and raisin, cheese, blueberry, and garlic varieties. Their wheat bagels are 100% whole wheat and no sugar, oil, preservatives, or bleached flours are ever used. Wholesale prices of $2.25 per doz. on fresh bagels (dozen-lots only) are available to nonprofit organizations who put in their orders at least 24 hours in advance.

Checks, Credit cards

Delphina's Thrift Store
Portland: 3310 N.W. Yeon St. ☎ 221–1829
Hours: Mon–Sat 10–4

Delphina's carries both day-old and freshly baked goods at prices below retail. Their day-old sourdough, whole wheat, and white breads all sell for 50% off the already-discounted fresh-bread retail prices. Fresh croissants, cinnamon rolls, and scones are sold at wholesale. For even bigger savings, watch for the periodic sales they hold to move occasional bakery overruns.

Checks

Franz Bakery

Aloha: 18075 S.W. Tualatin Valley Hwy ☎ 591–1414
Gresham: 331 N. Main ☎ 665–2152
Milwaukie: 15591 S.E. McLoughlin Blvd. ☎ 786–0394
Portland: 340 N.E. 11th ☎ 232–2191
    11540 S.E. Foster ☎ 761–2412
    4926 S.E. Division ☎ 236–3660
    14510 S.E. Stark ☎ 254–5476
Salem: 1220 20th St. S.E. ☎ 362–3606
Tigard: 10840 S.W. Cascade ☎ 639–6806
Vancouver: 6701 N.E. Highway 99 ☎ (206)696–2546
Hours: Generally, Mon–Fri 9–6, Sat 9–5, some locations open Sun
These outlets sell day-old breads at 50% or more off retail and fresh doughnuts and pastries at about 30% off. We found white bread at three loaves for $1.09, wheat at five for $3.70, and Country Hearth brand at five for $4.40. We noted that a dozen day-old doughnuts were $1.09, while the fresh price for the same was $1.59. Ask about their "production-goof" sales, when they sell fresh doughnuts that didn't quite turn out right for 59 cents a dozen.

Checks

Grandma's Foods Factory Outlet

Beaverton: 6220 S.W. 112th ☎ 643–4711
Hours: Mon–Fri 9–5
The store is located in the factory and offers its own fresh-baked cookies that are irregular, misshapen, or low in weight. Savings of up to 50% (and sometimes more) can be found here. Grandma's makes eight varieties of cookies that can be purchased in bulk or individually packaged. We noted that their 3-in. cookies (two per pack) that sell elsewhere for 59 cents each pack go for only 21 cents each when purchased by the box of 60 packs. If you need less than a box, you may get them here for 30 cents a pack. Grandma's is a great place to shop for school parties, not only for the great prices, but also because the cookies are individually wrapped—something 'that most school districts require for health reasons.

Cash only

Helen Bernhard Bakery
Portland: 1717 N.E. Broadway ☎ 287–1251
Hours: Mon–Sat 6–6, Sun 8–4

On Sundays only, the Helen Bernhard Bakery offers day-old breads, donuts, cakes, and Danish at 50% off retail. This premiere bakery offers quality made-from-scratch baked goods, including a scrumptious thick-crusted sourdough made from a sourdough starter that dates from the '20s.

Checks

Nature Bake
Portland: 7831 S.E. Stark ☎ 257–7167
Hours: Mon–Thurs 8–6, Fri 8–5, Sun 10–6

You'll find a variety of quality whole-grain products at great savings in Nature Bake's factory outlet. These are the same baked goods carried at Fred Meyer Nutrition Centers and Nature's. We found day-old breads and buns at one-third off retail, while frozen day-old breads were one-half off. Day-old cookies and muffins were going for one-third off. They also carry bread of the Mill Creek label.

Checks, Credit cards

New York Bagel Boys
Beaverton: 11667 S.W. Beaverton-Hillsdale Hwy (*Beaverton Town Square*) ☎ 641–3552
Hours: Mon–Fri 9–9, Sat 9–6, Sun 12–5

For great prices on day-old bagels, be sure to shop this store early—these bagels go fast. Day-old bagels run $1.25 per half-dozen (30% off the price of fresh) and come in plain, raisin, onion, poppy seed, sesame seed, and more. If you can't make it in early, call and they'll hold some for you. Their freshly made bagels go for wholesale prices when you buy at least five dozen.

Checks

Oroweat Bakery Outlet Stores
Beaverton: 10750 S.W. 5th ☎ 643–5541
Gresham: 2450 N.W. 11 Mile Ave. ☎ 666–3845
Hillsboro: 429 S.W. Baseline ☎ 648–0909
Lake Oswego: 17450 S.W. Boones Ferry Rd. ☎ 635–3796
Milwaukie: 16585 S.E. McLoughlin Blvd. ☎ 653–6138
Salem: 3393 Silverton Rd. N.E. ☎ 362–1415
Vancouver: 618 Grand Ave. ☎ (206)696–4251
Hours: Mon–Fri 9–6, Sat 9–5:30

You'll find great savings on both fresh and day-old baked goods when you shop at Oroweat's thrift stores. Expect prices at 30% to 50% off retail. Specialty breads, such as Brannola, which sold fresh for $1.79 at a major supermarket, were selling at Oroweat for $1.12 fresh or 92 cents day-old.

A six-pack of fresh English muffins retailed for 69 cents, while day-old English muffins were going for $1.15 for three six-packs. Also, Archway cookies, Keebler potato chips, and small bags of Frito Lay chips were available here at better-than-supermarket prices.

Checks

Otis Spunkmeyer Cookies
Tigard: 10170 S.W. Nimbus Ave. ☎ 620–5455
Hours: Mon–Fri 8–5

You'll save over 50% per cookie when you buy their pre-formed cookie dough. This is the same dough that Spunkmeyer distributes to convenience stores, delis, and hotel food services. You have to buy the dough by the case, which runs $40 and makes about 20 dozen cookies. It works out to about 16 cents apiece for these large 3-in. cookies when you bake them yourself as compared to the retail price of 35 cents each. They have butter sugar, chocolate chip, chocolate chip with walnut, chocolate chip with pecans, and, of course, a double chocolate chip that is richer than Donald Trump. Their cookie dough moves so quickly we suggest calling ahead.

Checks

Pierre's French Bakery
Portland: 1011 S.E. Oak ☎ 233–8871
Hours: Mon–Fri 7:30–5, Sat 9–4

Pierre's sells day-old French bread, rolls, and buns at prices 50% off. Their fresh breads go at prices 30% off retail. We noted that a loaf of fresh French bread at Pierre's was 85 cents; the same loaf was $1.20 at a chain supermarket.

Checks

Portland Bagel Bakery & Delicatessen
Portland: 222 S.W. Fourth ☎ 242–2435
Hours: Mon–Fri 6:30–4:30, Sun 8:30–12:30

Mixed bags of day-old bagels go for $1.50 a half-dozen, a savings of 30% to 40% off regular fresh bagel prices. In these mixed bags, you'll find whole wheat, raisin, plain, onion, poppy seed, and other left-over varieties. They offer wholesale prices to nonprofit organizations that may buy as few as one dozen at a time.

Checks

Quality Pie Bakery
Portland: 1111 N.W. 23rd ☎ 223–8112
Hours: Mon–Fri 6:30–5

Day-old cream pies, donuts, and muffins are sold at 50% or more off retail. We found custard and pumpkin pies that sold for $5.25 fresh available for

$2.75 each as day-old. Fresh muffins that sold for 95 cents each were going for 30 cents the next day. Day-old donuts were selling for $1 a six-pack (45 cents each when fresh). Quality Pie does not offer day-old products on Mondays, and suggest that you call ahead as to availability and variety of day-old items. They'll gladly set aside any day-old when you call.

Checks

Simply Divine Deli
Oregon City: 358 Warner Milne ☎ 657–7122
710 Washington ☎ 655–1130
Hours: Warner Milne, Mon–Fri 7:30–5, Sat 11–3; Washington, Mon–Fri 10–3

You'll save both time and money when you buy Simply Divine's cookie dough and make your own freshly baked cookies. We found six varieties of dough, including chocolate chip, peanut butter, and oatmeal raisin, ranging from $2 to $2.25 per lb. You save nearly 50% when you buy the dough and bake the cookies at home yourself. Eight cookies made at home from a pound of dough would run 25 cents each; the same eight cookies bought already baked at the store were 46 cents each. Buy as much dough as you need (one pound minimum); you can always freeze the leftovers. While the store on Washington always has cookie dough, the one on Warner Milne needs 24 hours' notice to get it.

Checks

Val's Bagels
Clackamas: 11525 S.E. Highway 212 ☎ 656–2777
Hours: Mon & Tues, Thurs–Sat 8–5

Unlike the automated, machine-made bagels seen elsewhere, Val's premier bagels are made fresh and by hand. They offer mini-bagels (13 to a bag) and regular bagels (six to a bag) in plain, onion, cinnamon raisin, poppy seed, sesame seed, jalapeno, whole wheat with honey, and sourdough with honey. You'll save at least 25% off retail if you buy five bags or more and at least 35% when you purchase 20 bags or more. They require 48-hour advance notice to fill orders.

Checks

Williams Bakery Thrift Store
Gresham: 17408 S.E. Powell Blvd. ☎ 669–7872
Milwaukie: 8440 S.E. 45th ☎ 774–2699
Portland: 4444 S.W. Multnomah Blvd. ☎ 452–1929
Hours: Generally, Mon–Sat 9–6, Sun 10–5

These thrift stores carry day-old breads, doughnuts, cookies, and pastries at prices well below retail. We found McKenzie Farm bread at four loaves for $3.69 and Williams Bakery bread at three loaves for $1.09. Mother's cookies, which retail for $1.59 per doz. fresh, were 99 cents per doz. Ruth Ashbrook pastries, which retail for 69 cents each, were only 47 cents here. Also, take advantage of their low prices on *Nabisco* and *Frito Lay* chips.

Checks

Wonder Bread Bakery Thrift Shops
Albany: 3511 S.W. Pacific ☎ 928–3527
Beaverton: 13227 S.W. Canyon Rd. ☎ 626–3306
Hazel Dell: 6301 N. Highway 99 ☎ (206)693–7034
Portland: 115 N Cook ☎ 282–7506
Salem: 3590 Portland Rd. N.E. ☎ 364–0568
Hours: Mon–Sat 9–6, Sun 11–5

These thrift shops stretch from Longview, Washington to Roseburg, Oregon and offer complete lines of Hostess and Wonder products at 50% off retail. We found boxes of fresh Twinkies (eight per box) for $2.09, while the same fresh products at the supermarket were $3.99. Both fresh-baked and day-old loaves of Wonder white bread sold for 37 cents a loaf here, while in the supermarkets they were $1.49 a loaf for fresh. Although it hasn't always been this way, 75% of Wonder Bread Thrift Shop products are now as fresh as the same items sold in supermarkets.

Checks

You've Got It Made
Portland: 4620 S.W. Beaverton-Hillsdale Hwy ☎ 244–1985
Hours: Generally, Sun–Thurs 11–10

Although You've Got It Made is primarily a supplier of fresh-baked cookies to schools, hospitals, delis, etc., they can save you more than 50% off retail cookie prices when you buy their cookie dough (in 5-lb. lots only) and bake your own. Cookie dough comes in chocolate chip, oatmeal raisin, oatmeal peanut butter, or snickerdoodle. You'll pay between $1.35 and $2.25 per lb., depending on the kind you choose. Five pounds too much? Use all the dough you need and freeze the rest.

Checks

Eggs & Dairy Products

If you've got a houseful of growing kids who down eggs, milk, and cheese almost as quickly as they're out of the grocery bags, you'll be delighted to know about the sources in this section.

Although the companies listed here require quantity purchasing, you'll find the savings so attractive you're bound to walk out with a case of eggs, a cheese block or two, dozens of ice cream treats, and a tub of ice cream. If you can't use it all, share with relatives or friends on tight budgets.

Alpenrose Dairy

Portland: 6149 S.W. Shattuck Rd. ☎ 244–1133
Hours: Mon–Fri 8–1

Alpenrose sells ice cream treats and frozen novelties just like those available in supermarkets, except at wholesale prices. We noted that ice cream sandwiches went for $2.70 per doz. at Alpenrose and $3.98 per doz. in the supermarket. Drumsticks (ice cream—not turkey legs) sold here for $3.20 per doz.; at the supermarket they were $5.10. You'll save from 20% to 25% off retail when you buy their milk in the half- pint or one-pint sizes. They require a minimum purchase of six dozen ice cream products or one case of milk (48 half-pints or 32 pints to the case). Orders must be placed at least 24 hours in advance.

Checks

Associated Food Service

Portland: 19099 N.E. San Rafael ☎ 666–3600
Hours: Mon–Fri 8–5

This wholesaler caters primarily to delis, pizza parlors, and restaurants, and offers a complete line of cheeses that come sliced, shredded, or in blocks. In the 5-lb. block, Jack cheese sells for $1.89 per lb., whereas supermarket prices were around $2.50. In the 40-lb. block, the price fell to $1.45 per lb. Sliced American cheese (120 slices in the 5-lb. weight) sold for $1.78 per lb. as compared to supermarket's *Kraft* brand, which sold for $3.89 per lb. Skim mozzarella was going for $1.25 per lb. Minimum order is 5 lbs., and orders must be placed a least an hour in advance of pick-up.

Checks

Chris' Poultry Farm

Hubbard: 30578 S. Meridian ☎ 651–2299
Hours: Mon–Fri 8:30–4:30

You'll find fresh farm eggs at about 10% off retail here, as well as "chex" eggs—eggs that are slightly cracked and cannot be sold to stores or restaurants. Large chex eggs sold for 55 cents per doz. and there is no minimum (over one dozen). We're told that chex eggs should be hard-cooked, fried, or baked and not eaten raw or soft-cooked.

Checks

Sunshine Dairy

Portland: 801 N.E. 21st ☎ 234–7526
Hours: Mon–Fri 8–4:30

Sunshine's excellent buys include ice cream sandwiches at $2.68 per doz.; Sunday cones (also known as "drumsticks") at $3.35 per doz.; and Nestle's Crunch bars at $4.35 per doz. These prices are 30% to 35% below retail. The minimum order is six dozen, and there is no need to call in advance to place your order.

Checks

Tillamook Ice Creamery
Lake Oswego: 37 S.W. A ☎ 636–4933
Hours: Sun–Thurs 11–9:30, Fri & Sat 11–10:30
Rub-a-dub-dub—three gallons of ice cream in a tub. Tillamook sells tubs of ice cream (about 14 pounds worth) for $22 a tub. We checked at Baskin Robbins and the same tub went for $27. Choose among 40 different flavors—brown cow, chocolate moose, root beer float, bubblegum, baseball nut, supermix, and a host of others. Call in your order in advance.

Checks

Willamette Egg Farm
Canby: 31348 S. Highway 170 ☎ 651–2152
Hours: Mon–Fri 8–4:30
Willamette sells fresh farm eggs at prices 20% below retail. The only catch is that they require a minimum purchase of one case (15 dozen eggs). Buy a case and split it up among friends or neighbors.

Cash only

Fruits & Vegetables

Always look for fruits and vegetables on special. Low prices are often an indication that fresh produce is in peak supply. Your taste buds will thank you for buying fresh, in-season fruits and vegetables.

For the absolute freshest and cheapest produce (unless you grow your own!), head out to the farm whenever possible and shop at U-pick farms, roadside stands, and farmers' markets.

Farmers' Markets

Visit a farmers' market and you'll find local farmers selling fresh produce (and other wares)—and lots of bargain shoppers snapping up bargain-priced fruits, vegetables, and other goodies.

Shop early in the morning and you'll get first pick of the crop. Shop an hour or so before they're ready to shut down (usually around noon to early afternoon) and you'll find incredible prices. Farmers slash prices near day's end because they don't want to take perishables back home with them.

Beaverton Farmers Market
Beaverton: Between Betts St. & Hall Blvd., on the south side of Farmington
Hours: Sat 8–1:30, second Sat in June thru October

This is one of the largest farmers' markets in Oregon, where about 50 farmers and vendors supply a wide selection of seasonal produce (some organically grown), plus honey, jams, jellies, baked goods, plants, herbs, and flowers. In addition, the market features freshly baked homemade breads, cinnamon rolls, fresh coffee, and German sausages served on buns—the crowds line up early in the morning. There are plenty of places to sit and relax while you munch on delicacies and soak in the sounds of a live band playing pop and country tunes. Most of the things you'll find here are locally grown or made, and by dealing directly with the farmer, you'll pay less than in the supermarkets.

Corbett's Village Marketplace
Corbett: Corbett Hill Rd. & Crown Point Hwy *(Corbett Grade School)*
Hours: Sat 11–4, second Sat in June thru August
  While touring the beautiful Columbia River Gorge, stop by this marketplace where dozens of vendors offer fresh local produce, nursery stock, and high-quality crafts. The kids will not only enjoy the live entertainment, they'll also be able to play on the school ground's covered area and playground while parents shop.

Gresham Farmers' Market
Gresham: Eastman Ave. between Burnside & Division *(City Hall Parking Lot)*
Hours: Sat 8–2, second Sat in May thru October
  About 40 farmers and vendors sell everything from apples to zinnias at prices well below supermarket prices. On a typical Saturday you might find fresh berries, stone fruits, gourmet coffee (roasted and ground there), honey, mushrooms, nursery stock and bedding plants, flavored vinegars and relishes, herbs (fresh, dried, and potted), pies, cakes, or savory blueberry cobblers. The market also features craft items such as wood carvings and toys, paintings, jewelry, and hand-painted T-shirts. Most of what you'll find here is locally grown or crafted

Hillsboro Farmers Market
Hillsboro: E. Main & N.E. Second Ave.
Hours: Sat 8–12, first Sat in June thru second Sat in October
  Adjacent to the county courthouse in Hillsboro you'll find a scenic square that comes to life with the colors, aromas, and sounds of 30 farmers and vendors selling fresh produce and wares. Discover the freshest in-season berries and other fruits, garden-fresh vegetables, potted plants, flowers (dried or fresh-cut), nursery stock, honey, and nuts. There's also an assortment of craft items, including clothes, clocks, and woodwork. A local coffee shop owner pulls out his tables and chairs and voila! a French sidewalk cafe complete with pastries and fresh-brewed coffee.

McMinnville Farmers Market
McMinnville: 2741 N. 99W
Hours: Sat 9–?, last Sat in August thru third Sat in September
If you're in the area, drop on by, but don't come much later than the market opening at 9 am—things go amazingly fast, and an hour later there might not be anything left! You'll find about 25 local farmers selling products from their farms: fresh produce, fresh and dried flowers, honey, herbs—even rabbits and puppies. You'll get fresh produce at prices below retail when you buy directly from these growers.

Salem Public Market
Salem: 1240 Rural St. S.E.
Hours: Sat 8:30–12, year round
A tradition since 1942, the Salem Public Market brings about 20 farmers and vendors together under one roof (a large roof to be sure!) selling fresh seasonal produce the whole year-round. Summer offers a cornucopia of fresh fruits and vegetables, and in winter you can find a wide variety of squash, celery root, carrots, potatoes, apples, garlic, and onions. Also, you'll discover ceramic craft items, cider, nuts, baked goods, bedding plants, and house plants.

Saturday Market
Portland: S.W. Ankeny & Front
Hours: Sat 10–5, Sun 11–4:30, first weekend in March thru Christmas Eve
Besides arts and crafts and food booths (see our listing under "Gifts"), you'll be delighted to find some of the best seasonal home-grown produce found anywhere. Though not a large operation (about five to ten vendors), Saturday Market offers produce that has been raised or gathered by the seller, including fruits, vegetables, herbs and spices, honey, nuts, and fresh and dried flowers, as well as orchids in summer and fresh wreaths in winter. And by dealing directly with the grower, you'll pay less and get only the freshest. Most of the produce is on Ankeny Street, although several vendors are located among the arts and craft booths.

Vancouver Farmers' Market
Vancouver: Fifth & Broadway Streets
Hours: Sat 10–5, June thru Oct
In its second year, this downtown Vancouver Farmers' Market features fresh fruits, vegetables, flowers (some edible!), bedding plants, baked goods, sweets, and agriculturally oriented craft items. There are workshops for cooks and gardeners, as well as children's story hours at 11 am and 2 pm. When your lunch bell goes off, try munching on a vegetable stir-fry, strawberry crepes, nut brownies, pies, or a host of other freshly prepared foods.

Produce Markets

Sure, every grocer sells produce—but not the way Comella's and Sheridan's do. You'll find an incredible selection of fresh fruits and vegetables both attractively displayed and priced at these two exceptional marketplaces.

Comella & Son & Daughter
Beaverton: 6959 S.W. Garden Home Rd. ☎ 245–5033
Hours: Mon–Sat 8:30–7, Sun 8:30–6

An extensive variety of quality produce and good prices awaits you when you pop into Comella's. The staff is friendly and you'll always find one of the Comellas around to answer questions or get what you want. Watch for their in-store produce specials, and for even bigger savings, ask about their bulk prices. Their selection of natural foods products is greater than that found in most full-line supermarkets. They offer wholesale prices when you buy cheeses in 5-lb. or 10-lb. bricks. Be sure to place your order by Monday in order to pick up your cheese later in the week.

Checks

Sheridan Fruit Co.
409 S.E. M.L. King Blvd. (Union) ☎ 235–9353
Hours: Mon–Sat 6–8, Sun 6–6

This store is a visual delight. It's chock full of beautifully displayed produce that is among the best anywhere—and at good prices, too. Wander down the aisles. In addition to all the regulars, there are winter banana apples, plantain bananas, bok choy, and nappa cabbage, as well as mint, baby dill, thyme, watercress, rosemary, sweet basil, sage, and oregano—all fresh! Pasta lovers will find below-retail prices on 5- and 10-lb. boxes of fettuccini, lasagna, egg noodles, regatoni, macaroni, and perciatelli. Over in the bulk foods sections are dried fruits, nuts, legumes, and institutional-size cans and jars of pickles, beans, ketchup, fruits, and vegetables.

Checks

U-Pick Produce

Pack up the car with family or friends and head into the country (some farms are not all that far away!) for some fresh air and "pick-your-own" fruits and vegetables. You'll find plenty of cheap, fresh produce at U-pick farms—and have a lot of fun to boot. It's also fascinating to see how your favorite fruits and vegetables are grown. Be sure to call ahead for picking times and available crops. Ask about containers—you might have to bring your own.

Bithell Farms
Boring: 28355 S.E. Kelso Rd. ☎ 663–6182
Season: June–August

Raspberries, marionberries, blueberries, loganberries, boysenberries, black-berries, gooseberries, red currants, and pie cherries.

Dave Jossi & Son
Hillsboro: Rt. 1 Box 706 ☎ 647–2158
Season: June
Strawberries (Shuksan).

Normandin & Sons
Forest Grove: Rt. 1 Box 334 ☎ 357–2351
Season: August–September
Pears (Bartlett) and peaches (Red Globe, Harken).

Pavlinac Farms
Oregon City: 19629 S. Meyers Rd. ☎ 656–8833
Season: June–October
Strawberries, red raspberries, Waldo blackberries, jubilee and white sweet corn, and pumpkins.

Sauvie Island Farms
Portland: 19730 N.W. Sauvie Island Rd. ☎ 621–3768
Season: June–September
Strawberries, raspberries, marionberries, peaches, and blueberries.

Taylor's Blueberries
Portland: 13325 N.W. Thompson Rd. ☎ 645–1643
Season: July–August
Blueberries and corn.

Van Buren Farms
Portland: 3001 N.E. 148th ☎ 253–7459
Season: June–August
Boysenberries, loganberries, cascadeberries, marionberries, and Fairview raspberries.

Ready Picked Produce

You'll always save when you eliminate the middleman and buy direct. The next best thing to picking your own produce is to head to your local farmer and buy ready-picked fruits and vegetables.

Barn Owl Nursery
Wilsonville: 22999 S.W. Newland Rd. ☎ 638–0387
Season: April–July, October–November

Many varieties of herb plants and scented geraniums, dried herbs, flowers, herb teas, and potpourri.

The Berry Basket
Portland: 15318 N.W. Sauvie Island Rd. ☎ 621–3155
Season: June–September
Strawberries, raspberries, marionberries, blueberries, peaches, apples, apricots, asparagus, beans, beets, broccoli, cabbage, carrots, cauliflower, cherries, corn, herbs, honey, onions, garlic, pears, potatoes, tomatoes, watermelon, and more.

Currant Ideas
Hillsboro: Rt. 5 Box 662 ☎ 647–5948
Season: July
Red and black currants.

Giusto Farms
Portland: 3518 N.E. 162nd Ave. ☎ 253–0271
Season: August–January
Basil, beans, beets, broccoli, brussels sprouts, cabbage, carrots, cauliflower, corn, cucumbers, eggplant, fennel, garlic, leeks, shallots, lettuce, onions, peppers, parsnips, potatoes (red, yellow, white), pumpkins, rutabagas, tomatoes, turnips, winter squash (five varieties), zucchini, fruit, and more.

Laurel Orchard
Hillsboro: 32866 S.W. Laurelview Rd. ☎ 628–2556
Season: June–December
Apples (Jonathan, Cox Orange, Liberty, Melrose Spitzenberg, Newton), blueberries, peaches (Red Haven, Veteran), pears (Asian, Bartlett, Winter), plums, hazelnuts, walnuts, candy, and jam.

Loughridge Farm
Hillsboro: 13300 S.W. River Rd. ☎ 628–1286
Season: July–December
Garlic (elephant, Italian), garlic braids, dried flowers, Indian corn, basil, wreaths, honey, walnuts, hazelnuts, apples, Christmas trees, pussy willow wips.

Mallers Mini Barn
Banks: Highway 26 & Maller Rd. ☎ 324–1072
Season: June–September
Apples (nine specialty varieties), fruits, vegetables, and nuts.

Mason Hill Farm

Hillsboro: Rt. 1 Box 481 ☎ 647–5669
Season: Mid August–October
Apples (Gravenstein, Jonagold, Mutsu, Melrose, Criterion), apple butter, chutney, jams.

Oregon Heritage Farms

Hillsboro: 22801 S.W. Scholls Ferry Rd. ☎ 628–3353
Season: Mid August–Mid December
Varietal apples, apple ciders, local produce, garlic, prunes, plums, squash, gourds, honey, peppers, pumpkins, walnuts, corn, filberts, peaches, flowers, melons, pears, potatoes, and tomatoes.

Parson Farm Greengrocer

Lake Oswego: 15964 S.W. Boones Ferry Rd. ☎ 635–4533
Season: Year–round; Mon–Sat 7–7, Sun 9–5
Produce market.

Peterson Farms Apple Country

Hillsboro: 4800 N.W. Glencoe ☎ 640–5649
Season: July–December
Apples (45 varieties), cider, corn, strawberries, pears, grapes, honey, squash, pumpkins, tomatoes, filberts, walnuts, gourds, jams-syrups, and apple butter.

Rosedale Orchards

Beaverton: 23100 S.W. Rosedale Rd. ☎ 649–7354
Season: May–December
Bedding plants, fresh and dried flowers, apples (eight varieties), peaches, pears, prunes, tomatoes, garden produce, cider, honey, pumpkins, and squash.

Rossi Farm

Portland: 3839 N.E. 122nd Ave. ☎ 253–5571
Season: August–January
Lettuce, tomatoes, cucumbers, peppers, corn (white, yellow), cabbage, cauliflower, broccoli, potatoes (red, white, yellow), carrots, squash, onions, garlic, parsnips, rutabagas, turnips, beets, zucchini, and greens.

Susie's Peaches

Hillsboro: 17500 S.W. Hillsboro Hwy ☎ 628–1353
Season: Mid July–September, November
Peaches and walnuts.

U-Pick & Ready Picked Produce

The following farmers offer both U-pick and ready-picked fruits and vegetables—so you can have it both ways. The farms may range from a few acres of one crop to hundreds of acres of many crops. You could be dealing with the farmer from his front porch or in a spacious, modern structure. One thing's for sure: you'll get great farm-fresh produce at rock-bottom prices.

Albeke Farms
Oregon City: 16107 S. Wilson Rd. ☎ 632–3989
Season: June–October
Strawberries, raspberries, blackcaps, marionberries, boysenberries, blueberries, loganberries, peaches, cucumbers, tomatoes, beans, pumpkins, concord grapes, broccoli, corn, cauliflower, apricots, pears, apples, cherries, and more.

Baby Gotter's Pumpkin Patch
Hillsboro: 24375 S.W. Scholls Ferry Rd. ☎ 628–1366
Season: October–November
Pumpkins, sweet corn, gourds, Indian corn, winter and turban squash, cider, fresh-cut flowers, and walnuts.

Barb's Peaches
North Plains: P.O. Box 136 ☎ 647–5657
Season: Mid July–Mid September
Peaches (Red Haven, Veteran, Elberta).

Blueberry Hill Farm
Sherwood: 16997 S.W. Beef Bend Rd. ☎ 639–1525
Season: July
Blueberries (Early Blue, Blue Crop).

Bonny Slope Blueberries
Portland: 3565 N.W. South Rd. ☎ 645–1252
Season: July–August
Blueberries (seven varieties).

B.F. Carson and Sons
Hillsboro: 7100 S.W. Straughn Rd. ☎ 640–5469
Season: July–December
Kiwi fruit and plants, blueberries, filberts, and walnuts.

Joe Casale & Son
Aurora: 13116 N.E. Denbrook Rd. ☎ 682–1760
Season: June–October

Strawberries, beans, cabbage, cauliflower, corn, tomatoes, carrots, beets, cucumbers, peppers, dill, squash, garlic, broccoli, potatoes (red, white), onions, and basil.

Chehalem Mt. Fruit & Nut Co.

Newberg: 20125 S.W. Hillsboro Hwy ☎ 628–1490
Season: June–October
Cherries, pie cherries, herb plants, dried flowers, beans, tomatoes, peppers, prunes, corn, filberts, and country bouquets.

Duyck's Peachy-Pig Farm

Cornelius: Johnson School Rd. ☎ 357–3570
Season: Year round; daily 8–dark
Apples, apricots, beans (pole, bush), asparagus, beets, berries (black, blue, blackcaps, chehalem, logan, marion, rasp, straw ,young and plants), carrots, corn, cucumbers (regular, lemon), corn, dill, eggplant, eggs, filberts, flowers, garlic, onions (regular, Walla Walla), peaches, pears, peas, peppers (bell, hot), popcorn, prunes/plums, pumpkins, rhubarb, squash, tomatoes, walnuts, weaner pigs, cherries, and freezer hogs.

Fir Point Farms

Auroa: 14600 Arndt Rd. ☎ 678–2455
Season: April–December
Everything from apples to zucchini, including corn, strawberries, cantaloupe, peaches, pumpkins, berries, flowers, trees, and wreaths.

The Flower Farmer

Canby: 2512 N. Holly ☎ 266–3581
Season: May–October
Flowers from astors to zinnias, including roses, carnations, and sweet peas; plus fragrant stock, herbs and spices, fruits, and vegetables.

Giles Farm

Forest Grove: Rt. 2 Box 347-C ☎ 357–3944
Season: July–October
Pie cherries, Red Haven peaches, Brooks prunes, and filberts. Ready-pick on order in Eastmoreland, 6812 S.E. 30th.

Golden Orchard

Hillsboro: Rt. 1 Box 332 ☎ 647–5769
Season: August–mid September
Peaches (Vivids, Veterans), peach marmalade, peach butter, peach conserve, red raspberry and marionberry preserves, and honey.

Gordon's Acres

Banks: HCR 61, Box 62-A ☎ 324–9831
Season: June–October
> Strawberries, raspberries, blueberries, tomatoes, peppers, cucumbers, picklers, squash, and pumpkins.

Grammas

Sherwood: 21235 S.W. Pacific Hwy ☎ 625–7104
Season: May–frost
> Bedding plants, hanging baskets, strawberries, corn, garlic, pears, peaches, onions, potatoes, pumpkins, apples, and flowers.

Tom Gregg Farm

Hillsboro: 31660 Hornecker Rd. ☎ 681–9851
Season: June–September
> Peaches (Red Haven, Veteran, Elberta).

Hartnell Farms

Milwaukie: 15000 S.E. Johnson Rd. ☎ 655–1297
Season: Year–round, Mon–Sat 8–6
> Produce stand, blueberries, strawberries, raspberries, pole beans, cucumbers, tomatoes, peaches, pears, apples, squash, corn, boysenberries, loganberries, carrots, beets, pumpkins, salad vegetables, and other fruits and vegetables in season.

Jaquith Family Farm

Newberg: 23135 S.W. Jaquith Rd. ☎ 628–1640
Season: June
> Strawberries (hoods and other varieties).

John's Peach Orchard

Canby: 7335 S. Fawver Rd. ☎ 266–9466
Season: Mid June–October
> Raspberries, peaches, nectarines, prunes (several varieties), tomatoes, peppers, squash (Danish, butternut, hubbard, sweetmeat), melons, eggplant, dill, beets, garlic, sweet corn, and cabbage.

Jossy Farms

Hillsboro: 31965 N.W. Beach Rd. ☎ 647–2136
Season: July–November
> Peaches (Veterans and other varieties), pears, apples, filberts, and walnuts.

Kelso Blueberries
Boring: 28951 S.E. Church Rd. ☎ 663–6830
Season: July–September
  Blueberries, boysenberries, raspberries, Suncrest peaches.

Kennedy Farm
Portland: 17035 N.W. Brugger Rd. ☎ 645–1416
Season: June–December
  Raspberries, blueberries, and dried walnuts.

Lakeview Farms
Cornelius: 31345 N.W. N Ave. ☎ 647–2336
Season: July–December
  Produce from A-Z, including corn, tomatoes, and a variety of berries;
  flowers, pumpkins, and Christmas trees.

Larson Farm
Corbett: Christensen Rd. ☎ 695–5882
Season: July–August
  Blueberries, raspberries, marionberries, boysenberries, early apples, and
  blueberry plants.

Lee Berry & Tree Farms
Tualatin: 6050 S.W. Borland Rd. ☎ 692–0275
Season: May–Christmas
  Strawberries, red and black raspberries, marionberries, loganberries, boysen-
  berries, fuschias, impatiens, vegetables in-season, cherries, peaches, apples,
  pumpkins, fresh and dried flowers, nuts, jam, honey, and Christmas trees.

The Frank Lolich Farm
Beaverton: 185th on Scholls Ferry Rd. ☎ 628–1436
Season: June–September 5 & October
  Blueberries, marionberries, boysenberries, strawberries, raspberries, apples,
  pears, pumpkins, cherries, peaches, garlic, nuts, and honey.

Lukas Blueberries
Portland: 9495 S.W. Moss St. ☎ 245–2116
Season: July–September
  Blueberries and honey.

McKnight's Blueberry Farm
Wilsonville: 24275 S.W. Nodaway Lane ☎ 638–4989
Season: Late June–August
  Blueberries (three varieties), cherries, and peaches.

Meyers Produce
Hillsboro: 2305 S.W. 325th Ave. ☎ 648–5251
Season: July–November

Tomatoes, peppers (hot, bell, yellow sweet), beans, beets, broccoli, cauliflower, cabbage, carrots, cucumbers, dill, onions, zucchini, pumpkins, peaches, apples, melons, and Christmas trees.

Nichols Orchards
Sherwood: Chehalem off 99W ☎ 538–2386
Season: August–December

Apples, filberts, peaches (Red Haven, Veteran), pears, prunes, plums, walnuts, dried prunes, and cider.

Oliphant Orchard
Sherwood: 23995 S.W. Pacific Hwy ☎ 625–7705
Season: July–October

Apples, cherries (sweet, pie), peaches, plums, prunes, pears, pumpkins, apple cider, and flowers.

Orca Farm
Forest Grove: Rt. 1 Box 348 ☎ 357–9116
Season: July–September

Peaches (five varieties), plums (Brooks, Parson), filberts, apples (Gravenstein, McIntosh), Bartlett pears, beans (Blue Lake, bush), garlic braids, corn, leeks, summer squash, and tomatoes.

Pruitt's Farm
Cornelius: Rt. 4 Box 304 ☎ 357–6981
Season: April–December

Bedding plants (annuals and perennials), hanging baskets, cut flowers, tomatoes, corn, beans, cucumbers, dill, garlic, potatoes, onions, peppers (hot, sweet), summer and winter squash, pumpkins, and house plants.

Pumpkin Patch Vegetables
Portland: 16511 N.W. Gillihan ☎ 621–3874
Season: June–November

Strawberries, raspberries, peas, greens, flowers, blueberries, cabbage, corn (Super Sweets, Jubilee, white, bi-color), beans (green, shell), beets, carrots, broccoli, cauliflower, apples, peaches, pears, honey, brussels sprouts, pickling cucumbers, squash, gourds, Indian corn, pumpkins, tomatoes, peppers, and Christmas trees.

Riley & Sons Oregon Blueberries
Aurora: 26022 N.E. Butteville Rd. ☎ 678–5852
Season: July 5–August 14
Blueberries.

Sara's Blueberries
Hillsboro: 24375 S.W. Drake Lane ☎ 649–6000
Season: July 5–August 15
Blueberries (four varieties).

Sauvie Island Blueberry Farm
Portland: 15140 N.W. Burlington Ct. ☎ 621–3332
Season: July–Mid August
Blueberries.

Sauvie Island Market
Portland: 13743 N.W. Charlton Rd. ☎ 621–3489
Season: May–November 7
Asparagus, beans, beets, broccoli, cauliflower, carrots, corn, cucumbers, dill, garlic, onions, peppers, potatoes, pumpkins, squash, tomatoes, apples, apricots, peaches, pears, blueberries, boysenberries, marionberries, raspberries, strawberries, and flowers.

Schwartz's Farm
Corbett: 34926 E. Crown Point Hwy ☎ 695–5428
Season: June–September
Produce stand, raspberries, blueberries, nectarberries, frozenberries, jams, and syrups.

Simantels Farm & Nursery
Hillsboro: 31665 N.W. Scotch Church Rd. ☎ 648–0925
Season: March–December
Apples, beans, bedding plants, blueberries, cucumbers, cut flowers, daffodils, dahlias, dill, hazelnuts, gladiolas, gourds, honey, nursery stock, peppers, plums, pumpkins, raspberries, squash, strawberries, sweet corn, tomatoes, tulips, and walnuts.

Smith Berry Barn
Hillsboro: 24500 S.W. Scholls Ferry Rd. ☎ 628–2172
Season: Call
Raspberries, boysenberries, marionberries, pickling cucumbers, corn, tomatoes, table and juice grapes, pears (Bartlett, Asian), apples, honey, jams, other fruits and vegetables.

Spada U-Pick Farm
Portland: 4939 N.E. 158th ☎ 253–2313
Season: May–November
Strawberries, fruit, peas, super sweet corn (white, gold), cucumbers, Japanese eggplant, cabbage, cauliflower, broccoli, tomatoes, zucchini, squash, kohlrabi, spinach, carrots, beets, Korean/Japanese radishes, melons, bitter melon, peppers (red, yellow), apples, bananas, and mangoes.

Thompson Farms
Boring: 24727 S.E. Bohna Park Rd. ☎ 667–9138
Season: June–August
Strawberries, raspberries, boysenberries, and marionberries.

Trapold Farms (The Barn)
Portland: 5211 N.E. 148th ☎ 253–5103
Season: June–December
Strawberries, raspberries, honey, salad vegetables, tomatoes, carrots, sweet corn, pickling cucumbers, green and shell beans, potatoes, cabbage, broccoli, cauliflower, brussels sprouts, summer and winter squash, eggplant, peppers, peas, flowers, pumpkins, Christmas trees, and wreaths.

West Union Gardens
Hillsboro: Rt. 1 Box 1068 ☎ 645–1592
Season: June–October
Produce stand, hood strawberries, raspberries (summer and fall), boysenberries, blackberries, loganberries, beans, pickling cucumbers, Roma tomatoes, basil, cantaloupe, flowers, and herbs.

Wilhelm Farms
Tualatin: 6001 S.W. Meridian Way ☎ 638–5387
Season: April–December
Produce stand, strawberries, raspberries, loganberries, boysenberries, marionberries, blueberries, beans, cucumbers, tomatoes, pumpkins, asparagus, rhubarb, bedding plants, broccoli, peaches, apricots, cherries, beets, carrots, pears, apples, cauliflower, honey, corn, filberts, flowers, plants, dried fruit, walnuts, jams, syrup, apple butter, and Christmas trees.

Organic Farms

Fruits and vegetables from the following farmers have been "organically grown"—raised on soil without the use of chemical fertilizers or pesticides. No sprays, dusts, or other chemical treatments are applied, so you won't find any waxes or coatings—just delicious produce.

While most of these farms are of the typical U-pick variety, several offer membership plans (fees required) that provide discounts and guaranteed crop availability for members.

Barb's Dutchmill Herbfarm
Forest Grove: Rt. 2 Box 190 ☎ 357–0924
Season: March–Christmas
> Herb plants, living wreaths (succulent and herbal), scented geraniums, lavender, basil, dried herbs and flowers, Indian corn, pumpkins, and Williamsburg-style evergreen Christmas wreaths.

Brentwood Park Organics
Estacada: 20301 S. Mattoon Rd. ☎ 631–8013
Season: June–September
> Beets, cabbage, corn, garlic, greens, herbs, leeks, summer squash, tomatoes, and bedding plants.

Dennis' Organic Farm
Wilsonville: 25006 S.W. Gage Rd. ☎ 638–4211
Season: May–December
> Pole peas (shelling, snap), lettuce, spinach, cabbage, carrots, cucumbers, corn, beans, broccoli, peppers, squash, brussels sprouts, garlic, shallots, onions, tomatoes, apples, cherries, prunes, plums, raspberries, basil, grapes, and potatoes.

Double Decker Acres
Portland: 16835 N.W. Pauly Rd. ☎ 690–6730
Season: July–September
> Blueberries and apples.

Hinsvark Farm
Portland: 2147 N.E. 10th ☎ 287–5215
Season: July–September
> Raspberries, boysenberries, loganberries, and marionberries.

Judy Farms
Sherwood: 19995 S.W. Chapman ☎ 625–7161
Season: August–September
> Brooks plums.

Johnson Farm
Estacada: 25271 S. Springwater ☎ 630–7177
Season: July–September
> Blueberries, marionberries, and raspberries.

Malinowski Farm

Portland: 13130 N.W. ☎ 642–1600

Season: June–October

Blueberries, raspberries, strawberries, broccoli, corn, cucumbers, greens, herbs, peppers, beets, summer squash, tomatoes, flowers, and vegetable, herb, and flower starts.

Nature's Fountain

Tualatin: ☎ 692–4877

Season: June–October

Apples, cherries, plums, pears, green beans, blueberries, cucumbers, herbs, summer squash, tomatoes, and strawberries.

Natural Harvest Farm

Canby: P.O. Box 1106 ☎ 266–9682

Season: May–October

Farm memberships, $25. Apples, raspberries, plums, Asian pears, persimmons, chestnuts, almonds, kiwi, gooseberries, figs, loganberries, boysenberries, raspberries, blueberries, grapes, rose hips, and currants.

Oerther Family Farm

Clackamas: 16168 S.E. Sunnyside Rd. ☎ 658–5132

Season: Year–round, daily 11–7

Garlic, greens, herbs, herb plants, parsley, peas, squash, turnips, broccoli, fertile eggs, pumpkins, cauliflower, dill, rutabagas, fresh and dried flowers, potatoes, and mint.

Simpleton Farm

Portland: 17136 N.W. Lucy Reeder Rd. *(Sauvie Island)* ☎ 621–3568

Season: June–December

Farm memberships, $25. Green beans, broccoli, corn, cucumbers, greens, herbs, onions, celery, peas, peppers, potatoes, cauliflower, tomatoes, Jerusalem artichokes, root vegetables, winter squash, seeds, and flowers.

Sublet Farms

Yamhill: 19155 N.W. Reservoir Rd. ☎ 662–4396

Season: July–September

Green beans, corn, cucumbers, greens, peas, peppers, tomatoes, and summer and winter squash.

Sunshower Orchard

Cornelius: Rt. 4 Box 139 ☎ 357–6423

Season: August–December

Apples (12 varieties) and Christmas trees.

Three Rivers Farm

Canby: 2525 N. Baker Dr. ☎ 266–2432
Season: June–October

Farm memberships, $25. Strawberries, apples, beans, broccoli, cabbage, carrots, cauliflower, corn, cucumbers, eggplant, eggs, flowers, lettuce, honey, lettuce, lamb, melons, onions, peas, peppers, potatoes, plums, pumpkins, squash, tomatoes, and walnuts.

Beverages

You can save money on soda pop by stocking up on it when local supermarkets or drugstores run specials. On coffee, juices, and alcoholic beverages, your best bet is to head to any of the distributors we've listed—the discounts can be substantial (and don't overlook Costco). Several water products companies offer good prices and service if fresh, pure water is your thing.

Aqua-Cool

Portland: 802 N.E. Davis ☎ 233–9991
Hours: Mon–Fri 8–5

If you're not sure what's coming out of your tap and would like the convenience of delivered bottled water, consider having your water brought to you in five-gallon bottles. Aqua-Cool sells two "types" of water. Their purified drinking water (charcoal filtered, which removes the chlorine and most other contaminants but leaves in beneficial minerals) goes for $4.75. Distilled water (steam distillation process, which takes out just about everything except the water itself) sells for $4.95. Basic water dispenser rental runs $3 per mo. The minimum water purchase is two five-gallon bottles each month.

Checks

Bonneau Products

Portland: 81 N.E. Columbia Blvd. ☎ 289–7181
Hours: Mon–Fri 8–5, Sat 8–2

For those opting for the taste and health benefits of pure distilled water, there's nobody around that beats Bonneau's prices. The one-gallon plastic bottles of distilled water that go for 99 cents to $1.09 in the markets sell here for only 50 cents. If you want even bigger savings, bring your own containers and they'll fill 'em up for 35 cents a gallon (and you don't even have to pump your own!). Some of the other products they carry are soup bases (chicken or beef), soy sauces, and vinegar. If you can use white vinegar in the one-gallon size, you'll find it here for $1.50; in the grocery stores, they sell for $3 to $4 each.

Checks

Brewed Hot Coffee
Portland: 802 N.E. Davis ☎ 233–9991
Hours: Mon–Fri 8–5

Brewed Hot Coffee carries premium gourmet coffees, canned soft drinks, and paper products in case-lot quantities. But the best prices we found were on their individually wrapped packets of hot tea, hot chocolate, hot spiced ciders, and soups and broths. You can buy these beverage mixes by the box and still get wholesale prices. There's a nice selection of teas, soups, and broths, plus sugar-free hot chocolate and spiced ciders.

Checks

Fresh Brewed Coffee
Clackamas: 9065 S.E. Jannsen Rd. ☎ 657–5004
Hours: Mon–Fri 9–4

Fresh Brewed Coffee sells individually wrapped packets of coffee for your coffee maker at wholesale prices—but you have to buy at least one case (42 packets). You can also pick up big savings off supermarket prices when you buy their individually wrapped packets of soup mixes, hot chocolate, hot and cold beverages, and tea blends, which come 25 to 100 per box. These are handy at school or work. Just add hot or cold water and—presto!—an instant meal or beverage. Call and place your order in advance.

Checks, Credit cards

General Distributing
Oregon City: 13895 Fir ☎ 656–9470
Hours: Mon–Thurs 8–5, Fri 8–5:30

This distributor carries a wide selection of imported and domestic beers, but no wines. The minimum purchase is three cases (24 cans to the case). We found Hamm's selling for $8.65 a case, including deposit. In the supermarket, that same case was going for $11.92 plus deposit (an additional $1.20). The case price of Coors was about 25% below grocery store prices.

Checks

Gourmet Coffee Catering
Portland: 1105 S.E. Morrison ☎ 234–4811
Hours: Mon–Fri 6–5

Gourmet Coffee Catering offers regular and gourmet coffee by the case (42 packets per case), as well as individually wrapped packets of hot and cold beverages, teas, hot chocolate, and soups and broths. You'll get wholesale prices when you buy at least one box of these instant beverage and soup mixes. The selection of soups and teas is good and you'll find several sugar-free hot chocolate and beverages mixes. Their 10-oz. bottles of *Very Fine* fruit juices, including apple blends, orange juice, grape juice, and grapefruit juice sell for 20% to 30% off supermarket retail. There's a one-case (24 bottles) minimum purchase.

Checks

King Harvest Natural Foods Kitchen

Portland: 1502 S.E. Morrison ☎ 239–6515
Hours: Mon–Fri 8–7

You can save 10% off retail if you buy freshly squeezed carrot juice, carrot-wheat grass juice, wheat grass juice, or green juice (spinach, celery, and parsley blend) directly from the King Harvest Kitchen. Juices come in 8-, 16-, 32-, and 48-oz. sizes. There's nothing like freshly squeezed, but plan to drink your juices within several days because they're quite perishable. The carrot juice has a surprisingly sweet taste, while the fragrance and gusto of the wheat grass juice will leave quite an impression! You'll find tasty apple-raspberry blends and protein shakes as well.

Checks

McClaskey's Wine Distributor

Portland: 930 N.W. 14th ☎ 224–3150
Hours: Mon–Fri 8–5

McClaskey's carries a large selection of wines, including *Christian Brothers, Robert Mondavi, Columbia Crest,* and *Hidden Springs.* You'll save 20% off retail when you order wine through McClaskey's. (There's a minimum order of one case, or 12 750-ml bottles.) After placing your order with McClaskey's, the wine will be sent to one of the Fred Meyer's stores, Kienow's Food Stores, or Harris Wine Cellar for pickup; McCaskey's does not sell directly. Call in your order several days in advance.

Mountain Fresh

Clackamas: 9065 S.E. Jannsen Rd. ☎ 657–5004
Hours: Mon–Fri 9–4

You'll save from 10% to 15% off the price of those one-gallon bottles of drinking water found in supermarkets when you have Mountain Fresh's five-gallon bottles of water delivered to you. You can buy regular drinking water (carbon filtered to remove chlorine and contaminants) in five gallon bottles for $4.75 each, or distilled water (steam distilled, which is probably the purest water around) in five-gallon bottles for $4.95. If you buy four or more bottles (20 gallons) each month, there's no charge for their basic water dispenser. In addition, you can buy individually packaged soup and tea mixes from Fresh Brewed Coffee, a division of Mountain Fresh; they will deliver the mixes with your bottled water. See their listing in the "Beverage" section.

Checks, Credit cards

Portland Distributing Co.
Portland: 2026 N.E. Columbia Blvd. ☎ 283–2471
Hours: Mon–Thurs 9–4:30, Fri 9–5

They carry a wide beer selection, including *Bud Light, Budweiser, Busch,* and *Michelob.* There's a three-case (24 cans) minimum, and you'll find their prices below those in the markets. We noted that *Busch Light* and *Bud Dry* were each selling for $7.20 a case here (which included deposits).

Checks

Candy & Snacks

By shopping the outlets listed below, we guarantee your wallet won't lose much weight—and neither will you! The selection of sweets and treats is mouth-watering—and the prices, irresistible.

Whether you're planning a party or just stocking up for your own enjoyment, you'll find everything from fine soft chocolates to mini meatballs in ten-pound boxes—and all at great prices.

Barlow Trail Farm
Portland: 4060 N.E. 158th ☎ 252–4150
Hours: Mon–Fri 8–5

Beef jerky, beef jerky, and more beef jerky, at prices 50% to 60% below retail, can be found at Barlow Trail Farm in 1- oz., 2-oz., 4-oz., 6-oz., 1-lb., and 5-lb. bags. Nonprofit organizations should inquire about how they can get even bigger savings.

Checks

Blue Bell Potato Chip Co.
Portland: 100 N.E. Farragut ☎ 289–8851
Hours: Mon–Fri 8–4:30

If your organization is having a fund-raiser or carnival—or if you just love to munch snack foods—you'll find what you need at Blue Bell. Although the majority of their business is in supplying a full line of snack food items to retail markets, they are open to the public for business. To get wholesale prices, you have to order at least one case of snack items (Blue Bell label), which include potato chips, cheese snaps, pretzels, popcorn, and dips. You must order several days in advance.

Checks

Candy Basket Factory Outlet
Portland: 2429 S.E. 11th ☎ 239–4447
Hours: Mon–Fri 8:30–5

At Candy Basket you'll find a wide assortment of hard candies and chocolate-covered candies. You can skip all these, as other shops have these candies at comparable prices, but race over and pickup their grab bags, which go for 60% off retail. These bags hold a pound apiece of scrumptious chocolate-covered seconds, such as misshapen or unevenly covered candies. You'll find nothing wrong with their taste as you wade through each bag of assorted chocolate-covered caramels, fruit creams, jelly sticks, almond clusters, beaver paws, and peanut butter nuggets. The regular price is $10.80 per lb., but when you buy these "imperfects," you only pay $4.25 for a 1-lb. bag.

Checks

Chocolate Express
Tigard: 17937 S.W. McEwan Rd. ☎ 636–8404
Hours: Mon–Fri 8:30–5

We've all seen chocolate-covered candies. But what about a chocolate-covered Oregon? At Chocolate Express you'll find all kinds of chocolate novelty items, such as solid chocolate maps of Oregon, Oregon-shaped mints, miniature chocolate apples, and chocolate spoons. If it's indescribably delicious handmade chocolate you're after, you'll find savings of 45% to 50% off retail on "seconds" (assorted chocolate creams, caramels, and other blemished or misshapen chews) and "break-ups" (chocolate pieces that once may have been a chocolate map or telephone).

Checks

Hoody's Outlet Store
Beaverton: 5555 S.W. 107th ☎ 646–0555
Hours: Mon–Fri 8:30–4:30

Hoody's sells bulk nuts and candies at prices much lower than in the grocery stores. And these are not seconds. The day we checked, their bulk peanuts were about 45% off retail; various other nuts and seeds ranged from 25% to 40% off. There is no minimum at Hoody's. Some of their scrumptious bulk items included: malt balls, yogurt clusters, pecans, almonds, filberts, Spanish and honey-roasted peanuts, walnuts, and nut mixes. For convenience, you'll find pre-packed 5-lb. bags of many of these bulk items. The handy ten-packs of bagged sunflower seeds, camper's mix, or dry roasted peanuts were $1.60—great for class parties, special events, or traveling. Also, those familiar bags of *Hoody's* sunflower seeds and unshelled peanuts seen in most groceries were 40% off.

Checks

Maui Maid Candies
Vancouver: 2707 N.W. Lower River Rd. ☎ (206)694–6289
Hours: Mon–Fri 8–4:30

Macadamia nut lovers, leap with joy! You'll find these tasty Hawaiian nuts smothered in chocolate at wholesale prices when you buy the one-pound bags of factory seconds. The regular retail price is $3.50 for eight ounces, but you'll pay only $3.50 per lb. when you buy these delicacies in the 1-lb. bags of broken pieces or otherwise slightly "imperfects"—and your taste buds won't know the difference. Take their free factory tour and see how these treats are made. Call ahead to schedule your trip behind the scenes—and don't forget to ask for sample munchies.

Checks

The Oregon Candy Farm
Sandy: 48620 S.E. Highway 26 ☎ 668–5066
Hours: Mon–Fri 9–5, Sat & Sun 12–5
This is not your typical farm. No animals here, just chocolates—in fact, about 100 different varieties of chocolates are made here. We found the best bargain was their "oops" bags. Each contained a pound of broken and imperfect assorted chocolates for $5.25—a savings of nearly 40% off the regular retail price of $8.50 per lb.

Checks, Credit cards

Poppers Supply Co.
Portland: 340 S.E. Seventh Ave. ☎ 239–3792
Hours: Mon–Fri 8–4:30
If you're putting on a party, here's the place to pick up many of the ingredients— at wholesale prices. But comparison shop; we found good buys on some items and not-so-good buys on others. For instance, you'll save 30% off retail prices on their red or black licorice ropes when purchased by the box (120 unwrapped ropes). But you'll pay regular retail prices on large 4½-lb bags of popcorn. Because they pop their own corn, the fresh taste is worth the price (already-popped corn in the markets can sit around for weeks). Besides traditional popcorn, they carry several mouth-watering varieties, including buttered, cheese, and white cheddar varieties. We also found better-than-retail prices on some paper goods (i.e., paper plates) but not on others (i.e., paper cups). They also rent popcorn poppers, cotton candy machines, and sno-cone equipment.

Sea Fresh Co.
Portland: 3303 S.E. 20th ☎ 231–7830
Hours: Mon–Fri 8–5, Sat 9–1
Sea Fresh (sorry—no seafood here) supplies taverns with all sorts of delectable snack-food items. Here you'll find wholesale prices on such bulk items as mixed nuts, pepperoni sticks, potato chips, and pretzels. Giving a large soiree? Discover better-than-retail prices on their ten-pound boxes of mini meat balls (320 balls to the box) and ten-pound boxes of smoked sausages (500 of these petite hot dogs per box).

Checks

Shorthill Candy Co.
Portland: 532 S.E. Clay ☎ 232–8962
Hours: Mon–Fri 7–3

Premium taffy anyone? Shorthill makes their own taffies and sells them at wholesale. You only have to buy a minimum of one pound of their assorted mouth-watering taffies (each twisted and wrapped). The price on these is $2 per lb. (30% to 50% off the regular retail price). For an even bigger savings, go hog wild and pick up a case of assorted taffies. You'll get 25 pounds for $28.50, which works out to $1.14 per lb.

Checks

Van Duyn Chocolate Shops
Beaverton: 10200 S.W. Parkway *(Cedar Hills Shopping Center)* ☎ 292–2121
3205 S.W. Cedar Hills Blvd. *(Beaverton Mall)* ☎ 646–0809
Portland: 12000 S.E. 82nd *(Clackamas Town Center)* ☎ 659–1031
739 N.E. Broadway ☎ 287–1256
Jantzen Beach Shopping Center ☎ 285–5300
12307 N.E. Glisan ☎ 252–5033
Hours: Generally, Mon–Fri 10–9, Sat 10–6, Sun 11–5; Broadway, Mon–Fri 9:30–5

The people at Van Duyn's have been making fine chocolate delicacies for decades. You'll find the best prices on their 1-lb. bags of irregular chocolates—the dipping might not go all the way around or the pieces might be misshapen. Their regular price is $8.99 per lb., but when you buy 1-lb. bagged irregulars, you'll pay only $4.50. All their outlets may not have irregulars at all times (so it's best to call ahead). If you're in the neighborhood of their Broadway store, just pop in. We're told they nearly always have these bags of luscious creams, caramels, and fudge irregulars.

Checks, Credit cards

Ethnic Foods

No need to brush up on your Spanish, Italian, or Japanese—though you'll think you're a half-world away from Portland when you shop some of the outlets in this section.

You'll find "flavored" pastas available in shapes from angel hair to lasagna; freshly made tofu bobbing in a water tank;, hot bean paste; 100-lb. sacks of imported rice; red bean ice cream bars; coconut syrup; freshly baked tortillas; and more.

We've even seen fit to consider salmon fishermen an ethnic group by including an outlet that custom cans fresh salmon catches.

An Dong Oriental Food Company
Portland: 5441 S.W. Powell ☎ 774–6527
Hours: Sun–Thurs 9–7, Fri & Sat 9–8

This large Asian food market stocks such exotic items as Thai eggplant, melon dunqua, szechuan, pickles, frozen fish balls, rabbit fish, and baby squid. You'll save on bulk fruits and vegetables found in large 3- to 6-lb. cans; on several varieties of soy sauce in gallon containers; and on noodles by the case. We found great prices on herbal tea (liquid), soy milk, and fruit juices in convenient aseptically six-packs, at $1.35 per pack. How about slipping a container of coconut milk into the kid's lunch box (a six-pack in aseptic packages runs $2.45)? Their many varieties of rice are always good buys, especially when you can use the 50-lb. sacks. Check out the gifts, tea pots, bowls, flasks, and cookers at the back of the store.

Checks

Anzen Importers
Beaverton: 4021 S.W. 117th Ave. *(Canyon Place)* ☎ 627–0913
Portland: 736 N.E. M.L. King Blvd. *(Union)* ☎ 233–5111
Hours: Beaverton, Mon–Sat 10–6:30, Sun 12–5; Portland, Mon–Sat 9–6:30, Sun 12–5

You'll think you stepped right into the Orient when you enter Anzen Importers. They carry a large selection of Oriental groceries, including frozen, dried, canned and packaged foods, condiments, teas, and fish. They offer a 10% case discount on all foods and drinks. We noted that the 16-oz. packages of tofu were priced 10% below the prices we found in other markets. If you have a yen for soy sauce, you'll pay less when you buy it in one-gallon size bottles. The 5-lb. boxes of Chinese-style dry noodles were also good buys. A few of the more exotic items we noted were azuki (red bean) ice "cream" bars, coconut syrup, lotus root, pickled ginger, and water chestnut powder. For a great price on rice, be sure to pick up one of their 50-lb. bags of homai rice (around $11). They also carry a wide and wonderful selection of Oriental gifts, Japanese books and magazines, and cookware. It's definitely the place to shop if you're looking for a rice cooker.

Checks

Bellissima Italia
Beaverton: 15075 S.W. Koll Parkway ☎ 646–5852
Hours: Mon–Fri 8–4

This factory makes fresh pasta and offers wholesale prices as long as you buy at least ten pounds. They make their own pesto and "red" sauces and give free tours. Call a day in advance to place your pasta order and to arrange for a behind-the-scenes look. Keep in mind that they make fresh pasta only on Mondays, Tuesdays, and Thursdays.

Checks

Cornell's Custom Canning
Portland: 5001 N.E. 82nd ☎ 252–9762
Hours: Mon–Sat 8–5:30 (April–October)

Salmon fishermen bring their catches in to this custom canner that cleans, prepares, processes, and cans the fish. Canning is 75 cents for eight ounces and 90 cents for 13. The process takes a couple of days; it's best to call before you head over with your salmon.

Checks

Dae Han Oriental Food & Gifts
Beaverton: 9970 S.W. Beaverton-Hillsdale Hwy. ☎ 646–1213
Hours: Mon–Sat 9–9, Sun 10–8

If you haven't shopped "oriental" before, you're in for a real eye-opener the moment you step into this shop. You'll find a wide selection of foods, cookware, and gifts from many nations of the Orient, all neatly displayed. Their inventory of frozen fish (some exotic) seemed endless. We found soy sauce in gallon cans ($5.99 each), hot bean paste ($4.29 for 2.2 lbs.), 100-lb. sacks of rice, and a wide array of noodles, including bean threads, rice sticks, and Korean vermicelli. In addition, the produce section featured not only fresh produce (broccoli was 25 cents per lb.) but also salted seaweed, pickled and salted radish, and sweetened and salted turnip in stay-fresh vacuum packs.

Checks

Dae Han Tofu
Portland: 737 S.E. Alder ☎ 233–8638
Hours: Mon–Fri 8–6

Dae Han makes and sells fresh tofu. You can buy the 16-oz. tofu in bulk (65 cents each) by bringing your own containers or already packaged (80 cents each)—25% to 35% off regular grocery store prices. They also make tofu burgers, smoked tofu, and teriyaki tofu. There's a case minimum on the burgers, so if you can use a dozen packs (two burgers per pack), you'll save a whopping 40% off retail.

Checks

Fong Chong and Co.
Portland: 301 N.W. Fourth Ave. ☎ 223–1777
Hours: Mon–Sat 9–7, Sun 10–6

This Asian grocery, one of the largest in the area, offers a mind-boggling array of fresh, frozen, dried and canned oriental foods at prices as low or lower than at other oriental groceries. Their bulk offerings are good buys, especially large sacks of long-and short-grain rice. In addition, they stock an enormous variety of dried Chinese noodles, cellophane noodles (a delightfully slippery noodle made from mung beans), fresh white rice noodles, and rice sticks (wiry dried rice noodles). Not to be missed are their fresh egg and rice noodles carried down from Vancouver, British Columbia.

Checks, Credit cards

Ota Tofu Co.
Portland: 812 S.E. Stark ☎ 232–8947
Hours: Mon–Fri 7–5, Sat 7–4

Soft or firm tofu is freshly made and sold here, both in bulk and pre-packaged. Bulk tofu is sold for 75 cents each (bring your own containers); 70 cents each when you buy more than 12. Their packaged tofu runs 85 cents each. You save 15% to 30% off retail grocery prices on tofu here. They offer a few other products at prices somewhat below retail, including fried tofu and soy milk.

Checks

Pasta Pazzo
Gresham: 229 N. Main Ave. ☎ 667–5617
Hours: Tues–Fri 10–7, Sat 10–5

Pasta Pazzo supplies grocery stores and restaurants with their freshly made pasta. But you too can take advantage of wholesale prices when you buy pasta in their 10-lb. lots. You'll find flavored pastas such as lemon thyme, orange basil, pinenut parsley, roasted pepper, spinach, jalapeno, garlic parsley, and chive. The pasta can be bought in a variety of shapes and cuts, ranging from angel hair to lasagna. Call the day before to place your order.

Checks

Pasta Works
Portland: 3731 S.E. Hawthorne Blvd. ☎ 232–1010
Hours: Mon–Sat 9:30–7, Sun 11–5

At Pasta Works you're going to find fresh-made pasta at wholesale prices when you buy in 10-lb. lots. "Flavored" pastas, such as spinach, whole wheat, garlic parsley, and red pepper, as well as filled ravioli and tortellini, are also available at wholesale. If you can use ten pounds or more, place your order a day in advance. Pasta Works' other shop on N.W. 21st does not sell at wholesale.

Checks, Credit cards

The Taco Shak
Portland: 239 S.E. Oak ☎ 231–1834
Hours: Mon–Fri 9–5

Attention Mexican food enthusiasts! Freshly made corn tortillas are sold here at below-retail prices. The $5\frac{1}{2}$-in. tortillas are packed three dozen to the bag and sell for $1 a bag. The thinner tortillas (also $5\frac{1}{2}$ in.), perfect for making your own chips (chop them up and pop into a 425-degree oven for a few minutes—presto, you have chips!), are packed five dozen to the bag and go for $1.25 a bag. While some grocery-store tortilla brands may come close in price, there are no tortillas to match the taste of Taco Shak's own freshly baked ones, which they make Tuesdays, Thursdays, and Fridays. They also carry chili pods and freshly ground masa to make your own tamales.

Checks

Natural and Bulk Foods

You can save up to 40% off retail when you buy in bulk. The selection of bulk foods includes dried fruits, nuts, seeds, grains, honey, pasta, flours, cereals, candies, herbs, spices, and teas—all in convenient tubs or bins. Scoop up as much or as little as you need.

Markets are able to pass along big savings on bulk foods because they eliminate packaging and greatly reduce handling costs. You can get an additional 10% off already low bulk prices by buying in large quantities—such as honey in 40-lb. tubs, 25-lb. bags of oats, or most anything else found in the bulk bins. Don't forget to check out the bulk food departments in local supermarkets, including Safeway, Waremart, and Fred Meyer Nutrition Centers.

A to Z Natural Nutrition
Portland: 822 S.E. 162nd Ave. ☎ 254–4466
Hours: Mon–Wed & Fri & Sat 9–5

This little shop has about the best prices around on vitamins, food supplements, and body care products such as creams, lotions, and toothpaste. All their products are 5% to 10% off retail, and if you become a "member" ($10 the first year, $5 thereafter), you'll get 10% to 20% off. Whatever they don't have in stock can be ordered. So you'll have access to all the product lines and national brands found in major markets, such as *Schiff, Twinlab, Richlife,* and *Nature's Plus*—except at lower prices. They also have access to a multitude of specialty formulations prepared by smaller natural foods companies that are not found in large stores. If you prefer, they'll mail your purchases to you without a handling charge (though you will have to pay the postage).

Checks

Dragon Herbarium
Portland: 4642 S.W. Beaverton–Hillsdale Hwy ☎ 244–7049
Hours: Mon–Fri 11–7, Sat 12–7

You'll find 300 kinds of herbs and 25 kinds of teas at 10% off retail in rows of glass gallon jars at Dragon Herbarium. Use the cellophane bags to buy what you need. You'll find even bigger discounts on their gourmet coffee beans.

Checks, Credit cards

International Food Bazaar
Portland: 915 S.W. Ninth ☎ 228–1960
Hours: Mon–Sat 11–7:30

International Food Bazaar specializes in Middle Eastern, Indian, and Greek foods. They carry a wide range of bulk food items ,including herbs, dates, apricots, pistachios, walnuts, and sunflower seeds. Pick up some popular snack foods enjoyed in India, such as roasted and salted watermelon seeds and squash seeds. Save 10% or more off retail when you buy 25 pounds or more of any of their bulk foods.

Checks, Credit cards

Loughridge Farms
Scholls: 13300 S.W. River Rd. ☎ 628–1286
Hours: Daily, 10–dark

Loughridge Farms offers filberts, walnuts, and several kinds of garlic at prices 30% to 40% below retail. Filberts were selling for 70 cents per lb., walnuts for 80 cents per lb., and elephant garlic was $2 per lb. They'll sack the products in any weight you want. If you can use 50 pounds of elephant garlic, the price falls to $1 per lb.

Checks

Moore's Mill
Milwaukie: 5209 S.E. International Way ☎ 654–4307
Hours: Mon–Sat 9–5

You'll pick up great savings when you buy their cereals, granolas, grains, legumes, candies, nuts, and dried fruits—all pre-packaged in 1- to 10-lb. bags, 25-, 50-, and 100-pound bags. Moore's freshly grinds their grains every day (and also sells these products under the Bob's Red Mill label in supermarkets). For even bigger savings, watch for their monthly in-store sales. We saw pancake mixes on sale: A 26-oz. bag was $1.29 (previously $1.55), and the 10-lb. bag was $5.99 (previously $7.20). Ask them about mail order purchases and special discounts to organizations.

Checks

Oregon Spice Company
Portland: 3525 S.E. 17th ☎ 238–0664
Hours: Mon–Thurs 8–5, Fri 8–4, Sat 9–2

You'll find nearly 150 culinary herbs and spices separately pre-packed in small cellophane bags, commercial-size bottles, or 5-lb. bags at wholesale prices in the Oregon Spice Company's warehouse outlet. Just like the restaurants, you can pick up spices in the large 1- and 5-lb. bottles or premium coffee beans (they carry 15 varieties) in 5-lb. bags. They'll even grind the coffee at no charge. For custom orders, there's a $50 minimum, and you'll have to give them 24-hour notice to fill your special order. The day we checked, a customer was picking up an order of orange-crate-sized boxes of pacilla chilepods. (They carry a whole line of chile pods, among other things.)

Checks

Pak-Sel
Portland: 7524 S.W. Macadam ☎ 244–9661
Hours: Mon–Thurs 9–4:30, Fri 9–2

Pak-Sel manufactures cellophane bags, which are made from wood cellulose and are ideal for hypo-allergenic or environmentally sensitive persons, at prices 40% or more off competitor's prices. Cellophane bags are available in boxes of 250 and 1000, and come in a variety of sizes. They are clear like glass, moisture-proof, biodegradable, non-toxic, and will keep food fresh and leave no odors. Also, Pak-Sel has the lowest prices around on the Champion juicer (ranked as one of the finest juicers made). Take advantage of their toll-free number (800–635–2247) and their service of shipping orders anywhere in the country.

Checks, Credit cards

Wholesome and Hearty Foods
Portland: 1416 S.E. 8th ☎ 238–0109
Hours: Mon–Fri 8–5

Some vegetarians coming to dinner? Treat them (and yourselves!) to a meal of garden burgers. These yummy burgers are made of mushrooms, onions, cheese, oats, rice, walnuts, and egg whites. You'll save about 20% off retail when you buy them by the case (one-case minimum) direct from this manufacturer. The big "quarter-pounders" (served in restaurants) come 48 to a case, and the smaller $2\frac{1}{2}$-oz. burgers (available in markets) come 60 to a case. It works out to about 87 cents each for the big ones and 67 cents each for the small ones. They also carry wholesome and hearty vegetarian garden sausages and garden tacos. You can freeze what you don't need immediately and later pop them in the microwave or oven for a quick meal. Nonprofit organizations should ask about the special discounts available to them.

Checks

The following natural foods stores also carry a wide assortment of bulk foods, herbs, spices, and teas. Ask about case discounts when buying fruits and vegetables in quantity. A 25-lb. bag of carrots, for example, sells for about one-third less than the regular price of carrots.

In addition, some of the stores listed below offer famous name-brand skin care lotions in bulk. Just bring in your own clean empty containers (or buy their empties) and buy as much as you want.

Comella & Son & Daughter
Beaverton: 6959 S.W. Garden Home Rd. ☎ 245–5033
Hours: Mon–Sat 8:30–7, Sun 8:30–6

Daily Grind
Portland: 4026 S.E. Hawthorne Blvd. ☎ 233–5521
Hours: Mon–Thurs 9–9, Fri 9–5, Sun 10–7

Food Front Cooperative Grocery
Portland: 2375 N.W. Thurman ☎ 222–5658
Hours: Daily, 9–9

Nature's Fresh Northwest
Beaverton: 4000 S.W. 117th ☎ 646–3824
Portland: 5909 S.W. Corbett ☎ 244–3934
   3449 N.E. 24th ☎ 288–3414
   6344 S.W. Capitol Hwy ☎ 244–3110
Hours: Generally, daily 9–9

People's Food Store Co-op
Portland: 3029 S.E. 21st ☎ 232–9051
Hours: Daily, 8–10

Gifts

Farm-fresh preserves and honey in attractive jars and gift packs make thoughtful gifts that are a delight to receive. You'll save 25% or more off retail store prices when you buy these sweet treats direct from the farmer.

Golden Orchards
Hillsboro: Rt. 1 Box 332 ☎ 647–5769
Hours: Mon–Fri 9–5

Golden Orchards' preserves, beautifully packaged (gold foil labels emblazoned with peaches or berries) in 5- and 12-oz. jars, make fine gifts for others—and for yourself. Their peach and berry preserves are sold throughout Oregon, including Made In Oregon shops and in many upper-end grocery stores. From their own peach orchards come the tasty ingredients for mouth-watering peach preserves, and superb Oregon raspberries and seedless marionberries are transformed into savory preserves. Three 12-oz. jars retail for $5 to $7 each, but you'll pay $4 a jar when you order one case (12 jars per case) or more from Golden Orchards. Call in advance and arrange a pickup time or have them ship your order to you for a small handling and shipping charge.

Checks

Hanna's Honey
Salem: 4760 Thorman ☎ 390–5104
Hours: Generally, Mon–Fri 9–5

Hanna's offers gourmet Oregon honeys in attractively packaged 1-lb. jars and gift packs that will both please the eye and delight the sweet tooth. They feature several varieties of honey, each from a different floral source, including clover, raspberry, blackberry, and wildflower. While Hanna's honey is sold at many groceries, you'll save up to 25% off retail when you buy a case or more (24 1-lb. jars per case) directly from Hanna's. Either order in advance and pick up your order yourself or have them ship it to you for a small handling and shipping charge. They also offer honey sticks (flavored honeys in straws), natural energy boosters for hikers, campers, and the rest of us when our batteries are low.

Checks

Mail Order Food

We've selected a couple of "local" mail-order farmers whose products are simply out of this world. Ordering by mail is a real joy—you don't have to brave the crowds or feel any pressure from salespersons. And without a retail outlet to run, most mail-order farms enjoy a lower overhead and can pass along the savings to their customers.

Henry's Farm
Newberg: 1216 E. Henry Rd. (97132) ☎ 538–5244

At Henry's you'll find high-quality, all-natural hazelnut products straight from the tree. They carry raw, dry-roasted, and honey-roasted hazelnuts (also called filberts), filbert butter, and hazelnut shortbread cookies. We found savings of about 25% off retail on their filbert butter in 8- and 16-oz. jars and about 33% off retail for their roasted hazelnuts in 1-lb. bags. Because Henry's is a mail-order company, you'll have to call them for an order form. Also inquire about their bulk wholesale prices. They charge a shipping and handling fee of $2.50 for products sent to Oregon and Washington ($4 to all other places).

Checks

Muirhead Canning
The Dalles: 5267 Mill Creek Rd. (97058) ☎ 298–1660

Caution: Once you taste Muirhead's naturally ripened canned fruits and vegetables, you won't want to buy anybody else's canned produce again! Muirhead offers cherries, apricots, applesauce, plums, peaches, pears, asparagus, peas, beans, and corn—in cans that are hand packed with more fruits and vegetables and less water than most other brands. The result is not only competitive prices, but also a superior quality of canned fruits and vegetables that will grab your attention with the first bite. There's a minimum order of a half case (12 28-oz. cans). You can pick up your order at the cannery or they'll mail or truck it to you for a small delivery charge. Be sure to place your orders in advance of heading to the cannery.

Checks

Personal Care

Beauty Supplies

Beauty supply stores are great places to pick up big savings on name-brand skin and hair care products and quality supplies and equipment. Their brushes, combs, clippers, and scissors are made for professional use, so you know they will deliver top-notch performance and last a long time.

Wigs are high style again with the young and trendy, so we've included a good source of low-priced hairpieces and wigs, as well as an outlet offering a full range of ethnic beauty products.

Several outlets offer bulk products—so bring your own containers for big savings on natural cosmetics and fragrances such as coconut milk soap, carrot moisture cream, frankincense, and rose petal. Be sure to check our section on Hair Salons for additional sources of bulk shampoos and gels.

The Body Shop
Portland: 700 S.W. Fifth Ave. *(Pioneer Place)* ☎ 226–7141
12000 S.E. 82nd Ave. (*Clackamas Town Center*) ☎ 653–8384
Hours: Mon–Fri 10–9, Sat 10–6, Sun 11–6
The first Body Shop opened in England in 1976. Now over 500 shops in 37 countries offer skin and hair care products made of natural ingredients that have not been animal-tested—and they're packaged in recyclable containers. You'll find coconut milk soap, honey water, aloe peel-off face mask, rhassoul mud shampoo, carrot moisture cream, and several hundred other products at prices lower than those found in the department stores. The Body Shop encourages recycling by crediting customers 25 cents for every bottle they return and have refilled.

Checks, Credit cards

Escential
Portland: 710 N.W. 23rd ☎ 248–9748
3638 S.E. Hawthorne Blvd. ☎ 236–7976
Hours: Mon–Sat 10–6, Sun 11–4

Put a little pizazz in your life by choosing from over 140 fragrances that can be added to a wide variety of unscented bath and skin care products. How about custom scenting your bubble bath or body lotion with a little frankincense, rose petal, or rain? One way the prices are kept low here is by offering simple packaging. You'll also find mineral bath crystals, glycerine soap, and $\frac{1}{2}$-oz. perfume oils—all at prices below those found in other specialty or department stores.

Checks, Credit cards

Garden Botanika

Tigard: 9508 S.W. Washington Square Rd. *(Washington Square)* ☎ 620–1975
Hours: Mon–Fri 10–9, Sat 10–6, Sun 11–6

Garden Botanika offers naturally based body, bath, skin, and hair care products made with botanical and mineral extracts at 50% or more off fashionable department store prices. They're able to offer low prices by avoiding the expensive "marketing hype" that usually goes along with cosmetics and by locating in high-traffic shopping malls, thereby not needing much advertising. The company does not use animal products or petro-chemicals and does not test its products on animals. They use recyclable materials and give a five-cent refund for returning used containers to the store. Go ahead and try their ivy and yarrow moisture creme, their linden flower cleansing milk, or their energizing hair conditioner with Ginseng—you'll be bestowing kindness to your body, wallet, and planet. The Clackamas Town Center and Lloyd Center stores are scheduled to open soon.

Checks, Credit cards

Ja-Bell's Beauty & Barber Supplies

Portland: 5287 N. Lombard ☎ 283–6085
5834 N.E. M.L. King Blvd. *(Union)* ☎ 281–6393
Hours: Mon–Sat 9:30–6

Ja-Bell's offers a wide variety of beauty, barber, and nail supplies, including a large selection of ethnic beauty products. You'll find big savings on their generic knock-offs of the major brands. Ensure conditioner from *Nexxus* usually sells for $13 for the 16-oz. container; its generic knock-off goes for $9.95 for a whopping 32 ounces—a savings of over 60%. Knock-offs are also available on *Redken* and *Paul Mitchell* products. We found good prices on their hair-cutting scissors, ranging from $7.95 to $17.95. *Wahl* clippers, usually around $50, were sale priced from $28 to $39. Ja-Bell's also carries a nice selection of *O.P.I.* and *Ultra* nail tips; a set of 20 were priced from $2.95 to $4.25.

Checks, Credit cards

Save More Beauty Products

Portland: 12415 N.E. Glisan ☎ 254–4773
Hours: Mon–Fri 9–6, Sat 9–5:30

Save More carries a large selection of competitively priced professional beauty products. You'll find savings of 20% or more on such brands as *Paul Mitchell, KMS, Focus 21, Peter Haus,* and *Sebastian* when you bring in your own bottles and fill them from the store's bulk containers.

Checks, Credit cards

Wells Hairgoods

Portland: 1960 S.E. Hawthorne Blvd. ☎ 234–0977
Hours: Mon–Sat 9–5:30

For anyone needing extra hair, Wells Hairgoods is the place to shop. Wells, in business for over 20 years, offers a full line of wigs and hairpieces for men and women, including styling and cleaning services. A large assortment of close-outs are priced at 50% off regular prices. *Eva Gabor* samples and close-outs start at $39.

Checks, Credit cards

Drugs & Sundries

When you go to the pharmacy to pick up your prescription drug, ask the pharmacist to fill it with the "generic equivalent." The generic will be safe, effective, and much cheaper than the prescribed name-brand drug. Better yet, when your doctor is writing out the prescription, ask him or her for a generic drug. It's your right to get the generic equivalent, so insist upon it.

Even though you're buying generic, it doesn't mean you're getting the lowest possible price. Prices on generic prescription drugs can differ measurably between pharmacies, so shop around before you buy.

Costco Pharmacy

Aloha: 15901 S.W. Jenkins Rd. ☎ 626–3200
Milwaukie: 13350 S.E. Johnson Rd. ☎ 654–9464
Portland: 4849 N.E. 138th ☎ 257–3935
Tigard: 18120 S.W. Lower Boones Ferry Rd. ☎ 684–9678
Hours: Mon–Fri 11–7, Sat 10–6

What else but great prices would you expect to find at Costco? This giant buys big and passes along the savings. We compared their prescription drug prices with those of several major chains and found Costco's prices to be 40% to 50% less. Their over-the-counter products such as aspirin, antacids, cough syrups, and cold remedies are also priced lower than at any other pharmacy.

Checks

Irving St. Pharmacy

Portland: 638 N.W. 23rd ☎ 223–6297
Hours: Mon–Fri 9–8, Sat 9–7

We found some of the lowest prescription prices around at this pharmacy. We compared the prices of several popular prescription drugs sold here and at the major chains. Irving St.'s prices were an amazing 40% to 50% less than those of the chains. Ask them about shipping your prescriptions to you.

Checks, Credit cards

Medic Pharmacy

Portland: 1016 S.W. Clay ☎ 222–9611
Hours: Mon–Fri 9–6

Put this pharmacy's phone number on your refrigerator door! Medic's prices on selected prescription drugs were a whopping 50% to 55% less than on those comparable items found at several major chains we called. Low overhead and volume purchasing enable Medic to offer low prices. For 50 cents they'll ship your order (regardless of how many items) to you.

Checks, Credit cards

Medicine Shoppe Pharmacies

Forest Grove: 2305 Pacific Ave. ☎ 357–7171
Gresham: 1855 N.E. Division ☎ 669–0473
Portland: 5534 E. Burnside ☎ 235–0164
Vancouver: 8606 E. Mill Plain ☎ (206)892–6700
Hours: Mon–Fri 10–6, Sat 10–1

These franchised pharmacies offer free health-care screenings, pre-schooler discounts, and prices on selected prescription medications from 30% to 35% less than the prices for those same products at several major chains. Medicine Shoppe will match any other pharmacy's prescription prices.

Checks, Credit cards

Northwest First Aid Supply

Portland: 10322 S.E. Holgate ☎ 761–0233
Hours: Mon–Fri 9–6, Sat 9–2

This company specializes in first aid kits and refills, emergency medical supplies, and products for diabetics (such as blood glucose monitors and test strips, insulin, needles, and swabs), all at low discounted prices. They stock a wide selection of over-the-counter medications and supplies that are available in large-quantity packaging at prices 10% to 30% off. Call for a price sheet and mail order form.

Checks, Credit cards

Portland Pharmacy
Portland: 4300 S.E. Hawthorne Blvd. ☎ 233–9634
Hours: Mon–Fri 9:30–6, Sat 9:30–4

This single unit pharmacy advertises that they'll match any other pharmacy's prices. We found that prices on selected prescription drugs were 15% to 25% lower than at the big chains.

Checks, Credit cards

Dental Services

The cost of dental care can be painfully high. Yet alternatives do exist for bargain shoppers determined to get the best price on everything. Portland-area residents are fortunate to live near a university dental school and two community college dental clinics where a variety of dental services, including exams, X-rays, cleaning, fillings, crowns, and root canals are performed at a fraction of the cost charged by dentists in private practice.

Work is performed by dentists-in-training and dental hygiene students under the supervision of their professors. Be patient, however; the services are likely to be quite thorough and much slower than those performed by a private dentist. But you'll love the prices.

Mt. Hood Community College Dental Clinic
Gresham: 26000 S.E. Stark ☎ 667–7176
Hours: Tues–Fri 8–4

Their specialty is cleaning teeth at low prices. For $20 you'll get an exam and a teeth cleaning. Six months later you can return for another cleaning for $15. Full-mouth X-rays are $10. You'll have to schedule your cleaning a month in advance. Dental hygiene students do all the work, and their skills are matched by the wonderful enthusiasm with which they go about their work. Low income and welfare clients can have fillings replaced or inserted for $10 to $25, and the work is performed by a dentist. The clinic is closed from the end of May to the beginning of October.

Checks, Credit cards

Oregon Health Sciences University School of Dentistry
Portland: 611 S.W. Campus Dr. ☎ 494–8867
Hours: Mon–Thurs 9–12 & 2–5

You'll save 50% or more on your dental bills when you bring your teeth here. An exam plus x-rays cost $42; a cleaning is $25. Fillings are from $20 to $40. (For more involved work such as crowns, or root canals, call for pricing.) The work is done by students under the supervision of dentists. Appointments must be made at least a week in advance. In addition, there's a pediatric department for youngsters (ages two to 13) where he or she can have an exam, X-rays, cleaning, and fluoride treatment for $20. Pediatric appointments must be made a month in advance; no appointments can be made in August or the first two weeks in September when the dental school is closed.

Checks, Credit cards

Portland Community College Dental Clinic

Portland: 12000 S.W. 49th *(Sylvania Campus)* ☎ 244–6111 x4909
Hours: Mon–Fri 9–3

This clinic offers low prices on a variety of dental services. The charge for teeth cleaning ranges from $8 to $15 (the dirtier the teeth, the higher the cost). For $4 you can have your bite wings X-rayed, and your full mouth X-rayed for $15. The clinic does not perform complicated dental work such as extractions or crowns, but sticks to routine, simple fillings; they charge from $5 to $12 for this service. All work is done by dental students under the watchful eyes of dentists. You'll have to make your appointments a month in advance. The clinic is not open from June through October.

Checks

Optical Services

Those of you who've been paying high prices for eyeglasses will be delighted with the outlets listed in this section. Eye exams, lenses (including contacts), and designer frames are all priced below the retail prices found at major optical chains. Be sure to ask about their fitting or exchange policies.

Beaverton Wholesale Optical

Beaverton: 3889 S.W. Hall Blvd. ☎ 626–2616
Hours: Mon–Fri 10–6, Thurs 10–7, Sat 9–2

Single-vision lenses with frames start at $52 (about 25% less than the chains) and the charge for an eye exam is $34. You'll find big savings off chain-store prices when you buy contact lenses here starting at $89 (includes an eye exam).

Checks, Credit cards

Costco Optvision

Aloha: 15901 S.W. Jenkins Rd. ☎ 641–6023
Portland: 4849 N.E. 138th ☎ 257–3557
Hours: Mon, Wed, Fri 11–7, Tues & Thurs 10–7, Sat 9:30–6, Sun 11–5

If you can break away for a while from all those good buys you're finding in the rest of Costco, be sure to stop by the in-house optical department, where you'll find prices below those at the chains. An eye exam, including glaucoma test, runs $34; single-vision lenses are $39.95. Frames are priced at $24.95 and up. Extended-wear contacts range from $79.95 to $149.95.

Although the rest of Costco doesn't accept credit cards, the optical department does.

Checks, Credit cards

Crown Optical and Safety Inc.
Portland: 2933 E. Burnside ☎ 232–5006
Hours: Mon–Fri 9–5, Sat 9:30–1
Crown's single-vision lenses and frames start at $60 (about 15% less than the chains) and exams at $45. There are hundreds of adult frames to choose from, including one of the largest selections of children's frames in Portland (over 300 in stock). Their daily-wear soft lenses (about 40% less than the chains) start at $120, which includes a $50 contact lens eye exam.

Checks, Credit cards

Eye-Land
Beaverton: 2680 S.W. Cedar Hills Blvd. *(Walker Center)* ☎ 626–2444
Portland: 11390 S.E. 82nd Ave. *(Clackamas Square)* ☎ 777–0361
Hours: Mon–Sat 10–6
Eye-Land is so sure of their low pricing that if you find a locally advertised lower price within 30 days of your purchase, they'll refund you the difference. Their single-vision glasses with frames (about 40% less than at the major optical chains) start at $39.95 for one pair; for $59.95, you can purchase two pairs. Fashion and premium-line frames add an additional $20 to $40 to the basic $39.95. Contact lenses start at $30 a pair, and eye examinations run from $29. There are hundreds of frames to choose from, each offering tremendous savings when compared to chain-store prices.

Checks, Credit cards

Nationwide Vision Center
Beaverton: 3780 S.W. Hall Blvd. ☎ 646–7711
Portland: 11211 S.E. 82nd *(Ross Center)* ☎ 659–3515
Hours: Mon–Thurs 9–8, Fri 9–6, Sat 9–5
You'll think you're seeing double—Nationwide's single-vision lenses with selected frames start at $39.99 for two pair. Prices for lenses with higher quality frames range from $59.99 to $89.99 a pair, with a second pair available for $10 to $30 extra. Eye exams for glasses are $22, while those for contacts range from $48 to $58.

Checks, Credit cards

Optical Brokers
Portland: 134 N.W. 21st Ave. ☎ 295–6488
7325 S.E. Milwaukie Ave. ☎ 238–9868
Hours: 21st, Mon–Fri 10–6; Milwaukie Mon–Fri 10–6, Sat 10–3

Single-vision lenses start at $32 a pair; designer frames, from $40 to $70. You'll find the biggest savings on their discontinued frames, which run as low as $5 – $10. Daily-wear contact lenses start at $52 a pair. The store on Milwaukee gives eye exams, but the one on 21st does not; you'll have to bring your own eyeglass prescription there.

Checks, Credit cards

Home Building & Remodeling

Whether your remodeling plans include a whole-house make-over, papering the walls, or just tiling around the tub, the best places to begin your comparison shopping are Builders Square, Fred Meyer Home Improvement Centers, Home Club, Pay 'N Pak, and Tualatin Valley Builders Supply. These well-known suppliers of building materials and tools offer both the serious and amateur do-it-yourselfer a good look at how the project can be done and at what cost. If the project is big enough, ask for a package discount, and by all means don't be shy about asking for detailed advice on how to do the job.

Building Materials, Hardware, and Tools

In addition to the stores listed below don't forget to check the section Surplus and Liquidators for some more good bargains.

Building Materials & Hardware

Builders City
Portland: 8905 N. Vancouver ☎ 285–0546
Hours: Mon–Sat 8:30–5, Sun 10–5
  Not quite as large as a city, but at least five acres of building materials, including close-outs, overstocks, and freight-damaged goods await the bargain shopper. Although the inventory is continually changing, you'll find a large selection of doors, siding, lumber, paneling, hardware, plumbing and electrical supplies, paint, and more. If you know what you can use and are

a good judge of quality, you'll certainly have a ball shopping here and picking up some incredible bargains.

Checks, Credit cards

Builders Lighting Inc.

Tualatin: 17571 S.W. 65th Ave. ☎ 639–8816
Hours: Mon–Fri 8:30–5, Sat 10–4

Builders Lighting offers one of the largest selections of decorative fixtures and table and floor lamps in Oregon. You'll find the best prices on their red-tag sale merchandise, mostly fixtures and some lamps, scattered around the showroom floor. Several times a year they have a "50/20 sale" in which hanging lamps are 50% off and floor lamps, 20% off. These 50/20 sales are well advertised about a week or so before they begin.

Checks, Credit cards

Builders Square

Portland: 2315 S.E. 82nd Ave. ☎ 775–0040
1160 Hayden Meadows Dr. ☎ 286–0074
Hours: Mon–Sat 7:30–9, Sun 9–6

Do-it-yourselfers will find a large selection of home improvement and organizing ideas at warehouse prices. Building materials, plumbing, electrical, decorating, tools, and garden and patio equipment are all good buys, but the competition is fierce and the smart shopper will compare prices. Watch for their periodic sales and promotions when prices on selected items are marked down 50% off their everyday low prices.

Checks, Credit cards

1874 House

Portland: 8070 S.E. 13th Ave. ☎ 233–1874
Hours: Tues–Sat 10–4

1874 House carries a good selection of antique and reproduction hardware, lighting fixtures and shades, windows, shutters, and mantels—all waiting to become part of remodeled old homes. We found a nice array of interior doors priced from $20 to several hundred dollars, plus door locks and plated hinges at $2 apiece. Don't miss their annual sidewalk sale each October (held in front of the store), where reproduction hardware is discounted at least 10%; even bigger savings can be found on selected old hardware and fixtures.

Checks, Credit cards

George A. Morlan Plumbing Supply

Portland: 5529 S.E. Foster Rd. ☎ 771–1145
Tigard: 12585 S.W. Pacific Hwy ☎ 624–7381
Hours: Mon–Fri 7:30–6, Sat 9–5, Sun 10–4

These stores are among the largest plumbing outlets in the area, offering a wide range of parts, fixtures, and related equipment at competitive prices. Several times a year they hold red-tag sales and selected items are marked way down. When you're doing a large remodeling job and buy a tub, toilet, sink, and faucet, for example, ask for their special "package price," which is also available on other "package" purchases. Frequent close-outs can also yield big savings; we found a pedestal and faucet marked down to $99.

Checks, Credit cards

Hippo Hardware & Trading Co.
Portland: 1040 E. Burnside ☎ 231–1444
Hours: Mon–Sat 10–6

Hippo is not your typical hardware store. Sure, they have new hardware, plumbing, lighting, and architectural items. But you'll also find original Victorian hardware, turn-of-the-century fixtures, plus whatever else they find when they go in and strip old houses before demolition. Some fixtures are bargain-priced, while Victorian and "antique" items can get pricey. Bring in your own fixtures and work out a swap with them (after all, they are a "trading" company) and ask about their 10% quantity buying discount.

Checks, Credit cards

Home Club
Beaverton: 11055 S.W. Canyon Rd. ☎ 643–3433
Portland: 1950 N.E. 122nd Ave. ☎ 252–9898
Hours: Mon–Fri 7–9, Sat 7–8, Sun 8–6

This giant warehouse operation stocks all sorts of remodeling and building project materials and supplies, including lumber, tools, hardware, fixtures, windows, doors, wall and floor coverings, and garden supplies. Home Club is open to everyone and separate prices for members and non-members are a thing of the past. Watch for their promotional flyers that are frequently inserted in *The Oregonian*. Home Club stores for Salem and Clackamas are scheduled to open soon.

Checks, Credit cards

Pay 'N Pak Home Center
Beaverton: 2595 S.W. Cedar Hills Blvd. ☎ 641–7430
  4955 S.W. Western Ave. ☎ 641–1939
Gresham: 2865 N.E. Hogan Rd. ☎ 667–4606
Milwaukie: 15550 S.E. McLoughlin Blvd. ☎ 654–5740
Portland: 7365 S.W. Barbur Blvd. ☎ 245–0714
  8900 N. Vancouver ☎ 285–4987
  5240 S.E. 82nd Ave. ☎ 777–4111
  750 S.E. 122nd Ave. ☎ 254–8287
Salem: 441 Lancaster Dr. N.E. ☎ 581–9771

Vancouver: 5411 E. Mill Plain *(Town Plaza)* ☎ (206) 699–5112
Hours: Mon–Fri 9–8, Sat 9–6, Sun 10–5

At Pay 'N Pak Home Centers you'll find a wide selection of self-service items, including lighting and plumbing fixtures, housewares, tools, electrical supplies, cabinets, water heaters, home security, building materials, and even kitchen sinks—all at competitive prices. Close-outs are always good buys, and several times a year their promotional sales are worth catching.

Checks, Credit cards

Ralph Miles Liquidators

Portland: 7639 S.E. Foster Rd. ☎ 775–1030
2601 N.W. Nicolai ☎ 295–0492
Hours: Mon–Sat 8–6, Sun 9–5

About 75% of their inventory consists of building materials, and the remainder is general merchandise, such as tools, housewares, kitchenwares, hardware, patio and gardening equipment, beauty supplies, and toys. Ralph Miles deals in wholesaler and manufacturer close-outs, offering great prices on new and used stock. Their 99-cent items include shampoos, trash bags, sunglasses, bottle openers, spatulas, pens and pencils, paper airplanes, stuffed dolls, and more. We found low prices on fan hoods, roofing materials, scroll and band saws, wood doors (pre-hung, with over 3,000 in stock), as well as on interior and exterior paint. Inventory continually changes, so get on their mailing list to hear about new stock and specials.

Checks, Credit cards

Rejuvenation House Parts Co.

Portland: 901 N. Skidmore ☎ 249–2038
Hours: Mon–Sat 9–5:30

Rejuvenation carries just about everything you need for remodeling your home. You'll find a wide variety of lighting, plumbing, and hardware items, as well as architectural elements and vintage doors. Salvage lighting fixtures and salvage plumbing parts are available at reduced prices, but often in "as-is" condition, so check them out carefully. Sometimes their refurbished original fixtures can be found at better prices than reproductions.

Checks, Credit cards

Truax Builders Supply

Portland: 10949 S.E. Division St. ☎ 256–4066
Hours: Mon–Thurs 8–5, Fri 8–6

Truax offers aluminum, wood, and vinyl windows, doors, and skylights at prices that beat those at most lumberyards. We found storm doors regularly priced at $114 marked down to $99. They take pride in the helpful service they offer before and after each purchase. Also, pre-hanging service is available. Although prices are competitive on most items, it's wise to comparison-shop when on large purchases.

Checks

Tualatin Valley Builders Supply

Aloha: 20945 S.W. Tualatin Valley Hwy ☎ 591–8827
Gresham: 905 E. Burnside St. ☎ 667–8827
Lake Oswego: 15700 S.W. Boones Ferry Rd. ☎ 636–8401
Hours: Generally, Mon–Fri 7–6, Sat 8–5, Sun 10–4

This company carries a complete line of building materials for both the serious do-it-yourselfer and the professional home builder. Hardware and lumber are their specialties. Several times a month the store runs ads in *This Week* magazine (delivered in the mail on Tuesdays) offering discounted prices on selected items. You'll appreciate their fine, friendly service, and they're happy to special order any item not in their regular inventory.

Checks, Credit cards

Tools

Black and Decker

Portland: 1640 N.W. Johnson St. ☎ 228–8631
Hours: Mon–Fri 8–5

This outlet carries a large selection of Black and Decker tools, including sanders, saws, drills, polishers, and mowers. All items are "blemished" or reconditioned and priced at 15% or more off the retail prices found at other stores for these same tools. Blemished tools are those that have been scratched or discolored; in most cases the only defect is a dent or tear in the packing box holding the tool. Black and Decker guarantees reconditioned tools with the same warranties carried by new tools. They also carry a large stock of reconditioned professional tools.

Checks, Credit cards

Bob's Rental and Sales

Portland: 8041 S.E. McLouglin Blvd. ☎ 233–4671
  14625 S.E. Stark St. ☎ 255–4671
Hours: Daily 7–7

Bob's rents a wide variety of tools, equipment, machinery, and gear. When normal wear and tear requires Bob's to purchase new rental stock, they sell the used items at 50% or more off new. We found used tractors, tillers, saws, sod cutters, concrete tools, a small selection of power tools, and sports equipment. Used lawn mowers were priced from $60 to $250, and several used four-person rubber rafts, which go for $190 new, were priced from $60 to $70 apiece. Because their used inventory is continually coming and going, call if you're looking for something in particular.

Checks, Credit cards

Griffin Tool
Cornelius: 2442 Baseline ☎ 693–0804
Hours: Mon–Sat 9–4

Griffin Tool carries a large selection of new and used tools, such as hoists, jacks, planers, band saws, welders, grinders, compressors, and compactors. The best prices are on their used power tools, which can be 50% or more below new prices. New drill presses run around $145, while an old bench model drill press with new motor was priced at $70. The used-equipment inventory turns over quickly, so call or stop by often.

Checks, Credit cards

The Tool Peddler
Portland: 11493 S.E. 82nd Ave. ☎ 653–7084
Hours: Mon–Fri 8–6, Sat 9–5

Tools are their only business, and they claim to offer the greatest selection of tools at discounted prices in the Portland area. They carry major lines and well-known brands, and gladly quote prices over the phone. In addition to low prices they offer friendly, helpful service that may not always be available at large chain operations. Watch for their spring and winter sales.

Checks, Credit cards

Paint & Wallpaper

Walls should do more than hold the ceiling up and the floor down. Whether you cover them with paper or paint, walls can brighten your spirits, make rooms look larger and lighter, help cut down the glare of sunlight pouring in, or make your home a cozy, welcoming haven. The stores listed below offer a large selection of wallpaper and paint, many of which are close-outs or discontinued patterns. The best prices are available on "goof" paints (mismatched colors, unclaimed custom tints, etc.) and on older or discontinued wallpaper patterns. Watch for newspaper ads or call your favorite store to see when the next sale is planned.

Imperial Paint Company
Portland: 2526 N.W. Yeon ☎ 228–0207
Salem: 4190 River Rd. ☎ 390–1613
Hours: Portland, Mon–Fri 8–5; Salem, Mon–Fri 8–5, Sat 9–1

These factory outlets offer premium paints available in 900 colors at prices from $5 to $12 a gallon less than competitors' prices. Additional discounts are available when you buy paint in 5-gal. cans. You'll also find a large variety of painting supplies here at competitive prices. The Salem store goes by the name of H and H/Imperial Paint; be sure to ask for "painter prices" when shopping there.

Checks, Credit cards

Portland Paint and Supply Co.

Portland: 11025 N.E. Halsey St. ☎ 252–2440
Hours: Mon–Fri 7:30–5:30, Sat 8–4

This store's premium interior and exterior paints are competitively priced starting at $21.95 a gallon. However, the big savings come on their "goof paints" (paints that were mis-mixed or tinted paints that were ordered by customers but never picked up). These "goofs" are actually top-of-the-line paints and are available in varying quantities and shades (a lot of off-whites!). They sell for an incredible $5 per gal. If you roll up your sleeves and dig through the piles, you may come up with anywhere from two to ten gallons of the same color and shade. If not, do what a lot of painters do—select a few close shades and mix them yourself. Your customized mixes made from these goofs would make great primers.

Checks, Credit cards

Rodda Paint

Beaverton: 3615 S.W. Hall *(Beavercreek Village)* ☎ 641–7750
   8614 S.W. Hall *(Progress Plaza)* ☎ 644–6188
Gresham: 2155 N.E. Burnside *(Oregon Trail Center)* ☎ 661–0400
Hillsboro: 2293 N.W. 185th Ave. *(Tanasbourne Village)* ☎ 645–1028
Oregon City: I–205 at McLoughlin *(Oregon City Shopping Center)*
   ☎ 655–7981
Portland: 11980 N.E. Glisan ☎ 255–3224
   1103 S.E. 7th Ave. ☎ 233–6016
   10309 S.E. 82nd. Ave. ☎ 788–0797
   6932 S.W. Macadam ☎ 245–0788
Salem: 2395 Lancaster Dr. N.E. ☎ 585–7900
Tualatin: 8365 Tonka ☎ 692–6699
Vancouver: 4710 E. Fourth Plain Blvd. ☎ (206)696–0300
Hours: Generally, Mon–Fri 7:30–6, Sat 8–6, Sun 12–5

Rodda offers a wide array of competitively priced interior and exterior paint, wallpaper, and window coverings. Their top-of-the-line flat interior paint runs $12.99 to $15.99 per gal., while the semi-gloss interior paint is priced from $16.99 per gal. However, you'll save several dollars per gallon by asking for their Master Painter paint (also known as "contractor grade.") This paint is not as high quality as their regular top-of-the-line products, but it still equals or exceeds many other manufacturers' top brands. You'll find even bigger savings on their "mistints"—in-store tinting goofs. These mistints are top-of-the-line products that go for as little as $3.99 per gal., and you can choose from hundreds of gallons of these paints (which are usually hidden away in their basements—so ask for them). Watch for their big January and July half-off sales.

Checks, Credit cards

Standard Brands
Beaverton: 13281 S.W. Canyon Rd. ☎ 626–6777
Portland: 20 N.E. Hancock ☎ 287–8098
11424 S.E. 82nd Ave. ☎ 653–5311
12339 S.E. Stark St. ☎ 253–5043
Hours: Mon–Fri 9–9, Sat & Sun 9–5:30
You'll find a wide range of paint to choose from at Standard Brands, from their plain labels starting at $6.99 per gal. to the Standard Brand premium at $18.99 per gal. In stock you'll find floor and wall coverings, including carpets, tiles, and blinds; something is usually on sale every day. When we checked they were closing out *Color Roll* wallpaper at $1.99 per roll. There was a terrific variety of art supplies at good prices, as well as remnants at bargain-basement prices. Watch for bulk mailings that announce their periodic sales promotions.

Checks, Credit cards

The Wallpaper Place
Beaverton: 9575 S.W. Beaverton-Hillsdale Hwy. ☎ 646–6016
Hours: Mon–Fri 10–6, Sat 10–5
The Wallpaper Place offers a nice selection of wallpapers and window coverings at 20% to 70% off suggested retail. We found the same wallpaper pattern that was priced at $17.99 per roll at one of the chain stores at only $10.99 per roll here. Several pattern books of supplier close-out wallpapers were priced at 60% off suggested retail, and a couple of bins of old-pattern wallpaper were priced from $1.50 to $2 per roll. They also carry adhesives and tools. For even bigger savings, watch for the store's frequent sales.

Checks, Credit cards

Wallpapers To Go
Beaverton: 10205 S.W. Beaverton-Hillsdale Hwy. ☎ 643–7523
Milwaukie: 15601 S.E. McLoughlin Blvd. ☎ 654–3149
Portland: 1182 N. Hayden Meadows Dr. ☎ 283–3039
Hours: Mon–Fri 10–8, Sat 10–6, Sun 12–5
You'll find thousands of in-stock and special-order patterns available at this national chain. A good selection of discounted patterns was available from $3.99 to $9.99 per roll. If you find the right discounted pattern but there are too few rolls, have them call around to their other stores to get you more. Check out the "gift wrap" bin, where you'll find various patterns in 1- to 2-roll quantities priced at $1.99 each (just enough to wrap your gifts). Watch

for their frequent sales, especially the semi-annual home sales where all in-stock wallpapers are up to 30% off. When we checked they were holding a 20% off sale on most patterns.

Checks, Credit cards

Wood stoves

The modern wood stove has shed its former smoky reputation and has become both an economical and environmental alternative to most other forms of home heating, especially nonrenewable fossil fuels. Current wood stove technology has reduced particulate emissions by over 85%, lowered operating costs, and improved the convenience of wood heat (to say nothing of helping us become "energy independent—especially important in this day and age of continual oil crises). Woodstoves are not the simple little fireboxes they once may have been. Be sure to get advice from your wood stove dealer about size, burn technology, and the wide range of available features. By tailoring your wood stove to your needs, you'll find the right model at the right price.

Cascade Fireplace & Stove Co.
Portland: 2222 N.W. Raleigh ☎ 241–8899
Hours: Mon–Thurs 8–6, Fri 8–7, Sat 9–5

At the Northwest's largest wood stove and fireplace warehouse (over 18,000 square feet of inventory), you'll find a complete selection of pellet stoves, wood stoves, and fireplace inserts in a variety of colors and available options, all at competitive prices. Check out their periodic sales and close-out merchandise for savings. If you're looking for quality stoves and don't mind a few blemishes or even minor damage, you'll find big savings on models that have been scratched or dinged in transport between the store and the several home shows at which the company displays its stock. Ask the salesperson to point out these home-show demos and any other models that the store's salespeople have used as field demos. You're guaranteed to save hundreds off regular retail. We found one such demo, a cast-iron from Ireland with a broken leg, that was marked down over $400.

Checks, Credit cards

Lisac's Discount Stoves
Milwaukie: 9035 S.E. 32nd Ave. ☎ 297–7815
Hours: Mon–Fri 11–6, Sat 11–5

Customers from as far away as California and the Oregon and Washington coasts come here to find the best buys in wood, gas, or pellet stoves. Lisac's offers such brand-name equipment as *Earth Stove, Jamestown, Quadra-Fire,* and *Oregon Stove* at prices from $100 to $400 less than competitors' prices. Lisac's has been in business for over 50 years and advertises that they will not be undersold. Watch for their seasonal sales.

Checks, Credit cards

Floor Coverings

Your choice of floor coverings can set the tone of your room, from softly romantic to old-world elegance, with a lot of mood in between. Whether you choose the plushest carpet, an exotic wood, natural brick, or stone, it's wise to consider durability, ease of care, beauty, and, of course, price! Carpeting just happens to be the most popular floor covering in the typical American home. The first step in finding that dream carpet is to browse around the better retail and department stores to get a close up look (and feel!) at what's available. Ask employees about the quality and differences between the styles you like. In short, find out as much as you can. Armed with your new-found carpet knowledge, start calling and visiting the stores listed below, and you'll find that beautiful floor covering at a price you'll be happy to pay.

B & E Home Furnishers
West Linn: 19155 Willamette Dr. ☎ 636–0636
Hours: Mon–Fri 8–5:30, Sat 10:30–4

Attention do-it-yourselfers! B & E offers a "no-frills" deal that shaves several dollars or more a yard off such fine name brands as *Evans and Black, Philadelphia, Salem,* and *Cabin Crafts.* After you make your selection from among the hundreds of their display samples , B & E places your order, and two weeks later you pick up your own carpet (direct from the mills) at the docks on Swan Island. By picking up your own carpet and making your own installation arrangements, you'll pay only from $7 to $9 per yd. for your carpet. B & E also offers a regular full-service carpet business, and you'll find low prices based on their pricing formula of charging their cost plus 10% plus freight. Also, you might have them finish off a remnant, which makes a nice area rug at a great price.

Checks, Credit cards

Buccella's Hilltop Interiors
Oregon City: 2264 Molalla Ave. ☎ 655–0784
Hours: Mon–Fri 9–5, Sat by appointment

While this shop carries only a small in-store stock of carpets, it has access to all the same brands such as *Armstrong, Philadelphia,* and *Salem* sold by the major stores. Carpets that run from $13 to $25 elsewhere are priced from $10 to $18 at Buccella's. A plush, usually priced at $33 per yd., was everyday priced at $22. Good quality 100% nylon carpets range from $7.50 to $8.50.

You'll find the service excellent here—after all, you'll be dealing with the owner of the store.

Checks, Credit cards

Carpeteria

Beaverton: 4800 S.W. Western Ave. ☎ 643–0115
Clackamas: 9064 S.E. Sunnyside Rd. *(Clackamas Promenade)* ☎ 653–5943
Portland: 16022 S.E. Stark St. ☎ 255–4997
Hours: Mon & Fri 9–9, Tues–Thurs & Sat 9–6, Sun 10–6

With over 80 stores in the chain, Carpeteria buys in bulk and passes along the savings to their customers. They carry most of the major brands and prices start out at around $13.99 per yd., which includes pad and installation. We spotted a nice selection of 5'x8' Oriental rugs from $99 to $199. Don't be afraid to negotiate. One salesperson confided that the pad and installation can usually be worked in for free. Watch for periodic sales where the savings can be significant, with such items as close-out carpets priced from $9 per yd.

Checks, Credit cards

Carpet City

Portland: 1511 S.E. Holgate Blvd. ☎ 231–4944
Vancouver: 2113 E. Fourth Plain ☎ (206)696–1106
Hours: Mon–Fri 9–6, Sat 9:30–4:30

At Carpet City you'll find carpets from such nationally known companies as *Philadelphia, World, Armstrong,* and *Salem* at prices between wholesale and retail. Plushes start at $11.99 per yd., and these prices include pads. Beautiful 2'x4' Oriental-looking rugs (each with fringes on the edges) were priced at $39. They have a large room full of remnants priced from $5.99 to $13.99 per yd. (including pads). When we checked, thick plush friezes were sale priced at 30% off retail.

Checks, Credit cards

Carpet Mill Outlet

Portland: 8300 S.E. McLoughlin Blvd. ☎ 233–6071
Hours: Mon–Fri 9:30–7:30, Sat 9:30–5:30, Sun 12–5

Carpet Mill Outlet offers a wide selection of competitively priced carpets, but you'll find the best deals in their remnants department. First-quality, brand-name remnants (Grade A) are 50% off retail and range from $6.99 to $12.99 per yd. The store buys remnants directly from the mills and can sell the customer enough to fill anyone's house. They also find remnants that make great low-priced area rugs. Remnants come and go quickly, so give one of their decorators your name and phone number and they'll be on the lookout for the style and color you need. Watch for their periodic sales and save up to 30% off retail on their stock of competitively priced carpets. Ask for a preferred customer card and save from 5% to 10% off all carpets (except remnants).

Checks, Credit cards

Carpet Place
Portland: 8112 S.E. Foster Rd. ☎ 775–4391
Hours: Mon–Sun 9–6

Since 1967, Carpet Place has been offering great selection and great prices. As wholesale carpet brokers, they offer any of the major brand names for about one-half the price of many retail stores. Their showroom holds over 10,000 samples from such leading American mills as *Salem, Queen, Galaxy, Cabin Crafts, Monticello,* and *Cascade.* From two days to two weeks after you place your order, the carpet is ready for you to pick up at the warehouse on Swan Island. Their commercial grades start at $4 per yd., while their major brands of quality residential, including plushes, range from $5 to $15 per yd. By keeping their overhead low (i.e., no warehouse or storage expenses, no vehicles, no commissioned salespeople, and no credit cards), they're able to pass on great prices to their customers.

Checks

Carpet World
Portland: 7126 N.E. Sandy Blvd. ☎ 287–2290
Hours: Mon–Fri 9:30–6, Sat 9:30–5, Sun 12–5

This family-owned business has been offering first-quality name-brand carpets at discount prices for over a quarter of a century. They stock hundreds of rolls and remnants in all colors, sizes, and prices. Commercial-grade carpets start at $5.99 per yd. and good-quality residential carpets, such as *World* and *Evans-Black,* can be found for under $7 per yd. We found many good buys in their huge inventory of remnants.

Checks, Credit cards

Color Tile
Beaverton: 3300 S.W. Cedar Hills Blvd. ☎ 643–7471
Gresham: 1108 N.E. Burnside ☎ 667–9474
Milwaukie: 16025 S.E. McLoughlin Blvd. ☎ 659–5134
Portland: 10114 S.E. Division St. ☎ 760–3232
 7461 S.W. Barbur Blvd. ☎ 246–7733
Salem: 1110 Lancaster Dr. N.E. ☎ 371–9291
Tigard: 11940 S.W. Pacific Hwy. ☎ 684–2527
Vancouver: 6718 N.E. Fourth Plain Blvd. ☎ (206)695–9288
Hours: Mon–Fri 8–8, Sat 9–6, Sun 10–5

There are over 735 Color Tile stores nationwide offering an extensive selection of ceramic, vinyl, and wood floor coverings at prices in just about everyone's range. Slow-movers are tagged as close-outs and drastically reduced in price. Their frequent clearance sales, as well as the remnants section, produce incredible savings. When we checked, over 40 floor coverings were being cleared out, and odd-sized lots of sheet vinyl were marked down in the remnants department. They also sell all the supplies necessary for do-it-yourselfers and rent ceramic tile cutters.

Checks, Credit cards

Chase International

Portland: 2730 N.W. Vaughn ☎ 222–1444
Hours: By appointment only

This large wholesale carpet buyer deals mostly with designers and builders. They open their showroom to the public on an appointment only basis except for their quarterly blow-out sales, when most carpets are discounted from 50% to 70% off retail. Their regular stock includes plushes, wool berbers, textures, commercial grades, remnants, and gorgeous hand-made Oriental rugs. Plushes start at $7.99 per yd. They claim that they're rarely undersold, and suggest that customers comparison shop, then make the last stop at Chase International for the best price around. Charge card purchasers pay $3\frac{1}{2}$% extra.

Checks, Credit cards

Crown Carpet

Gresham: 21655 S.E. Stark St. ☎ 655–4162
Hours: Mon–Fri 9–6, Sat 9–5:30, Sun 12–5

Commercial-grade carpets start at $5.99 per yd.; first- quality name-brand residential carpets go for about twice that. We found *Lees* carpets priced about 30% off retail. Their large in-stock supply of remnants makes it easy to find what you're looking for at good prices. In addition to their occasional store-wide sales (watch for their ads), there's always an un-advertised sale going on where you can save from 20% to 30% off retail.

Checks, Credit cards

Floor Covering Distributors

Tigard: 16112 S.W. 72nd ☎ 639–1700
Hours: Mon–Fri 9–4:30, Sat 9–1

This wholesale carpet dealer sells to distributor sand a specially targeted market segment—credit union members. Bring in proof of your member-ship and you can expect to pay from 30% to 50% off retail on first-quality carpets from most of America's largest mills, such as *Lees, Philadelphia, Salem, Cabin Crafts,* and *Monticello.* Although there's a small stock of in-store carpet rolls, you'll be looking through hundreds of samples. Within two weeks of your order, your carpet arrives directly from the mills in original factory wrappers. They also carry a small inventory of remnants at discounted prices.

Checks, Credit cards

Great Floors
Clackamas: 10315 S.E. Highway 212 ☎ 657–7896
Portland: 2818 N.E. 82nd ☎ 255–7896
Hours: Mon–Fri 9–6, Sat 10–4

At Great Floors you'll find wholesale prices and hundreds of full-carpet rolls on display from such well-known companies as *Philadelphia, Burlington,* and *Monticello.* Their good- grade short plushes start at $8.99 per yd.; top-quality plushes go for around $14 per yd. When we checked, they had 25 varieties of vinyl flooring in 12-foot roll ends at discounted prices. Their stock of carpet remnants was low, so best to call if you're shopping remnants.

Checks, Credit cards

Huggers Carpets
Oregon City: 812 Molalla Ave. ☎ 655–9421
Hours: Mon–Fri 8–6, Sat 8:30–5:30

Do-it-yourselfers can save 20% or more off name-brand carpets by picking them up at the store and doing the delivery and installation work themselves. Huggers carries a wide selection of in-stock carpet rolls and samples. Choose among a large inventory of remnants and save 50% or more off retail. The store holds numerous holiday sales, with savings of 20% to 30% off retail, and specials advertised in the *Nickel* ads. Their current special was on a 100% nylon sculpture texture *Philadelphia* carpet for $10.95 per yd., with no charge for pad and installation.

Checks, Credit cards

Linoleum City
Portland: 500 N.E. M.L. King Blvd. *(Union)* ☎ 234–7271
Hours: Mon–Thurs 8:30–5:30, Fri 8:30–7, Sat 9–5

Linoleum City offers name-brand carpet and vinyl floor coverings at prices from 10% to 50% off retail. Looped commercial-grade carpet runs from $5.50 – $8 per yd. plus pad and installation. We saw a looped carpet with a commercial-grade look priced at $3.99 per yd.; and lots of carpet remnants in the $3 to $4 range. Solarian vinyl remnants, and carpet remnants in plushes and level loops were priced up to 60% off regular prices. Be sure to check out their bins of close-out laminate in patterns, solids, and woods priced at up to 70% off retail.

Checks, Credit cards

Macadam Carpet Warehouse
Portland: 6100 S.W. Macadam ☎ 246–9800
Hours: Mon–Fri 9–5:30, Sat 9–5

Macadam buys carpet in volume directly from the mills and passes along the savings to customers. They offer hundreds of full rolls in stock in most styles, including berbers, thick plushes, and commercial grades. We found over 100 remnants in stock at 50% off retail, and lots of area rugs that ranged from $20 for a simple 2'x4' acrylic to the stately Persians priced at $7,500. Macadam sells only first-quality carpet and close-outs—at savings up to 55% off regular prices. Get on the mailing list to find out in advance about specials or close–outs.

Checks, Credit cards

Marion's Carpets
Beaverton: 3625 S.W. Hall Blvd. ☎ 643-5470
Portland: 6817 S.W. 52nd ☎ 771–8554
Tualatin: 8355 Tonka ☎ 692–7014
Hours: Mon–Fri 9–6, Sat 10–5

Marion's prices include pad and installation—so their *Dupont* StainMaster 30-oz. carpet at $11.99 per yd. is a great buy. This carpet is a residential-grade plush that comes with five-year wear and stain warranties. Ask about their "no-risk" plan that provides guarantees on installation, price, quality, and wear of their products.

Metropolitan Floors
Portland: 10708 N.E. Halsey ☎ 256–5234
Hours: Mon–Fri 8–5, Sat 10–3

Metropolitan Floors' complete showroom holds a huge selection of rolls and samples from all nationally known mills, including *Cabin Crafts, Salem, Philadelphia*, and *Lees*. First-quality name brands start at $6.85 per yd.; with remnants priced at up to 50% off retail. Because Metropolitan does considerable business with property management firms and builders, they purchase in huge volumes from the mills and pass along the savings to the customer.

Checks, Credit cards

Self-Service Furniture & Carpet Center
Gresham: 19240 S.E. Stark St. ☎ 665–3133
Hillsboro: 6101 S.W. Tualatin Valley Hwy. ☎ 642–5663
Salem: 3540 S.E. Commerical ☎ 585–7810
Tigard: 14255 S.W. Pacific Hwy. ☎ 620–8445
Vancouver: 7407 N.E. Vancouver Plaza Dr. ☎ (206)254–6786
Hours: Mon–Fri 9–9, Sat 9–5:30, Sun 12–5

This 26-store chain offers low prices by minimizing the number of employees in each store, by combining warehouse and sales operations on the same floor, and by buying carpet by the mile. You'll find major-brand carpets in hundreds of styles and colors starting at $8.95 per yd. (usually $17 to $18 per yd., plus pad and installation. Room-size remnants in a good variety of colors go for around $70 to $80 apiece. These remnants are first-quality carpets left over from customer carpet installations. Area rugs were priced from $119 to $200, while samples, which are great for door mats or pet bedding spots, were $2 each. Ask about their 30-day price guarantee policy. (See the Self-Service listing under our section on furniture.)

Checks, Credit cards

Sneed's Carpet & Interiors
Beaverton: 10115 S.W. Hall Blvd. ☎ 245–7500
Hours: Mon–Fri 10–6, Sat 10–5

You'll find hundreds of samples here of competitively priced carpets—from commercials to plushes and berbers. Occasionally, a mill will pass along a good deal to them, and Sneed's will hold a sale and knock 20% to 30% off retail on selected name-brand carpets. Watch for their ads or call the store to find out in advance about these sales. Also, choose between a good selection of first-quality name-brand remnants priced as low as $5 per yd.

Checks, Credit cards

Tile For Less
Beaverton: 11135 S.W. Canyon Rd. ☎ 643–7968
Portland: 1718 N.E. 122nd Ave. ☎ 252–4127
Hours: Mon–Fri 10–6, Sat 9–5, Sun 12–4

Over 150 types of tile to choose from here, including quarry, ceramic, mosaic, glazed, and unglazed, all for under $2 per sq. ft. There's no ordering and no waiting. Just pick out your tiles, borrow some expert advice and a tile cutter at no charge, and get started on your project. They don't do installations, but will gladly recommend companies that do. Although their supply of discontinued tile fluctuates, you'll pay $1 per sq. ft. if you find what you can use.

Checks, Credit cards

Warehouse Floors
Portland: 1235 S.E. Division ☎ 235–2128
Hours: Mon–Fri 7:30–6, Sat 8:30–5:30

At Warehouse Floors you'll find commerical-grade carpets from $5 per yd., and plush-style residential carpets from $7 a yard. Because they're a discount retail store, you'll find everything here below list prices. We found good prices on carpet close-outs and remnants, as well as discounts of up to 70% on vinyl remnants. They claim the best prices around on vinyl floors from *Mannington, Armstrong,* and *Congoleum.*

First-quality brand-name carpets are 50% off regular retail, and range from $6.99 to $12.99 per yd. Warehouse Floors buys remnants directly from the mills and can sell the customer enough to fill anyone's house. They also find remnants that make great low-priced area rugs. Their remnants come in and go out quickly, so give one of their decorators your name and phone number and he or she will be on the lookout for the style and color you need. Watch for their periodic sales and you'll save up to 30% off retail on their stock of competitively priced carpets. Ask for a preferred customer card and save from 5% to 10% on all carpets (except remnants).

Checks, Credit cards

West Valley Ceramic Tile Co.
Hillsboro: 1823A S.E. Tualatin Valley Hwy. ☎ 640–9727
Hours: Mon–Fri 8:30–5:30, Sat 10–4

You can choose tile from hundreds of manufacturers around the world here at Oregon's largest retail ceramic tile store. West Valley handles only top-of-the-line quality tile for kitchens, baths, floors, and other remodeling projects. Wall tile is priced from under $2 per sq. ft., while floor tile goes for around $33 per ft. (and much less when the store finds distributor close-outs).

Checks, Credit cards

Window Coverings

Window dressings are a lot like salad dressings: Both are available in such a wide variety of choices that, whatever your taste, you'll find something you like. Whether you prefer drapes, blinds, shades, duettes, or verticals, the outlets we've listed are sure to offer what you want—at a price you'll be happy with.

Comparison shopping for window coverings is easy. Measure a window and call the outlets for price quotes. Some will even come to your home or office and provide free measurements and estimates.

Be sure to ask about the annual "blow-out" sales common to most window-covering shops. Also, ask them about their "reject blinds," such as unclaimed merchandise, wrong color or size, etc. If you can make use of any of these, you'll find exceptional savings. Another money-saving hint: If you're having a bunch of windows covered, ask for a quantity discount; an additional 10% off might just come your way. (Also refer to the section on Arts, Crafts, & Fabrics.)

American Drapery & Blind
Portland: 607 N.E. Grand Ave. ☎ 234–6868
Hours: Mon–Fri 9–5:30, Sat 9–5

This company makes window coverings and sells them at reduced prices. The prices on their one-inch blinds are probably the lowest around. And they use strong .008 slats and include two extra slats in every blind. All this and in three days, too! They don't operate as a warehouse, but instead offer full-service one-to-one assistance in choosing your window coverings. You'll find even bigger savings on their "unclaimed" draperies and blinds that were made especially for apartment buildings and offices.

Checks, Credit cards

Blinds, Etc.
Tigard: 10240 S.W. Nimbus Ave. ☎ 639–8592
Hours: Mon–Sat 10–6

Their low-priced *Graybar* economy blinds are available in 40 colors and come with a lifetime warranty. Blinds, Etc. takes the worry out of making incorrect measurements by offering free in-home measurements and estimates. The store carries a large selection of competitively priced pleated shades, duettes, and verticals. When your order is ready, they ship it to your home or office at no charge.

Checks, Credit cards

Design Linens
Beaverton: 8775 S.W. Cascade Ave. *(Cascade Plaza)* ☎ 626–8057
Clackamas: 11211 S.E. 82nd Ave. *(Ross Center)* ☎ 654–2290
Gresham: 100 N.W. Burnside *(Gresham Square)* ☎ 667–1917
Portland: 32 N.W. 5th ☎ 223–5070
Vancouver: 8101 N.E. Parkway Dr. ☎ (206)256–9583
Hours: Mon–Fri 10–7, Sat 10–6, Sun 12–5

Design Linens offers a good selection of competitively priced mini-blinds, wood blinds, duettes, and verticals. Their Royale mini-blinds are priced very low, and one or more of their window coverings is always on sale. If you don't feel like going to their store to shop, you can arrange to have one of their decorators bring "the store" out to you, at no charge and without obligation. Watch for their annual sidewalk sale (usually in July), where huge savings can be realized. Shop, compare, then take them up on their offer: "If you find lower prices anywhere, we'll beat them."

Checks, Credit cards

Park Window Designs
Milwaukie: 17703 S.E. McLoughlin ☎ 659–8151
Hours: Mon–Fri 9–5, Sat 10–4

They offer competitive prices on Bali mini-blinds, vinyl vertical blinds, pleated shades, and duette classics. Vinyl verticals are made for windows or patio doors and are easy to clean and repair. They're also more energy efficient than mini-blinds. For big savings in vertical blinds, select one of their in-stock fabrics and receive a 55% discount off list price. These fabric verticals take two weeks to make. Install them yourself or, for a small charge, you can have them installed.

Checks, Credit cards

R.M. Dietz Co.

Beaverton: 14673 S.W. Teal Blvd. *(Murrayhill Marketplace)* ☎ 626–1065
Portland: 1212 S.E. Powell Blvd. ☎ 239–9014
Hours: Mon–Thurs 10–5, Fri 10–6, Sat 10–5

At R.M. Dietz you'll find competitively priced mini-blinds, pleated shades, duettes, wood blinds, and verticals. On orders of $300 or more, they'll come to your home or office and do the measurements for free, and there's never a delivery charge. Don't miss their annual one-day blow-out sale, where you'll find prices at 60% to 75% off retail—and all sizes of already-made blinds and shades go for the incredible price of $5.99 each. This sale usually takes place in October or February; call the store for the exact date.

Checks, Credit cards

Shade Specialties

Portland: 11302 S.W. Barbur Blvd. ☎ 245–9337
Hours: Tues–Sat 9–5, Fri 9–7

Because Shade Specialties is a factory, they are able to offer direct prices on a large selection of window treatments. Pleated shades, made with Kirsch materials, are 20% less than at other places, and are made in one to two weeks. Their *Kirsch* and *Bali* classic mini-blinds were priced well below most of the competitors we checked. For some incredible finds, ask them about their unclaimed blinds, shades, and duettes, where prices will be 50% or more off retail. Make your own measurements and call the store for a free estimate—they'll come out and take final measurements for free before starting on your order. They do charge for installation.

Checks, Credit cards

3 Day Blinds

Beaverton: 3905 S.W. 117th *(Canyon Place)* ☎ 646–1159
Clackamas: 8862 S.E. Sunnyside Rd. *(Clackamas Promenade)* ☎ 652–0044
Hours: Mon–Sat 10–6

In addition to their competitively priced pleated shades, woods, and duettes, you'll find super low prices on their mini-blinds (available in 35 colors). Six-foot vinyl verticals, available in ivory only, are $39.95. Verticals in other colors are priced higher and are competitive with other window covering shops. With over 100 stores in the Western states, and their own factory in Southern California, they're able to ship completed orders in about eight working days (it takes only three days if you live in Southern California).

Checks, Credit cards

Wallpapers To Go

Beaverton: 10205 S.W. Beaverton Hillsdale Hwy. ☎ 643–7523
Milwaukie: 15601 S.E. McLoughlin Blvd. ☎ 654–3149
Portland: 1182 N. Hayden Meadows Dr. ☎ 283–3039

Hours: Mon–Fri 10–8, Sat 10–6, Sun 12–5

At Wallpapers To Go you'll have the opportunity to coordinate wallpapers and window fashions to complete the perfect look. They offer pleated shades, duettes, and *Levolor* and *Del Mar* window fashions. All *Levolor* products are guaranteed to be at the lowest prices around—find it for less within 14 days of order and they'll pay you the difference. (Also see the Wallpapers To Go listing in this chapter under Paint and Wallpaper.)

Checks, Credit cards

Wells Interiors

Portland: 10075 S.W. Barbur Blvd. ☎ 244–0043
Hours: Mon–Fri 9:30–6, Sat 9–5, Sun 12–5

Definitely put this store on your list when comparing prices on window coverings. They advertise "the lowest prices in town" and offer a price guarantee to beat any competitor's advertised prices. We found great prices on their *Levolor* Riviera and Economy mini-blinds, and incredible deals on their "reject blinds" that are either unclaimed, wrong color or size, etc. They offer a large selection of name-brand mini-blinds, duette and pleated shades, verticals, wood blinds, and draperies. When we checked, they were holding a Levolor "everything on sale" sale and offering a free valance with each purchase of *Levolor* verticals. If you have five or more windows to be measured, they'll come out and measure them at no charge (there's a nominal charge for fewer than five windows). Also, you'll have your mini-blinds shipped from the factory in five working days instead of the typical several weeks it takes at many other places.

Checks, Credit cards

Window Wear

Beaverton: By appointment only ☎ 641–3169
Hours: Mon–Fri 9–6

Window Wear offers low prices and fast service on top-quality factory-direct custom blinds. Their vertical blinds are available in over 150 fabrics including ten colors in vinyl. Because they're a factory, they are sometimes able to have the vertical blinds made the next day. They also offer *Bali* mini-blinds at competitive prices. Window Wear does not have a showroom. The owner will come to your home or office with sample materials and take measurements without charge. When your order is ready, they'll even do the installation for free. If your job includes ten or more windows, you'll get a 10% discount.

Checks, Credit cards

Home Furnishings

All too often, your budget will play a big role in how you choose to furnish your home. But if you shop wisely, you can do some remarkable things in outfitting a house with an extravagant look on a small budget.

After you've decided what you need, how you're going to use it, how much space you have to work with, and last but not least, how much you can afford, you'll be ready to charge out and get the best for less.

When buying any big-ticket item, don't be afraid to do a little horse trading. You'll be pleasantly surprised at how quickly an instant-discount can appear when you ask for one. Some stores offer discounts to customers who pay with cash. If you're furnishing several rooms at once, ask about "package discounts." Find out from store staff about upcoming sales and promotions. A small wait can mean big savings.

You'll get the best value for your money when you buy furnishings that are not "here today and gone tomorrow." Good furnishings are those that are not only good looking, but also well built and designed. Go for furnishings that will stand the test of time.

Furniture

Many furniture stores offer used furniture, floor models, freight-damaged furniture, and returned items—all at great savings. Head straight for the "budget corner" or "scratch 'n dent room." Because the inventory of flawed or used furniture is constantly changing, it's not a bad idea to call the store if you're looking for a specific piece.

If you have an hour or so you don't mind spending with a screwdriver, pick up some "knock-down" furniture and save.

"Knock-downs" are ready-to-assemble pieces that are low priced because you provide the labor in transforming a bunch of components in a flat carton into an attractive and functional piece of furniture. You're provided with the necessary nuts, bolts, parts, and instructions to do the assembly yourself.

When you shop for furniture, don't forget to take a tape measure along. You'll save a lot of grief by not buying a piece of furniture that's too big for that special place you've reserved for it.

For other sources of furniture-for-less, refer to the sections on Office Furniture, Surplus & Liquidators, Estate Sales, & Mass Merchandisers.

Applecrate
Portland: 4528 S.W. Woodstock ☎ 775–6735
Hours: Mon–Sat 10–7, Sun 12–5

This mom and pop store keeps its overhead very low and passes along the big savings to its customers. You'll find famous brand name sofas, sleepers, bedroom sets, mattresses, futons, dinettes, desks, and more at prices up to 30% below those of other furniture stores. We spotted a Yugoslavian hardwood dinette set (with four chairs) at $199 and six-foot solid oak bookcases for $99 apiece. Whatever's not displayed can be ordered from their furniture catalogs (allow one to four weeks for delivery) at the same large discounts found on all in-stock furniture. Occasionally, freight-damaged items will be on the floor (clearly marked) at incredible bargains.

Checks, Credit cards

Asia America
Portland: 9590 S.W. Barbur Blvd. ☎ 244–8124
Hours: Tues–Sat 10–5:30, Sun 11–5

You'll save thousands of dollars by not going to China and Hong Kong because you can buy fine, elegant, imported Chinese furnishings here at Asia America. You'll find rosewood dining room sets, lacquered chests, lamps, porcelain fish bowls and vases, accessories, and many one-of-a-kind pieces at reasonable prices.

Checks, Credit cards

Banner Furniture and Carpet Outlet
Hillsboro: 4871 S.E. Tualatin Valley Hwy. ☎ 648–6028
Hours: Mon–Sat 9–6, Sun 12–5

This block-long discount store offers a huge inventory of furniture at prices that beat most of the competition. Cloth recliners start as low as $168 and queen sleeper-sofas, under $500. Dining sets, beds, mattresses, and chests of drawers are also low priced. If you wander through this long and narrow store all the way to the back, you'll find a treasure trove of quality used furniture, including tables, lamps, mattresses, box springs, couches, beds, and more. We spotted a flex-steel recliner in great shape for $85 and several hide-a-beds at $100 apiece. Watch for their occasional TV and local newspaper ads, and ask about a package discount when you furnish several rooms at a time.

Checks, Credit cards

Carey's Unfinished Furniture
Gresham: 22321 S.E. Stark ☎ 661–7026
Hours: Mon–Fri 10–6, Sat 10–5

Carey's offers a large selection of unfinished furniture for both home and office, and specializes in bookcases, chests, entertainment centers, table and chair sets, and bunk beds. Their all-wood unfinished furniture sells for less than the same items finished, although prices for furniture made from particle board do not differ much between finished and unfinished. We spotted a well-made birch bookcase for $95, as well as many pieces of kids' furniture (rockers, table and chair sets, and toy boxes) at good prices. To have them finish the furniture you select, you'll be charged an additional 40%, so best to do it yourself; it will cost only about $10 in supplies.

Checks, Credit cards

Dania
Beaverton: 13150 S.W. Dawson ☎ 643–6604
Portland: 1905 N.E. 41st ☎ 284–0880
Hours: Mon–Fri 10–7, Sat 10–6, Sun 12–5

This chain (there are 30 stores nationwide, with two in Oregon) carries a huge selection of contemporary Scandinavian-design home and office furniture. Because their furniture is "knock-down" (which means the customer does the assembly), they're able to hold own their prices. If you're not into assembly, for a small charge they'll do it. Adjustable desk chairs start at $39 and desks at $79. When we shopped, they were holding one of their two annual clearance sales (January and July), with many items discounted an additional 15% to 20%. Check out their "scratch 'n dent" room, where damaged and closed out items are marked down an additional 10% to 20%, depending on condition.

Checks, Credit cards

Designer Outlet
Portland: 40 S.W. Third ☎ 222–1559
Hours: Wed–Sun 10–6

This outlet specializes in contemporary designer lighting at affordable prices. You'll find probably the largest selection of halogen lighting here, as well as a small stock of furniture (mostly desks and tables) and accessories. Designer Outlet purchases in large lots and keeps the overhead down (by having only a small staff) in order to pass along the savings. We found four-foot track lighting, $69 elsewhere, priced at $29 here; a three-pull brass table lamp priced at $179 here was selling at a competitor's for $497. Watch for their periodic sales and get on their mailing list for advance notice of upcoming sales and specials.

Checks, Credit cards

Furniture Club

Milwaukie: 13720 S.E. Johnson Rd. ☎ 654–0558
Hours: Mon–Fri 10–8, Sat 10–6, Sun 12–6

At Furniture Club you'll find a large selection of national brand-name furniture at prices that beat most of their competitors'. Sleepers, sofas, bedroom sets, formal dining room sets, kids' bedroom furniture, recliners, entertainment centers, and more sell for hundreds less than other furniture stores. By keeping the overhead low, by not advertising, and by paying for their own volume purchases in cash, they're able to pass along the savings to their customers. Call or visit the store to find out about their occasional sales, when discounts of 10% to 20% off their regular low prices can be found.

Checks, Credit cards

GranTree Furniture Rental Clearance Center

Portland: 3232 S.E. 82nd ☎ 777–1067
Hours: Mon–Fri 10–8, Sat 10–6, Sun 12–5

Being the leading rental company in the Western states generates a huge inventory of quality rental-return office and home furniture. They steam-clean all return furniture and provide 30-day warranties. We found a bunch of couches that ranged from $88 to $298, and several brand-new recliners for $78 each. File cabinets ranged from $38 to $198. Although they had a nice selection of desks, chairs, and tables on the day we checked, the quantities on hand may be much smaller at times due to seasonal slow-downs, so best to call if you're looking for something in particular.

Checks, Credit cards

Hotel Motel Sales Inc.

Oregon City: 610 Main St. ☎ 657–9209
Portland: 439 S.E. Grand ☎ 235–7100
7020 S.E. Foster Rd. ☎ 777–2277
Hours: Oregon City, Mon–Fri 9–6, Sat 9–5, Sun 10–5; Portland stores, Mon–Fri 9–9, Sat 9–5, Sun 10–5

Chances are, the bed you slept in a few years back while staying at a west coast hotel is now for sale here. You'll find all kinds of furniture, as well as lamps, linens, and drapes (some less than one year old) at super prices. Couches from major hotels are priced as much as 75% off original, while sofas start at $144 and dinette sets at $189. Prices vary depending on the condition of the item. Generally, the stock is about three or more years old, but much of it is in surprisingly good condition. A large selection of used television sets (about five to eight years old) with prices from $99 to $129 are spread out throughout the store. Ask about package discounts.

Checks, Credit cards

The Leather Furniture

Beaverton: 1040 N.W. Murray ☎ 626–0707
6800 S.W. Beaverton-Hillsdale Hwy ☎ 297–1034
Portland: 311 S.W. Alder ☎ 224–0272
Hours: Generally, Mon–Sat 10–6, Sun 12–6

The Leather Furniture guarantees the lowest advertised prices on the largest selection of leather furniture in the Northwest. Although the store on the Beaverton-Hillsdale Highway is the largest, each of their warehouse showrooms has over one thousand leather furniture items in stock. Leather sofas that sell for around $1,100 elsewhere go for $549 here. In addition to a huge inventory of vintage, transitional, and contemporary home furnishings, you'll discover office furniture as well. Their best prices can be found on floor stock that, after sitting for several weeks on the floor, is discounted up to 35% off retail. Watch for their anniversary sale each spring and save an additional 10% to 20%.

Checks, Credit cards

Lloyd's Furniture Outlet

Portland: 337 N.E. San Rafael ☎ 281–4268
Hours: Mon 10–4:30, Tues–Sat 10–5, Sun 12–5

Lloyd's carries a huge inventory of higher-quality furniture just like you'd find in the department stores but at prices below list. All items are tagged showing both the list price and selling price. There's always a sale on selected things, so watch for special sale tags. We spotted solid hardwood dining tables from $149, and six-foot teak bookcases at $99 each. Watch for their special promotions featured in Saturday ads in *The Oregonian*'s Living Section.

Checks, Credit cards

Meier & Frank Warehouse Sale

Portland: Warehouse at N.W. 14th & Irving
Hours: Periodic sales

Of course it's a mob scene at each of their five annual three-day sales (in January, May, August, and September)—but that's what happens when fantastic warehouse-sale savings are made available. Take the free shuttle buses from the downtown store to the warehouse, then ride the freight elevator up to the fourth and fifth floors. You'll find discounts of 50% or more on a wide selection of home furnishings, including furniture, mattresses, linens, rugs, cookware, lamps, luggage, electronics, gifts, place settings, and more. The merchandise may be floor samples, returns, or discontinued styles, and includes "as-is" pieces and famous brand names. Full factory warranties come with all electronics. Call Meier & Frank at 241–5171 for specific dates or other information.

Checks, Credit cards

Montgomery Ward Clearance Outlet

Portland: 5905 N. Marine Dr. (near Terminal 6) ☎ 286–1228
Hours: Mon–Sat 9:30–5:30

This large retailer's clearance outlet is stocked with a huge selection of furniture and appliances, including tables, loveseats, mattresses, dinette sets, sofas, washers, dryers, refrigerators, microwave ovens, and more, at prices from 10% to 20% off retail. TVs, stereos, VCRs, and other electronics come with full warranties. Just about everything here is a floor model, returned merchandise, discontinued, "as-is," or overstock, so when you see what you like, grab it! They'll help you load your selection, but delivery is up to you. Watch for their holiday sales and save even more.

Checks, Credit cards

Mr. D & Sons

Portland: 8114 S.E. Division ☎ 775–4124
Hours: Mon–Sat 10–8, Sun 12–6

This large discounter stocks a nice selection of brand-name dining, bedroom, and living room furniture and accessories—all at super savings. Three-position vinyl recliners start at $127; complete seven-piece living room groups at $488; and a five-piece bedroom set at $477. When we shopped, we found store-wide clearance prices of up to 40% off retail.

Checks, Credit cards

Murphy's Furniture

Cornelius: 2962 Baseline ☎ 640–1124
Hours: Mon–Fri 10–6, Sat 10–5, Sun 11–5

Murphy's carries about 95 manufacturers' lines of unfinished furniture. Usually you'll save $100 or more on such things as tables, entertainment centers, and hutches when you purchase them unfinished. You'll find even bigger savings on their custom-made unfinished bookcases, tables, desks, headboards, and other furniture. We also found some terrific discounts of $400 off their solid oak (finished) roll-top and flat-top desks.

Checks, Credit cards

Nationwide Warehouse

Portland: 6338 N.E. Halsey ☎ 281–3456
Hours: Mon, Tues & Fri 10–8, Sat 10–6, Sun 12–6

This 83-unit chain buys in volume and passes the savings along to its customers. Many items are priced from 30% to 70% lower than their competition. When we shopped, we found a five-piece dinette set at $178, brass headboards at $38, bed frames starting at $19.95, and a bedroom suite (including headboard, frame, mirror, and double dresser) for under $300.

They carry brand-name furniture, as well as a huge offering of contemporary and traditional styles, at rock-bottom prices.

Checks, Credit cards

Natural Furniture

Portland: 800 N.E. Broadway ☎ 284–0655
Hours: Mon–Sat 10–6, Thurs 10–7, Sun 11–5

Natural Furniture carries a good selection of unfinished furniture for the home and office, including children's tables, chairs, and rockers. You'll save 10% or more on the same furniture here when you buy unfinished. Four-foot-high unfinished bookcases of solid pine were priced at $65 apiece, and oak TV carts (with cabinet), usually priced around $145 at other stores, were going for $99.

Checks, Credit cards

The Oak Mill

Portland: 11015 S.W. Capitol Hwy ☎ 244–0000
Hours: Mon–Fri 9–6, Sat 10–5:30, Sun 11–5

You'll like the selection and competitive pricing of their quality-made unfinished furniture for home and office. Big savings can be found on their in-store sale items that are either slow-movers or manufacturers' close-outs. We spotted an oak desk (four feet wide and with four drawers) that was reduced by about 30% to move it out. A solid wood table with four chairs that had not sold quickly enough was similarly reduced. Don't miss their fabulous "blow-out" summer sidewalk sale that takes place for one weekend only. You'll have to call the store because this is an unadvertised event; you're sure to find prices up to 50% off retail on bookcases, entertainment centers, and custom-made pieces.

Checks, Credit cards

RB Furniture Clearance Center

Gresham: 18201 S.E. Stark St. ☎ 667–1550
Hours: Mon–Fri 10–9, Sat 10–6, Sun 12–6

This clearance center features a huge selection of quality name-brand furniture and accessories at low clearance prices. The merchandise looks brand new and includes sofas, loveseats, sectionals, dining rooms, chinas, dinettes, game tables, recliners, chairs, bedding, and lamps that were floor samples, discontinued, or blemished. Stock is limited, so if you see something you like—grab it!

Checks, Credit cards

Scan Design

Beaverton: 10760 S.W. Beaverton-Hillsdale Hwy ☎ 644–4040
Lake Oswego: 333 S. State St. ☎ 636–7890
Hours: Mon–Sun 10–6

Scan Design offers contemporary Danish and Norwegian home and office furnishings in a wide range of prices. Furniture is sold "knock-down," so you'll be doing the assembly (although for a nominal charge they'll put the thing together for you). You'll find the best prices on furniture in their "budget corner" (also known as the clearance room), where you'll find fully assembled dressers, tables, desks, and other odds 'n ends that were floor models with slight damage. Their clearance inventory is constantly changing, so best to call the store to see if they have what you're looking for. Watch for their Saturday promotional ads in *The Oregonian.*

Checks, Credit cards

Self-Service Furniture & Carpet Center

Gresham: 19240 S.E. Stark St. ☎ 665–3133
Hillsboro: 6101 S.W. Tualatin Valley Hwy ☎ 642–5663
Salem: 3540 S.E. Commercial ☎ 585–7810
Tigard: 14255 S.W. Pacific Hwy ☎ 620–8445
Vancouver: 7407 N.E. Vancouver Plaza Dr. ☎ (206)254–6786
Hours: Mon–Fri 9–9, Sat 9–5:30, Sun 12–5

As their name implies, you won't be bothered by salesmen as you wander around their large showroom floor, which contains a large selection of contemporary home furniture from many well-known national manufacturers. All items are tagged, and you'll find prices here to be about 15% to 30% lower than at other stores. Ask about their 30-day price guarantee and you'll be sure to pay the lowest prices around. Also see the Self-Service listing under Floor Coverings in this book.

Checks, Credit cards

Smith's Home Furnishings Liquidation Center

Portland: 10544 S.E. Washington *(Plaza 205)* ☎ 256–2311
Hours: Mon–Sat 10–9, Sun 10–6

At this huge warehouse, you'll find a large selection of name-brand merchandise being cleared out from Smith's Home Furnishings stores. Furniture, appliances, and electronics that are floor models, dented, scratched, returns, discontinued, or overstocks are sold at cost—meaning savings of 20% to 60% or more. We spotted brand new washers, dryers, TVs, VCRs, and other electronics that were discontinued models at great prices. Watch for their newspaper ads for periodic sales.

Checks, Credit cards

Stanton Unfinished Furniture

Beaverton: 10175 S.W. Beaverton-Hillsdale Hwy ☎ 644–7333
Portland: 10800 S.E. 82nd ☎ 654–5282
Hours: Mon & Fri 10–9, Tues–Thurs & Sat 10–6, Sun 11–5

Stanton's showroom floors are full of quality unfinished furniture for every room in the home. Although savings vary among manufacturers, generally you'll find that unfinished furniture costs about 5% to 10% less than for comparable finished furniture. Call or visit to find out about their frequent in-store sales. When we dropped by, we found a sale in progress and noted that an unfinished bookcase (four feet high), usually $169, was sale-priced at $110. Occasionally, you'll find a close-out item on the showroom floor at an incredible discount.

Checks, Credit cards

Bedding & Linens

Futons make nice fits in homes with small rooms and for people on tight budgets! They're easy to move around, make great sofa-bed combinations, and are among the best buys you'll find when shopping for bedding.

Big savings can be found on rebuilt mattresses (they're made to be as good as new and come with guarantees!), and on "generic" mattresses, which are name-brand products—minus the label. Also, watch for year-end mattress clearance sales.

Your best bet to save money on linens is to consider factory-irregular bedspreads and comforters. Some linen outlets have "clearance corners" where rugs, chair pads, sheets, comforters, towels, and pillows are marked down. Don't forget to check out the August "white sales" at most department stores for quality bedding and linens at great prices.

Beaverton Futon Factory

Beaverton: 4021 S.W. 117th *(Canyon Place)* ☎ 646–7114
Hours: Mon–Sat 10–7, Sun 1–5

Because they make their own frames, Beaverton Futon Factory is able to offer special wholesale prices to their customers. The $179 futon package price includes a double, in unfinished pine, with frame and futon. A double in oak will run $479. Covers are an additional $49. Bean bag chairs and related accessories are available from time to time.

Checks, Credit cards

Bits & Pieces

Portland: 1420 N.W. Lovejoy ☎ 222–1549
Hours: Mon–Sat 10–5, Sun 12–5

As their name might suggest, this outlet offers fabric "bits and pieces," including quilt material at 50 cents per lb. and upholstery fabric at $1 per lb.

We found remnant fabrics priced as low as $1.50 per lb. and others at 99 cents per yd. Their factory irregular bedspreads and comforters were super-priced, starting at $30. Decorator pillows, bed ruffles, and placemats were priced up to 50% off regular retail. Check out their "odds 'n ends" (mostly returns) window coverings, where you can find name-brand mini-blinds and woven woods at $20 each.

Checks, Credit cards

Design Linens
Gresham: 100 N.W. Burnside ☎ 667–1917
Hours: Mon–Fri 10–7, Sat 10–6, Sun 12–5

Of all their stores (five in the area), only the Gresham location has a clearance corner offering incredible savings on bedspreads, down comforters, pillows, rugs, towels, kitchen items, accessories, and more. We found woven bed-spreads at $9.99 (originally $20); thermal blankets, usually around $45, at $19.99; and percale sheets (fitted styles), originally $12 to $50, for $4.99. Watch for their frequent sales and save up to an additional 50% off already discounted clearance prices.

Checks, Credit cards

Futon Gallery
Portland: 20 N.W. 2nd Ave. ☎ 227–3378
Hours: Mon–Fri 11–6, Sat 10–5, Sun 11–5

At Futon Gallery you'll find futons, frames, covers, pillows, end tables, coffee tables, and many accessories. Their basic economy-model futon (double, three positions, unfinished pine) sells for $169. There's always something on sale here. Frames are also available in oak, maple, teak, and mahogany. Covers are $49 if you buy the futon here; $55 and up if you're only buying a cover.

Checks, Credit cards

Luxury Linens/Burlington Coat Factory
Beaverton: 8775 S.W. Cascade *(Cascade Plaza)* ☎ 646–9900
Hours: Mon–Sat 10–9, Sun 11–6

Name-brand linens and accessories can be found here at prices from 20% to 60% below department-store prices. We noted big savings on a huge selection of famous brand comforters, duvet covers, blankets, and towel ensembles. Other products include: lace tablecloths, bedrests and floor cushions, sheet sets, chair pads, aprons, bath rugs, and more. Watch for their seasonal sales and special promotions.

Checks, Credit cards

Pacific Linen
Beaverton: 9009 S.W. Hall Blvd. ☎ 624–9340
Clackamas: 8624 S.E. Sunnyside Rd. *(Clackamas Promenade)* ☎ 652–0125
Hillsboro: 2421 N.W. 185th ☎ 690–7788
Salem: 3892 Center St. *(Evergreen Plaza)* ☎ 362–7979
Vancouver: 7809 N.E. Vancouver Plaza Dr. *(Vancouver Plaza)*
   ☎ (206) 892–6154
Hours: Generally, Mon–Fri 10–9, Sat 9–6, Sun 11–6
   Pacific Linen offers a great selection of items, in basic to fashionable styles, for the bed, bath, or kitchen. You'll find down comforters, flannel sheets, accent rugs, kitchen helpers, sleep sets, quilted chair pads, elegant tablecloths, brand-name towels, futons and frames, and a wide assortment of gift items—all at 30% or more off department-store prices. Watch for their periodic month-long sales for incredible bargains.

   Checks, Credit cards

PJ Sleep Shop
Portland: 1625 S.E. Hawthorne Blvd. ☎ 232–5222
Hours: Mon–Sat 9–6
   PJ, in business since 1977, tears down old mattresses to the springs, then rebuilds them using materials that may be even better than new. You'll pay less for these rebuilt mattresses than for new ones. A rebuilt twin set runs $69 and comes with a one-year guarantee. New twin sets range from $89 (smooth) to $129 (quilted,) and are guaranteed for two years. Delivery is extra, but they'll pick up your old mattress at the same time without charge.

   Checks, Credit cards

Sarna's Sleep Center
Portland: 14712 S.E. Stark ☎ 253–4947
Hours: Mon–Fri 10–6:30, Sat 10–6
   Generic mattresses, anyone? Name-brand mattresses (without the labels) can be found for up to one-third off retail. Mismatched twin sets sell for $100, while matched sets are $120. Sarna's offers ten name-brands and hundreds of mattresses to choose from at prices that are hard to beat. In business for nearly 48 years, Sarna's advises the bargain shopper to shop around and then come to Sarna's for even better prices. This no-frills warehouse operation has few employees, so bring a pickup and cart your good buys home yourself.

   Checks, Credit cards

Sleep-N-Aire
Beaverton: 8907 S.W. Canyon Rd. ☎ 297–2293
Portland: 10505 N.E. Sandy Blvd. ☎ 255–7500

Tigard: 11567 S.W. Pacific Hwy ☎ 624–1883
Hours: Mon & Fri 10–8, Tues–Thurs 10–6, Sat 10–5, Sun 12–5
> *Sealy* and *Simmons* mattress sets go for $50 to $100 less than at the department stores. Even better savings can be found on factory-direct *Sleep-N-Aire* label mattress sets made locally. Watch for their year-end clearance sales, where *Sealy* and *Simmons* sets are priced $100 to $200 below regular prices. If you like the clearance prices but don't immediately need a new mattress set, they take a $20 deposit to hold the set (and lock in the low prices) until you're ready. They have free delivery, free removal of old bedding, and a free 30-night comfort guarantee. Occasionally, they'll run sales on their large stock of adjustable beds.

> Checks, Credit cards

St. Vincent de Paul
Portland: 2740 S.E. Powell Blvd. ☎ 234–0598
Hours: Mon–Sat 10–6, Sun 12–5
> St. Vincent de Paul tears down old mattresses and completely rebuilds them using all new padding, batting, topping, and other materials—in effect, creating new mattresses but priced much less. Rebuilt twin mattresses sell for $59 each; twin sets are $99; and deluxe twin sets, $139. Be sure to call about availability of the deluxe sets—they come and go at a quick pace. Even if these aren't rock-bottom prices, remember that the proceeds go to a worthy cause.

> Checks, Credit cards

Household Appliances

By shopping around you can usually find the appliance you're looking for on sale somewhere at just about any time of year. In addition to following the sales timetable listed in this book's Introduction, some department stores hold appliance clearance sales after Easter, the Fourth of July, and Christmas.

A great way to compare major appliances is to use *Consumer Reports* magazine. This can save you a lot of money and grief and help you choose what will best work for you.

Used and reconditioned appliances can be a bargain sometimes—especially when backed by a warranty or guarantee. But, as with any used item, scrutinize carefully before buying.

Refer to the chapter Something For Everyone for additional sources of low-priced appliances.

Appliance Connection
Portland: 1 S.E. 28th ☎ 236–5769
Tigard: 11606 S.W. Pacific Hwy ☎ 639–0155
Hours: Mon–Fri 10–6, Sat & Sun 9–5

This store specializes in fully reconditioned appliances at 50% or more off original prices. All appliances have warranties, typically for one to three months, and extensions are available at $5 per mo. The inventory here is mostly made up of washers and dryers, stoves, refrigerators, ranges, freezers, and dishwashers. Besides used stock, you'll find some new appliances that have been scratched or slightly damaged that are priced from 20% to 40% off retail. Watch for their occasional sales and save an additional 10% to 15% off selected items. One such sale was in progress, and "off-color" (i.e., gold, avocado, and other slow-moving appliances) were being discounted.

Checks, Credit cards

Cynthia's Sewing Machine & Learning Center
Gresham: 2033 E. Burnside ☎ 661–2102
Hours: Mon–Fri 9:30–6, Sat 9:30–5

This family-operated business carries the *New Home* and *Elna* sewing machine lines. We noted that all machines carried everyday discounted prices. An *Elna* that regularly retailed for $499 was priced at $199. When you buy one of their machines, you're entitled to orientation classes on that machine. In addition, they sell used machines (trade-ins such as *Viking, Bernina,* and *Ward's*) that range from $59 to $1,200.

Checks, Credit cards

George Smith Warehouse Sales
Portland: 5010 N.E. Oregon ☎ 281–2100
Hours: Mon & Fri 9–8, Tues–Thurs & Sat 9–6, Sun 11–6

When the founder of Smith's Home Furnishings sold his stores in 1982, he kept one of them, which he renamed George Smith Warehouse Sales. This giant showroom, with attached warehouse, offers an incredible selection of electronics, appliances, and furniture. Name-brand washers, dryers, refrigerators, microwave ovens, VCRs, TVs, stereos, ranges, camcorders, sofas, rockers, and more can be found at everyday low warehouse prices. Watch for their big "blow-out" sales in the spring and around Christmas. And ask about their package discounts when you buy two or more items.

Checks, Credit cards

Sewing Machine Parts Co.
Portland: 3317 S.E. 21st Ave. ☎ 235–6165
Hours: Mon–Fri 9:30–5:30, Sat 9:30–3:30

Serving Portland for nearly a century, Sewing Machine Parts Co. offers broker prices on a big selection of name-brand sewing machines, including *New Home, Elna, Brother, Bernina, Singer, Viking,* and others. We noted a baby lock machine, suggested retail $399, priced at $199, and a considerable inventory of quality used machines starting at $50 apiece.

Checks, Credit cards

Silo
Beaverton: 9575 S.W. Cascade Ave. ☎ 626–2899
Portland: 11211 S.E. 82nd Ave. ☎ 659–4991
    1900 N. Hayden Island Dr. ☎ 286–9991
Salem: 1841 Lancaster Dr. N.E. ☎ 363–6806
Hours: Mon–Sat 10–9, Sun 11–6

Silo guarantees to have the lowest prices on a wide variety of audio/video equipment, name-brand appliances, and electronics. With their 30-day price guarantee, they'll reimburse you the difference plus 10% if somebody else has a better price on a product you've purchased at Silo. Every week they have different products on sale, so it's wise to pop in and check prices or give them a call for a price quote. Watch for the special tags on stock that have been scratched, dented, returned, or freight damaged and you'll save 10% to 20% more off their already low prices.

Checks, Credit cards

Standard TV & Appliance
Portland: 4804 S.E. Woodstock ☎ 777–3376
Hours: Mon & Fri 9–9, Tues–Thurs 9–7, Sat 9–6

For over 48 years, Standard Appliance has been offering some of the best prices around on major brand appliances. You'll pay the same low prices on *Maytag, Whirlpool, Tappen, Amana,* and other brands as do all those builders, remodelers, and contractors who regularly shop here. Ask about their guaranteed lowest prices on washers and dryers, ranges, dishwashers, refrigerators, TVs, VCRs, and other household appliances.

Checks, Credit cards

Stark's Vacuum Cleaner
Beaverton: 12625 S.W. Canyon Rd. ☎ 626–3699
Clackamas: 11750 S.E. 82nd Ave. *(Clackamas Corner)* ☎ 654–1517
Gresham: 240 N.W. Division ☎ 661–0128
Portland: 107 N.E. Grand ☎ 232–4101
Vancouver: SR500 & Thurston Way *(Vancouver Park Place)*
    ☎ (206)254–2661
Hours: Generally, Mon–Fri 9–6, Sat 9–6, some stores Sun 12–5

This family owned and operated business carries the area's largest inventory of vacuum cleaners (over 30 brands) at the lowest prices. You'll also find floor polishers, carpet sweepers, industrial-strength cleaning chemicals, and rental carpet cleaning equipment (more powerful than those found in supermarkets). Save about 50% on vacuum cleaner bags when you buy the generic brand (made by DVC) available in a wide variety of sizes.

Checks, Credit cards

West Coast Training

Milwaukie: 2525 S.E. Stubb ☎ 659–5181

Hours: Mon–Fri 8–2:30

Refrigerators and freezers that are donated to West Coast Training are repaired and reconditioned by their students and then sold for about $50 to $100 each. There are usually a few refrigerators or freezers available each week at this vocational school, but best to call before you head over there.

Checks

Kitchen & Restaurant Equipment

Serious cooks love shopping restaurant supply stores, where they can find a wide range of nearly indestructible pots, pans, and utensils, as well as restaurant-quality gas ranges, huge refrigerators, and dishwashers.

Bargains abound at these places, especially on used items. Restaurant glassware and silverware can be quite attractive and sturdy—they're built to last!

You may just get the urge to stock up as you wander the aisles chock-full of neatly displayed professional-grade gadgets. Even those who aren't serious chefs, but who love quality merchandise at good prices, will always find something at these kitchen emporiums.

Boxer-Northwest Co.

Portland: 438 N.W. Broadway ☎ 226–1186

Hours: Mon–Fri 8–5

This huge, block-long store is packed with over 10,000 quality restaurant equipment and supply items, including freezers, coolers, ovens, mixers, glassware, utensils, mops, and brooms. All products are out on the shelves or floor and individually priced, so no need to buy them by the case (except glassware and china in case lots). You'll find good buys all over as you wander up and down the neat aisles. To name a few bargains: Cooks' and bakers' caps were $5.50 apiece; bib aprons, in a variety of colors, were $7.95 each; pizza trays started at $2.40; and ketchup/mustard squeeze bottles were 70 cents. Be sure to wander back to the bargain room for their small stock of china and glassware (which doesn't have to be purchased by the case in the bargain room), chairs, and tables.

Checks, Credit cards

The Cook's Corner

Beaverton: 11777 S.W. Beaverton-Hillsdale Hwy *(Beaverton Town Square)*
☎ 644–0100

Hours: Mon–Fri 10–9, Sat 10–6, Sun 12–5

At Cook's Corner you'll find kitchen gadgets and cookware of every kind, as well as free baking, cooking, and food decorating demonstrations (held on

Saturday afternoons) and usually conducted by specialists. No need to register for these demonstrations—just come when you want. The selection of quality kitchenware is excellent and prices are competitive. We noted a table of sale items where colanders, baskets, and assorted knick-knacks were 50% off retail, and Gerber knives were also on sale.

Checks, Credit cards

Economy Restaurant & Bakery Equipment
Portland: 1001 S.E. Water Ave. ☎ 236–1459
Hours: Mon–Fri 8:30–5

Whether you're thinking about going into the food business or just plain looking for cookware, you're bound to find what you want among the thousands of items in this sprawling warehouse located on the third floor of the Portland Liquidation Center. We found a good selection of used equipment for bakeries, restaurants, and delis, including dough mixers, yogurt machines, soda fountains, salad bars, refrigerators, sinks, dishwashing machines, and gas ranges, as well as cups, mugs, plates, trays, and a wide assortment of table candles. If you're after new equipment, there's a small amount on display in their second floor office location along with new-equipment catalogs to peruse. When you're ready to go up to the warehouse, you'll have to ask to be escorted.

Checks, Credit cards

Golden's, Inc.
Portland: 910 S.E. Stark St. ☎ 233–6593
Hours: Mon–Fri 9–5

Golden's offers a large selection of restaurant, bar, and paper supplies. Their stock of glassware (from such manufacturers as *Anchor Hocking* and *Libbey*) includes cups, mugs, champagne glasses, goblets, decanters, and more. Glassware must be purchased in case-lot minimums (with one to six dozen pieces per case), although many other items are available in smaller quantities. When we checked, Mr. and Mrs. T bar mixes were sale priced at $1 per bottle; a case of cooking wine (12 16-oz. bottles) was $5; and a case of fruit nectar (24 cans) was also sale priced at $5.

Checks

Kershaw Knives Warehouse Sale
Wilsonville: 25300 S.W. Parkway Ave. ☎ 682–1966
Hours: Annual sale

Just in time for Christmas, the manufacturer of world-famous *Kershaw Knives* holds its annual warehouse sale. For three days only (usually the last weekend in each November), you'll find big savings on a huge inventory of overstocked or discontinued kitchen knives, scissors, flashlights, and hunting, fishing, utility, and pocket knives. Watch for the ads in *The Oregonian* and local papers or call for sale dates and hours.

Checks

Pitman Liquidators Inc.

Portland: 1535 S.E. Third Ave. ☎ 238–0634
Hours: Mon–Fri 8–5, Sat 9–2

Pitman specializes in such new and used restaurant equipment as coffee urns, ice machines, soda dispensers, freezers, ovens, and ranges. Bargain shoppers (with large families) who want to mass-produce their morning toast would appreciate the four-slot commerical toasters available here. How about a little "art deco" in the kitchen in the form of a refrigeration unit with sliding glass doors just like the kind the corner deli uses? Head upstairs where you'll find trays, plates, cups, glassware, and lots of chairs and stools. Ask about quantity discounts.

Checks, Credit cards

Tri-Star Restaurant Equipment

Portland: 721 S.E. Morrison ☎ 234–6222
Hours: Mon–Fri 10–5

New and used commerical equipment for restaurants, delis, and bakeries such as slicers, mixers, refrigerators, freezers, sinks, and cash registers fill Tri-Star's small store. There's a separate warehouse crammed with used equipment, so if you have something specific in mind, ask and they'll check for you. If you want to start a little business in your kitchen, we noted some good prices on four-slot toasters, yogurt and espresso machines, soda dispensers, and a chuck wagon salad bar (on wagon wheels and covered with a canvas canopy). Spice up your window decor with one of their neon signs, a few of which read: "We Deliver"; "Deli"; "Travel"; and "Fax."

Checks, Credit cards

Gifts & Decorative Accessories

Whether you're in the market for wedding or anniversary gifts or shopping for accessories to give your home a spectacular look—you'll find bargains galore at the outlets below.

Some of the gifts available at these outlets include silk flowers and plants; fine china and silverware; trophies and awards; ceramics, dinnerware, and cookware; a marketplace full of arts and crafts; and a store offering novelties and unusual gift items.

You can add pizazz to your personal interior decorating dreams with framed art prints and posters or vintage appliances and furniture. Some shops will even help you do your own art framing, thereby cutting down on the expense.

Discount Silks

Beaverton: 8775 S.W. Cascade Ave. *(Cascade Plaza)* ☎ 644–9228
Hours: Mon–Fri 10–9, Sat 10–6, Sun 11–5

Discount Silks offers a complete selection of silk flowers, plants, and trees, as well as planters and accessories. Silk flowers start at 99 cents per stem, and there's no charge for arranging your selections. There's usually something on sale here every day, and much of the time the store holds a 50% off sale on selected items.

Checks, Credit cards

Downstairs Attic

Portland: 825 N.W. 23rd ☎ 223–5046
Hours: Mon–Sat 11–4:45

Don't look down or up for Downstairs Attic, because this chinaware matching service is actually at street level. This shop offers discount-priced replacement pieces for china and flatwear. It's ideal for those needing to complete a set and who only need a few pieces. Be sure to check out the basket of stainless, where you'll find pieces priced at two for 25 cents.

Checks

Cook's China, Crystal & Silver Shop

Beaverton: 8538 S.W. Apple Way ☎ 292–4312
Hours: Mon–Thurs 10–5:30, Fri 10–6, Sat 10–5

Cook's is a perfect place for wedding and anniversary gifts. Choose your china patterns from such well-known companies a s *Lenox, Noritake, Royal Doulton, Royal Copenhagen, Dansk, Villory & Boch,* and *Gorham.* The selection of sterling and stainless flatware includes *Lunt, Towle, Wallace, Oneida,* and *Reed & Barton.* All their lines are permanently discounted, and at their frequent sales you'll find additional savings of 20% to 40%.

Checks, Credit cards

Harbromania

Portland: Store, 316 S.W. 9th; Warehouse, 1211 N.W. 17th ☎ 223–0767
Hours: Store, Mon–Fri 11:30–6:00, Sat 12–6; Warehouse, periodic sales

If you'd like to recreate the "I Love Lucy" or "Leave It to Beaver" look in your own home, you'll find everything you need at Harbromania. Vintage appliances, toasters, blenders, radios, phones, lamps, toys, furniture, and more—from the '20s to the '60s— fill up their store. One day each month, they cart a lot of this merchandise over to their packed warehouse and hold a sale, with everything 15% or more off their regular prices. Their furniture includes deco, over-stuffed, sectionals, formica and chrome dinette sets, blond end tables, big square chairs, and a lot of other things reminiscent of grandma's house at prices grandma probably paid. Their vintage stock is reconditioned and comes with 30-day guarantees. Get on their mailing list to find out more about the warehouse sales.

Checks, Credit cards

Mamma Ro

Portland: 1801 N.W. Upshur ☎ 274–0687
Hours: Mon–Sat 10–5
This distributor keeps his prices down by cutting out the advertising. On display in their showroom is a selection of fine imported Italian dinnerware, ceramics, and cookware. You'll find the best prices during their periodic sales, and discounts will vary from piece to piece. Be sure to call the showroom from time to time to find out in advance about their sales.

Checks, Credit cards

Portland Saturday Market

Portland: Under the Burnside Bridge at Front ☎ 222–6072
Season: First Sat in March until Christmas Eve
Hours: Sat 10–5, Sun 11–4:30
Since 1974, Portland Saturday Market (actually should be called Portland Saturday and Sunday Market) has been a major attraction for locals and tourists alike. Three hundred arts and crafts merchants offer a large selection of high-quality handmade items, including jewelry, stained glass, wool hats, backpacks, wine glasses, sweaters, furniture, rugs, quilts, music boxes, folk and fine art, cosmetics, and even gyroscopes (for those of us trying to regain our balance). By dealing directly with the makers, you'll pay less for their products than if bought in the stores. Some vendors also wholesale their wares to the major department and gift stores and will pass along those wholesale prices to Saturday Market shoppers. While bargain shopping, you'll be entertained by street entertainers who could be singing, dancing, playing the guitar, bagpipes, or steel drums, juggling, and maybe (when it's not raining) eating fire. Talking about eating, there are food booths (follow your nose to their area) offering Middle Eastern, Thai, Oriental, vegetarian, and Polish food. The Polish perogies (a round pasta filled with potato, cheese, and onion and then deep fried) go well with the freshly squeezed watermelon or pineapple juice or even the homemade root beer from the next booth. With 5,000 to 10,000 shoppers to mingle with, Portland Saturday Market is not a bad place to do your weekend people-watching, either.

Spencer's Gifts

Portland: 12000 S.E. 82nd *(Clackamas Town Center)* ☎ 654–0335
Hours: Mon–Fri 10–9, Sat 10–6, Sun 11–6
Spencer's is a great place to find novelties and unusual gifts—and at great prices to boot. We spotted inflatable 27" hearts, stationery gift baskets,

boxed rose bouquets, and lots of stuffed animals, all marked down 50%. Even bigger discounts of 60% to 70% off retail were available on a large stock of gold chains and bracelets. If you're into memorabilia, you'll find lots of it, with Bart Simpson, Dick Tracy, Garfield, Hulk Hogan, New Kids on the Block, and others emblazoning posters, hats, dolls, pictures, sneakers, mugs, and more—again, with big discounts. And of course, who could do without a hat with attached fish or the ever-popular life-size rubber chicken?

Checks, Credit cards

Trophies & Awards

Bardy Trophy Company
Portland: 1440 N.E. Broadway ☎ 282–7787
Hours: Mon–Fri 9–5:30

Bardy's smallest trophies are four inches tall with a 2"x3" marble base and come with 50 engraved letters for $4 per trophy. The minimum quantity ribbon prices (with eight free lines of gold stamping) are 28 cents each. They also do plaques, awards, certificates, custom certificates, and buttons.

Checks, Credit cards

Discount Trophies
Portland: 11107 N.E. Halsey ☎ 254–9216
Hours: Mon–Fri 7:45–5

This mom and pop trophy shop hasn't raised engraving prices in the 14 years they've been in business! Their smallest trophies (six to nine inches tall with a 2"x2" base) are $2.50 each with the engraving priced at five cents/letter. Gold-stamped ribbons start at 28 cents each. They also offer certificates, medals (made in the U.S.A.), and neck ribbons. Talk about old-fashioned service! If you're unable to make it to their shop before closing time, call ahead, and they'll stay open just for you!

Checks

J's Ribbons & Awards
Portland: 8123 S.E. 17th ☎ 238–3784
Hours: Mon–Fri 9–5:30, Sat 10–3

When the youngsters are done with baseball, soccer, basketball, or whatever, it's time to present the trophies—and J's is the place to get them. J's smallest trophies (perfect for small budgets) are three inches tall, cost $2.35 apiece, and include each player's first name and team year. Gold-stamped satin ribbons (2"x8") are 21 cents each, while acetate ribbons are 18 cents each.

Checks

Framed Art, Posters, & Frames

Artists and Framers Outlet

Portland: 6639 S.W. Macadam ☎ 245–1000
Hours: Mon–Fri 9–7, Sat 9–6, Sun 10–5

This outlet for Beard Frame Shops offers discount prices on frames, tools, glass, posters, and supplies. You'll find some incredible prices in their bargain bins, where frames start as low as 50 cents apiece and bags of goof-mats go for 99 cents (we counted 30 mats in our bag). Practically every month they have a sale going, and its not unusual to find discounts of 50% on thousands of frames and up to 80% on framed art. They're also set up to assist do-it-yourselfers who want to cut down on the cost of custom framing.

Checks, Credit cards

Beard Frame Shops

30 locations. Check yellow pages.
Hours: Generally, Mon–Fri 10–9, Sat 10–6, Sun 12–5

At Beard's you can bring in your poster or print and they'll help you pick out the mat and molding, cut the glass, mat, and frame, then schedule you to return to do the framing yourself at their store. You'll save considerably by doing it yourself this way. They offer a really inexpensive framing concept called "uniframe," which is nothing more than glass, backing, and mounting—but you save up to 75% off regular framing when you use this "frameless" framing. Their discount "goof" frames and returns are sent over to their outlet store, Artists and Framers Outlet.

Checks, Credit cards

Chrisman Picture Frame & Gallery

Beaverton: 12970 S.W. Canyon ☎ 626–2088
    4711 S.W. Beaverton-Hillsdale Hwy ☎ 245–7401
Gresham: 1446 E. Powell ☎ 667–7037
Hillsboro: 375 S.E. Oak ☎ 640–6748
Lake Oswego: 480 Second St. ☎ 635–5326
Portland: 8002 S.E. 13th Ave. ☎ 235–3287
    12843 N.W. Cornell Rd. ☎ 646–4286
    2912 E. Burnside ☎ 231–7462
Hours: Generally, Mon–Sat 10–6, Tues & Thurs 10–9, Sun 12–5

Do-it-yourselfers like the great prices they find at Chrisman's. The store will cut the frame, mat, and glass and show you how to frame your artwork at the store. They have a big selection of competitively priced ready-made frames, as well as the inexpensive "uniframe," where the poster or print is clipped on the glass without a frame. Check out the box of goof mats. You might find a mat you can use priced as low as 50 cents. Watch for their frequent sales and you'll save 20% or more on custom framing.

Checks, Credit cards

The Great Frame Up
Beaverton: 8120 S.W. Beaverton-Hillsdale Hwy ☎ 292–1875
Portland: 128 N.W. 23rd ☎ 221–0075
Hours: Mon–Fri 10–9, Sat 10–6, Sun 12–5

Save up to 30% on custom framing when you do-it-yourself. They'll do all the cutting and show you the whole process at their store. They promise you'll be able to do a framing job just like the professionals. Small ready-made frames (made from their molding scraps) are priced from $7 to $15, and goof-mats from $1.50 to $2.50.

Checks, Credit cards

Oregon Art Institute Rental/Sales Gallery
Portland: 1119 S.W. Park ☎ 274–4121
Hours: Mon–Fri 11–5, Sat 12–5, Sun 11–4

Cover your home or office walls with original art from Oregon artists for a fraction of the cost of purchasing the artworks. The gallery rents artwork for three months at a time, and the rental fees are based on the artwork's purchase price. If you later want to buy the artwork, you can have your rental payments applied towards the purchase price. To rent art you must be a member of the Art Institute (a nominal annual fee).

Checks

Picturemart
Portland: Janzten Beach Center ☎ 289–1950
10160 S.E. Washington *(Mall 205)* ☎ 255–5308
Hours: Mon–Fri 10–9, Sat 10–6, Sun 11–6

Picturemart offers terrific prices on a huge selection of quality framed prints. The frames look so good you'll be tempted to buy the framed prints for the frames alone. Mylar-framed (10"x16") prints are $5; posters in sleek black frames (with glass), usually $60 elsewhere, are priced $25; (22"x28") prints in dark-oak washed frames are $16; and various-sized dark-oak frames range from $3 to $10. The store is bright, cheerful, and fun to shop. Its large inventory of prints, posters, and collage collections (with openings for photos or baseball cards) with frame and glass make excellent gifts.

Checks, Credit cards

Pratt's
Portland: 2710 N.E. Broadway ☎ 287–7807
Hours: Tues–Fri 10–5:30, Sat 10–4

Do-it-yourself framers can save by taking home and assembling their own framed art after having Pratt's cut the glass, mat, and frame. You'll find even bigger savings by having your poster or print shrink-wrapped—a heat-set process that prevents the artwork from warping. Pratt's offers a good selection of frames, posters, and prints, including many fine art reproductions.

Checks, Credit cards

West Coast Picture Corp.

Portland: 5805 N.E. Skidmore ☎ 282–7295

6339 S.W. Capitol Hwy ☎ 245–2088

917 S.W. 16th ☎ 233–9954

Hours: Skidmore, Mon–Sat 8–5; Capitol & 16th, Mon–Fri 10–6, Sat 10–5

West Coast has about the best prices around for those not wanting to do the framing themselves. You'll find over a hundred different moldings here at prices that start at $1.70 a foot. Unfinished moldings are even less. The Skidmore store carries lots of odd-sized frames and returns priced from 49 cents to $5. West Coast sells frames and supplies at wholesale prices to artists, framers, and decorators who show their business licenses.

Checks, Credit cards

Plants, Flowers & Greenery

As certain as spring follows winter, the desire to buy plants, flowers, and greenery is a hardy perennial! However, smart shoppers know that the best buys appear at certain times of the year. March is a great time to buy bare-root roses; by June, most annuals have had their prices slashed; bulbs that flower in spring go on sale in July; a cornucopia of low-priced spring-blooming bulbs, perennials, and roses is available in September; and fruit and shade trees, including shrubs, can be found at great prices in October.

By making use of your master gardener and county extension services (discussed in this chapter), you'll be able to learn a lot about plants. You'll know how to "rescue" a sickly sale plant and spot a terrific buy (or a terrible one!) when you see it.

If you have a green thumb and are really serious about saving money, you can grow your own annuals and perennials from seed. You'll save 90% or more off the prices of bedding plants when you raise them yourself.

Nurseries

The Portland area is home to a multitude of fine nurseries offering plant lovers an abundance of quality selections at great prices.

Generally, the large garden centers buy in huge quantities directly from the growers and are able to pass on larger savings than can the smaller nurseries. The small nurseries rely on quality, service, and exotic offerings to entice customers their way.

One thing's for sure: Inventory is constantly and rapidly changing, so stop by your favorite nurseries often to take advantage of new items coming in and price reductions on those being moved out.

C & J Nurseries
Gresham: 4001 N.E. Division ☎ 665–3874
Portland: 16931 S.E. Foster ☎ 661–5957
Hours: Daily, 9–6

This large one-stop landscaper has acres of trees (shade, fruit, pine, spruce, maple, and cedar), as well as a large assortment of usual and unusual plants and shrubs, to choose from. If you're going to do some major landscaping around the house, be sure to ask about their special quantity prices. The Portland location is the larger of the two stores.

Checks

Cornell Farm
Portland: 8212 S.W. Barnes Rd. ☎ 292–9895
Hours: Mon–Fri 9–6, Sat & Sun 9–5:30

Cornell Farm specializes in perennials, annuals, nursery stock, and trees. There are lots of unusual and exotic plants and trees that will liven up any part of your yard that needs a boost. Wander through their eight greenhouses and you'll find azalea trees, dogwood trees, and many kinds of Christmas trees, such as pine, fir, and hemlock. You'll also find such vines as honey-suckle and jasmine, and magnolia trees trained on a stake that will bloom up in a ball shape (no leaves on the bottom, only on the top!). In spring and summer you'll be delighted by their fresh-cut flowers and beautiful hanging baskets. Contact the store to find out about their plant-of-the-week sale.

Checks, Credit cards

Country Gardens
Hillsboro: 4825 N.W. 253 ☎ 648–1508
Hours: Daily, 9–6

This country/Victorian shop offers fresh and dried flowers, bedding plants, and Christmas trees. They specialize in hybrid lilies, blooms, and bulbs, with hundreds of perennials and annuals to choose from. Pick up some attrac-tively priced "U-cut" flowers in summer.

Checks, Credit cards

Larsen Farm Nursery
Wilsonville: 25935 S.W. Stafford Rd. ☎ 638–8600
Hours: Mon–Sat 10–5

Open only from April until the end of October, Larsen Farm Nursery offers a large selection of annuals and perennials, as well as fresh cut flowers, in the summer months. Small plants are priced under $2, while the one-gallon perennials start at $3.99. The nursery hosts a large arts and crafts festival in May, and an antique fair and strawberry festival in June.

Checks, Credit cards

Midway Plant Farm
Hillsboro: 14900 S.W. Hillsboro Hwy ☎ 628–3232
Hours: Sun–Fri 9–6

This wholesale grower sells to both the trade and the public. Midway runs weekly sale advertisements in *This Week* magazine (comes in the mail on Tuesdays) offering great prices and selection on a wide variety of greenery. In addition, their weekly unadvertised specials are good buys. In late winter we found such unadvertised specials as blueberry bushes, usually around $15, priced at $6.99; begonias at $3.69 (over twice that cost at supermarkets); and a wide array of plants at over 50% off retail. A large selection of spring bulbs were discounted and fruit trees galore were priced from under $10. With three to four acres of trees, shrubs, ground covers, plants, and bulbs to choose from, you'll not only easily spend half your day here, you'll also spend a lot less money.

Checks, Credit cards

Portland Nursery
Portland: 5050 S.E. Stark ☎ 231–5050
Hours: Daily 9–6

Unquestionably, this is one of Portland's finest nurseries, where you'll find about five acres of quality plants, trees, seeds, bulbs, tools, and supplies. The staff is friendly and quite helpful—especially good news for those of us without "green thumbs." Several times a year, selected items are put on sale and, depending on the size of your order, you may be able to work out a special quantity price. Talk to the store manager.

Checks, Credit cards

Rancho Nursery
Beaverton: 8605 S.W. Beaverton-Hillsdale Hwy ☎ 292–0154
Lake Oswego: 599 A Ave. ☎ 636–8909
Portland: 3575 S.E. Division ☎ 232–7204
Hours: Daily, 9–6

At each Rancho Nursery you'll find over an acre of plants, annuals, perennials, and supplies—with lots of unusual stock items. Conifers abound, as do cypress (we counted five kinds), witch hazel, and deciduous trees. There's usually a sale on and we noted that azaleas were $2.99 and bulk rosemary, $2.69. It's a good idea to stop by often, as the inventory is continually changing. Get your name on their mailing list for their big semi-annual sale notices.

Checks, Credit cards

S & J Nursery
Tualatin: 21550 S.W. 108th ☎ 692–4267
Hours: Mon–Sat 9–6

Open only from April through July, S & J Nursery specializes in high-quality bedding plants at competitively low prices. You'll find such items as geraniums, perennials, annuals, patio planters, and more in three greenhouses covering over 8,000 sq. ft. We found gorgeous geraniums in five-inch pots, from $2.95 to $3.25 elsewhere, priced at $2.40 here.

Checks, Credit cards

Garden Ornaments

Carillon Wind Chimes Factory Outlet
Banks: 121 Banks Rd. ☎ 324–9460
Hours: Mon–Fri 9–5, Sat (usually) 10–4

Make your garden look and sound great with tuned wind chimes, bird houses and feeders, statuary and fountains, ceramic sundials, thermometers, and clocks. Wind chimes are priced about 30% less than at the garden centers, ranging from $10 to $100. Wind chime seconds can be found at even bigger savings. First-quality bird houses that sell for $20 elsewhere go for $12.50 here, and are further reduced by about 50% for factory seconds. Overall, you'll find the prices and selections of all their garden ornaments quite good.

Checks, Credit cards

Sol's Garden Decorations
Milwaukie: 18501 S.E. McLoughlin Blvd. ☎ 654–5359
Hours: Mon–Sat 8–5, Sun 12–5

There are over 4,000 garden decorations to choose from here, from inexpensive bird baths and benches to elaborate multilevel fountains with waterfalls and lights. Sol's display lot is covered with concrete planters, fountains, bridges, stepping stones, and lots of animals, such as deer, lions, bear, bunnies, and even a large life-sized moose. The statue collection ranges from classical Greek pieces to grizzled old prospectors and even mermaids. Prices start at around $9.95, and there's something here for everyone's garden or lawn. Although most items can easily be taken home, delivery and set-up is available on larger pieces.

Checks, Credit cards

Indoor Plants

Debbie's Discount Plants
Portland: 2101 S.E. Powell Blvd. ☎ 232–5863
Hours: Tues–Sat 11–5:30

Debbie's is packed to the rafters with indoor tropical plants—so much so that one customer blurted out upon entering: "Wow, it's like a jungle in here." Spiders and ferns (in six-inch pots) are $6.99, while the bigger floor plants start at around $20. Overall, Debbie's plants are top quality (and beautiful!) and her prices are among the lowest in town. We spotted a gorgeous rubber tree (in a ten-inch pot) on sale for $15. You'll also find a nice selection of clay pots and baskets here.

Checks, Credit cards

Michael's Discount Plants
Tigard: 12620 S.W. Main ☎ 639–9739
Hours: Tues–Fri 12–6, Sat 10–6

This indoor tropical plant specialist offers a large plant inventory of over fifty varieties, with attractive low prices. Although the six-inch potted spiders and ferns are priced at $6.99, the bigger plants frequently offer the biggest savings. Eight-foot bamboos, usually $150 elsewhere, are $79; evergreens and canes are about 50% off the retail prices found in florists' shops. Every three months the owner holds a giant liquidation sale prior to heading down to California, Florida, and Texas to stock up on new plants. Call about their close-outs on plants or trees that are getting too big for the shop—you'll get a beauty as well as a steal.

Checks, Credit cards

Plant Peddler
Portland: 1001 E. Burnside ☎ 233–0384
Hours: Daily, 11–6

At Plant Peddler, ferns and spiders in six-inch pots are $5.99 apiece; for an additional 99 cents, they'll wrap the plant with foil, add a bow, and attach a card—a gorgeous gift for under $7. Because they buy in large quantities, they're able to pass on low prices to their customers. Plant Peddler also does a thriving business selling to florists, and on orders of $150 or more, you can take advantage of those same wholesale prices. In addition to having lots of potted flowers in stock, Plant Peddler has one of the biggest cactus inventories around.

Checks, Credit cards

Florists

Besides the sources we've listed below, be sure to check out the floral departments popping up in many of the large supermarkets.

In addition, refer to the chapter on food, which lists some of the U-pick and ready-pick produce vendors that sell fresh flowers—at among the lowest prices around.

Flower Bill's
Portland: 6405 N.E. Glisan ☎ 238–0167
Hours: Tues–Sun 9–7
Flower Bill's has about the lowest prices around on cut flowers and plants. Long-stem royalty roses are priced under $20 a dozen; carnations run $7.99 a dozen; and mums (six-inch pots) are $4.99.

Checks, Credit cards

Rancho Flowers
Beaverton: 8605 S.W. Beaverton-Hillsdale Hwy ☎ 292–6090
Lake Oswego: 599 A Ave. ☎ 636–8909
Portland: 3575 S.E. Division ☎ 232–7204
2010 W. Burnside ☎ 227–2950
10625 N.E. Halsey ☎ 256–1144
Hours: Generally, Mon–Sat 8–8, Sun 9–6
Being Oregon's largest volume florist enables Ranch Flowers to offer a large selection of fresh, quality, low-priced flowers and plants. Their popular mixed flower bouquets are $7.98, and there's usually no waiting for them, because Rancho keeps them in stock. Roses are under $20 per doz.; mini-carnations go for $6.98 per bunch (many more than a dozen); and six- and eight-inch potted indoor plants range from $6.98 to $16.98. You'll probably find the biggest markdowns right after holidays, when their huge pre-holiday inventories have to be moved out quickly.

Checks, Credit cards

Community Gardens

Portland Parks and Recreation
Portland: Office, 6437 S.E. Division ☎ 823–1612
Have a green thumb and no place to use it? You do now. Community Gardens is a city-wide program for gardeners who need space to raise produce or flowers. Gardeners are assigned plots of 400 sq. ft. (within one of the 20 neighborhood locations) on which they must do all the gardening. Water is provided. Fees for year-round plots are $15 (no tilling provided); summer garden plots are $20 (tilling included).
Locations:
Northwest: Cornell Rd. near Audubon Society, upper Macleay
North: N. Edison & Johns; Strong St. & Van Houtan
Northeast: N.E. 27th & Everett
Southeast: 90th & S.E. Taylor; S.E. 18th & Oak; 20th & S.E.Taylor; S.E. Center & 16th; S.E. 38th & Ivon; S.E. Gladstone & 34th; next to 1983 S.E. Locust; 88th & S.E. Steele; S.E. 31st & Market

Southwest: South of Lair Hill Park; S.W. Miles on 3rd & 4th; 41st & S.W. Canby; 55th & S.W. Iowa; S.W. Water & Gibbs

School Plant Sales

Once a year, some of the area colleges and schools hold large fund raiser sales featuring a wide selection of plants, shrubs, and trees at prices usually below retail.

Although we've mentioned a few sources here, you might call any of the other area colleges and schools with horticultural departments to inquire whether they hold any plant sales.

Clackamas Community College
Oregon City: 19600 S. Molalla ☎ 657–6958 x389
Hours: Annual Sale

The horticultural department holds a big annual sale in the greenhouses that starts at noon on the Friday before Mother's Day. The sale, advertised only by word-of-mouth, features all the left-over plants not used in the college landscaping. You'll find a nice selection of annuals, perennials, and shrubs, and lots of rhododendrons—all at reasonable prices.

Checks

Mt. Hood Community College
Gresham: 26000 S.E. Stark ☎ 667–6422 x7477
Hours: Annual Sale

On the last Saturday in April, the Mt. Hood Community College Department of Horticulture puts on a big shrubbery sale featuring many different shrubs at great prices. Watch for sale information in the local Gresham newspaper, or call the college.

Checks

Operation Green Thumb
Portland: 6801 S.E. 60th ☎ 280–5818
Hours: Wed 8:45–10:45 & 12:45–2:45

From January to June, the Portland City School horticulture program holds mid-week plant sales, offering a good selection of house plants ranging in price from $1 to $6 each, and bedding plants starting from $1 for a six-pack. High school and middle school students staff these sales, and proceeds benefit the schools. The best time to shop is mid-April to mid-May, when you'll find the best-looking varieties.

Checks

Portland Community College/ Rock Creek Campus
Portland: 17705 N.W. Springville Rd. ☎ 244–6111 x7242
Hours: Annual Sale
   The horticultural department here puts on a big plant sale the weekend before Mother's Day. Sales are held in the green house and include a large stock of rhododendrons, azaleas, geraniums, and others—each in gallon containers and priced well below retail. Watch for their ads in the *Beaverton Times* or call for more information.

Checks

Master Gardener Program & Benefit Sales

Find out more about gardening and share that knowledge with neighbors and friends by taking a free ten-week Master Gardener course. You'll learn everything about gardening, from soil chemistry to plant pests, and be thoroughly amazed at the depth of your new-found gardening "expertise."

   Master Gardener graduates promise to "pay back" some time for the training they've received by volunteering a few hours in the county extension offices answering phone inquiries or doing office work, or at garden centers answering questions.

   Benefit sales are held by a variety of plant and tree societies to raise funds that allow these groups to continue the valuable work of educating the public on a wide range of gardening issues and in preserving the genetic diversity of old plant varieties.

Master Gardeners

For information on how to become a Master Gardener or if you need help or answers to garden questions, just call or visit the following Oregon State Extension Service office nearest you.

Clackamas County
Oregon City: 200 Warner-Milne Rd. ☎ 655–8631
Hours: Mon–Fri 9–12

Multnomah County
Portland: 211 S.E. 80th Ave. ☎ 252–5386
Hours: Mon–Fri 9–12 & 1–4

Washington County
Hillsboro: 2448 S.E. Tualatin Valley Hwy ☎ 681–7007
Hours: Mon–Fri 9–12

Benefit Sales

To find out about any of the following plant or tree societies or the sales they hold, call your nearest Extension Service office. These societies frequently advertise their sales well in advance, so watch for their ads.

American Rhododendron Society
Early show first weekend in April; big sale Mother's Day weekend at the Crystal Springs Rhododendron Gardens.

Home Orchard Society
Scion and root stock sale in March at Portland Community College/Sylvania Campus; fall show at Canby Fairgrounds.

Oregon Cactus and Succulent Society
Fall and spring show and sale.

Oregon Orchid Society
Spring show and sale.

Oregon Fuchsia Society
Plant auction the third Tuesday in April.

Oregon Association of Nurserymen
Plant and tree auction in June.

Portland Bonsai Society
Show and sale in May.

Portland Chrysanthemum Society
Fall show and small sale; sale last week of April.

Portland Dahlia Society
Tuber auction and sale in April.

Portland Rose Society
Show and sale of miniature roses in June at Lloyd Center.

U-Cut Christmas Trees

For a real old-fashioned Christmas that you'll remember for a long time, why not cut your own tree? You can pick up a Mount Hood National Forest tree-cutting permit for $5 at the U.S. Forest Service office, located at 2955 N.W. Division (phone 666–0771), or at any ranger station. Permits, available after

Thanksgiving, include a map of the area.

Over 100 U-cut Christmas tree farms in Oregon and Washington are listed in a free guide prepared by the Northwest Christmas Tree Association. The guide is available at G.I. Joe's, the YMCA, AAA, U.S. Forest Service, and Chambers of Commerce.

For additional sources of U-cut or pre-cut trees, check out the classified ads early in the holiday season. You'll find a whole forest of private tree farms stocked with trees of all sizes—from tabletops to the really big ones.

Finally, refer to our U-Pick Produce section for even more sources of Christmas trees. Whichever of these resources you use, you'll have a lot of fun and save up to 50% off the price of pre-cut trees found on typical urban tree lots.

Office Needs

Whether your office is in the home or in a business setting, you can give it a professional look at a reasonable price when you shop the outlets listed in this section. Attractive desks, chairs, bookcases, and accessories are easy to find—even for those on tight budgets.

Also refer to the Home Furnishings and Something For Everyone chapters for additional sources of quality office equipment.

Office Furniture, Machines, & Supplies

For some super buys, consider purchasing used desks, files, chairs, bookcases, and office equipment. Discounts on used merchandise are often substantial, and the discriminating bargain shopper knows how to zero in on the gems hiding out among the used goods, factory seconds, and freight-damaged merchandise.

Don't forget to ask about quantity discounts on both new and used inventory when you're buying a bunch of things.

Bizmart
Portland: 10319 S.E. 82nd *(Southgate Center)* ☎ 788–9234
10546 S.E. Washington (*Plaza 205*) ☎ 254–2927
Hours: Mon–Fri 8–9, Sat 9–9, Sun 12–6
This office products super center promises that "we won't be undersold" and guarantees to meet or beat any currently advertised price on any of the 7,000 office products they stock. You'll find everyday low prices on quality name-brand office supplies, furniture, lamps, planners and books, binders, calculators, computers and printers, typewriters, Fax machines, phones, and copiers—at savings from 40% to 60% off suggested retail. There are no membership fees, and for a small charge they'll deliver your order the next day. Sign up for the free Advantage Card and receive cash rebates of 1% to 2% per quarter based on your total dollar amounts spent at Bizmart.

Checks, Credit cards

Krueger's Supply

Portland: 720 S.E. Sandy Blvd. ☎ 233–7791
Hours: Mon–Fri 9:30–6

This liquidator specializes in used office furniture, including desks, cabinets, partitions, metal bookcases, file drawers, and typewriter tables. Four-drawer file cabinets are priced from $85 to $100; desks from $100 (we spotted a beautiful solid oak desk with linoleum inlaid top for $100); and typewriter tables from $10 to $35. Wander upstairs and check out the selection of office chairs priced from $5 to $45. Be sure to ask about a quantity discount when purchasing several items. In one of the back rooms, you'll find huge baskets (just dive in!) filled to the brim with old rubber stamps, rulers, stamp pads, and staplers.

Checks, Credit cards

Office Club

Portland: 323 S.E. M.L. King Blvd. *(Union)* ☎ 234–CLUB
Salem: 2949 Liberty Rd. S. ☎ 370–7700
Tigard: 10520 S.W. Cascade Ave. ☎ 620–CLUB
Hours: Mon–Fri 8–7, Sat 9–5, Sun 11–5

This office products chain offers low prices on thousands of items, from pens, pencils, folders, and staples to office machines, computers, and furniture. Office Club buys directly from manufacturers, thereby cutting out the middlemen. This enables them to offer significant discounts, ranging from 15% to 70% off retail. If this one-stop office products shopping center doesn't overwhelm you, there are over 30,000 additional products that can be ordered from their catalogs at 25% off list price. We found big savings on storage cabinets, chairs, typing stands, desks, copiers, Fax machines, typewriters, phones, and calculators. Although the public may shop here, non members pay 10% over posted prices. Membership is $10 per year (waived for nonprofit groups).

Checks, Credit cards

The Mart

Portland: 2202 E. Burnside ☎ 233–7665
Hours: Mon–Fri 8:30–5:30, Sat 10–4

A wide variety of basic office furniture, including file cabinets, desks, and chairs, can be found at prices 20% to 30% off suggested retail at The Mart. They offer quite a selection of file cabinets—many at especially good prices. Ask about their quantity discounts on chairs and desks. Wander back to their special discount room where close-outs, discontinued items, and freight-damaged merchandise are priced to move quickly. Watch for their bi-weekly newspaper ads featuring everyday low prices on file cabinets, as well as promotional sales items. Pick up a catalog when you visit to help in making price comparisons.

Checks, Credit cards

Remarketing Concepts
Portland: 1039 S. E. Water Ave ☎ 231–8828
Hours: Mon–Fri 9–5

This firm, located in the Portland Liquidation Center building, markets previously leased equipment that it has picked up through bankruptcies, foreclosures, and liquidations. You'll find near-new and used printing equipment, copiers, computers, cash registers, machine tools, forklifts, food service equipment, phone and fax systems, medical equipment, furniture, electronics, and more, available either in their showroom or 20,000-sq.-ft. warehouse—all at prices 10% to 60% below retail.

Checks

Surplus Warehouse
Portland: 100 S.E. Alder ☎ 232–0336
Hours: Daily, 9–6

This liquidator carries both used and new office furniture. Used four-drawer file cabinets (lettersize) go for $79 to $90; two-drawer models are priced from $49 to $69. Standard-size wood desks (30"x60") range from $99 to $249. From their huge inventory of secretarial chairs, you're sure to find what you need for $10 to $60 apiece. Take advantage of their "package deal" discounts: Buy a used desk, cabinet, and chair "package" and have 10% to 20% knocked off. Occasionally, they get in a batch of electric typewriters and office supplies, but best to call about these if that's all you're looking for.

Checks, Credit cards

Computers

Computer shoppers can take the byte out of high computer prices by doing a little homework before setting out to make their purchases. Decide what you want in your computer, then spend a few hours of research to help you locate the system that will deliver these needs.

A good place to start is at the library or a large bookstore. Look for books with recent copyright dates, since the technology changes quickly. A computer book several years old is probably out of date.

Read the ads that the computer stores run in the newspaper. This will give you a good idea of current prices. If you've decided on an entry-level computer that won't require much dealer assistance, be sure to check out the computer discount stores and stores that don't sell computers as their main business. You'll find some great buys this way.

If you're looking at an *IBM* computer, you can save a lot of money by considering a clone instead. Often, clones can offer the same package as an *IBM* product—for less money.

We've included several sources for those interested in renting computer systems, printers, scanners, and modems. A rental plan with option to buy can be a good choice for those wishing to try out a system before buying.

Computer Hardware

Advanced Computer Systems
Hillsboro: 2401 N.E. Cornell Rd. ☎ 648–2090
Hours: Mon–Fri 10–7, Sat 10–6
> They manufacture a wide variety of low-priced IBM clones and offer one of the best warranties around (two years on parts and one year on labor). Just about any software is available here at prices lower than at large retailers. Prices are for cash and checks; (add 4% for credit cards).
>
> Checks, Credit cards

Bridgeway Computer Center
Portland: 905 S.W. 16th ☎ 228–7220
Hours: Mon–Fri 8–8, Sat 9–5, Sun 12–5
> A wide selection of compatibles, including peripherals and software, can be found at Bridgeway. Their best-priced system is the Unitron, an IBM clone that goes for around 50% off name-brand systems. All systems purchased here come with complete one-year warranties and two-hour training classes. Additional classes are available, and any software not in stock can be ordered from catalogs.
>
> Checks, Credit cards

Buggs Warehouse Computers
Portland: 12730 N.E. Marx *(Parkrose Business Center)* ☎ 257–8136
Hours: Daily, 10–6
> Buggs carries a wide variety of IBM compatibles, software, and peripherals. During their occasional weekend sales, you can save 5% to 10% on selected computer systems. Sign up for the *Buggs* newsletter and find out in advance about sales and special promotions. All prices are for cash or check; credit card purchases, add 3%.
>
> Checks, Credit cards

Compuadd Superstore
Beaverton: 4005 S.W. 117th *(Canyon Place)* ☎ 627–0431
Hours: Mon–Thurs 9–6, Fri 9–9, Sat 9–5, Sun 12–5
> This company manufacturers IBM compatibles under its *Compuadd* name.

Their huge, 15,000-square-foot superstore contains PC systems, printers, software, and accessories. They also carry *Macintosh* peripherals and accessories. You'll pay the same low prices whether you use cash, check, or credit card.

Checks, Credit cards

Computer Link
Beaverton: 8362 S.W. Nimbus ☎ 644–8300
Hours: Mon–Fri 8–5, Sat 10–4
The prices on their half-dozen lines of IBM compatibles are among the lowest in town. All systems are protected by full one-year warranties, and the store's phone support is extensive and helpful. (Use their toll-free number (800) 441–8457 if taking your system out of the area.) You'll also find a full range of peripherals, a small stock of software, and an occasional used system. There's no added charge for credit cards.

Checks, Credit cards

The Computer Store
Portland: 700 N.E. Multnomah ☎ 238–1200
Hours: Mon–Fri 10–6, Sat 10–5
The Computer Store is the place for Macintosh, including a large inventory of peripherals and accessories. All of their systems have full warranties and come with several free home-use training disks. Watch for their semiannual clearance sales, where you'll find big savings on demos, discontinued systems, and older software. Occasionally there's a used system for sale. You'll pay the same price whether you use cash, check, or credit card.

Checks, Credit cards

Computer Warehouse
Vancouver: 5620 Gher Rd. ☎ (206)253–4350
Hours: Mon–Sat 9–6, Sun 12–5
You'll find a big inventory here of IBM clones and accessories at low prices. Every Saturday is "weekly special" day and selected systems are further discounted 10%. All systems are protected by standard warranties and come with two hours of free training. Their $25 per hr. fee for on-site maintenance and service is one of the lowest around. Prices shown are for cash or check; add 3% for credit cards. Show them your Oregon driver's license (or other I.D.) and Washington State sales tax will be waived.

Checks, Credit cards

Lucky Computer Company
Beaverton: 10773 S.W. Beaverton-Hillsdale Hwy ☎ 671–0961
Hours: Mon–Fri 9–6, Sat 10–5
This nine-store nationwide chain has been manufacturing IBM clones since

1984. All systems are protected by a warranty for two years on labor and one year on parts. During their occasional "add-on" sales, you can save up to one-third on accessories and peripherals with the purchase of any system. You'll pay the same low prices here whether you pay by cash, check, or credit card.

Checks, Credit cards

Mac Friends

Portland: 10540 S.E. Stark ☎ 254–6800
Hours: Mon–Fri 7–5

This "Mac only" showroom stocks a full range of systems, peripherals, and accessories. Occasionally a used or discontinued model will be available at terrific prices. We found several discontinued new SE models, usually around $2,000, priced $1,375, which included the standard warranty. Credit card users add 3%.

Checks, Credit cards

P C Supply

Tigard: 11507-A S.W. Pacific Hwy ☎ 246–9259
Hours: Mon–Fri 9–6, Sat 10–4

This local manufacturer does most of its business selling IBM clones to computer retailers, but also opens up its small showroom to the public offering systems, accessories, and software at wholesale prices. Purchases include warranties of one year on parts and two years on labor. Credit card users, add 3.7%.

Checks, Credit cards

MasterTech Computers

Beaverton: 4265 S.W. Cedar Hills Blvd. ☎ 627–0909
Hours: Mon–Sat 10–7

This company builds a wide variety of IBM-compatible systems that include complete warranties (one year on parts and two years on labor), three hours' free training, and free phone support. Watch for their sale ads several times a year and save around 15% off retail on all their systems. They always sell software below list prices. Credit card purchasers, add 2%.

Checks, Credit cards

Omnitek Computers

Beaverton: 12024 S.W. Canyon ☎ 626–9718
Portland: 9848 E. Burnside ☎ 253–1330
Hours: Beaverton, Mon–Fri 9–7, Sat 10–5, Sun 12–5; Portland, Mon–Fri 9–6, Sat 9–5

Omnitek is Oregon's largest independent retailer of IBM compatibles, with over 30,000 computer systems sold. They claim the lowest prices on such brands as *Hyundai, Leading Edge,* and *Leading Technologies.* All systems are protected by warranties (which vary from brand to brand) and come with about six hours of training. Omnitek also carries generic clones and used systems at great savings. You can rent a system either instead of or before buying it. The monthly rental is computed by taking 11% of the system's selling price, and two-thirds of each monthly rental applies toward the purchase.

Checks, Credit cards

Sunrise Computers
Beaverton: 2865 S.W. Cedar Hills Blvd. ☎ 626–2311
Hours: Mon–Fri 9–6, Sat 9–2, Sun 12–5
This computer manufacturer supplies IBM clones to many Federal, State, and local government agencies, as well as to the public, at wholesale prices. All systems come with warranties, unlimited free training, and free software copying. (Bring in your disks and they'll copy the programs of your choice— word processing, data base, spreadsheets, general education, and hundreds more.) Also, there's no labor charge for upgrades during your system's first year. Watch for their big ads every Sunday in *The Oregonian.*

Checks

Computer Hardware Rentals

Bit-By-Bit Computer Rentals
Tigard: 10220 S.W. Nimbus, Suite K-8 ☎ 639–5467
Hours: Mon–Fri 9–5
This nationwide computer rental store rents used Apple and IBM compatible systems, plus printers, scanners, modems, and more. Computer prices vary depending upon model, with your basic IBM compatible system (XT hard drive) renting for $90 per mo. plus an additional $50 per mo. for a printer. The monthly rental includes free delivery and pick-up. If you want to purchase the model you're renting, you may do so by paying $72 per mo. (plus $40 per mo. for the printer) for the next 15 months. Rentals for less than one month are also available, although you'll find the best prices on monthly rentals.

Checks, Credit cards

Computer-Rent, Inc.
Portland: 4300 N.E. Broadway ☎ 282–5534
Hours: Mon–Fri 9–5
Dual floppy XT IBM compatibles rent for $49 per mo. and hard drives for $78 per mo. Dot matrix printers are $29 per mo. Computer-Rent requests a $50 deposit (refundable) and first month's rent when you rent a system. Rentals can be purchased at any time. When we checked, several XT dual floppy

systems were priced at $350 apiece. There's a $25 per hr. delivery and pick-up service available.

Checks, Credit cards

Micro-Rentals Inc.

Portland: 825 S.W. 14th ☎ 273–8787
Hours: 8:30–5

Micro-Rentals carries a good selection of IBM compatibles along with a few Apples. The XT dual floppy rents for $70 per mo.; hard drives, $100 per mo.; and dot matrix printers, $40 per mo. There's a $25 (each way) delivery and pick-up service available. Call ahead to see if they have the system you're looking for. Rentals may be purchased at any time.

Checks, Credit cards

National Rent-A-Computer

Portland: 10243 N.E. Clackamas ☎ 256–5630
Tigard: 16192 S.W. 72nd ☎ 620–8944
Hours: Mon–Fri 9–6, Sat 10–5

At National Rent-A-Computer you'll find a wide range of IBM compatibles, printers, and peripherals. An XT with dual floppies runs $59 per mo.; one with a hard drive rents for $78 per mo. A dot matrix printer rents for $29 per mo.; and if you want delivery and pick-up, add $20. There's a $50 deposit and a 3% add-on charge for using credit cards. Ask about their rent-to-own plan if you'd like to keep the computer after renting it. (It usually takes from 17 to 20 months to pay off a system).

Checks, Credit cards

Third Wave Management, Inc.

Portland: 7227 S.W. Terwilliger ☎ 244–6128
Hours: Mon–Fri 8–5

Third Wave carries mostly IBM compatibles along with a few Apples. An XT dual floppy runs $99 per mo. (the hard drive is $125 per mo.; and a printer, $45 per mo). There's a $35 delivery and pick-up charge if you can't make it in to get your system. You can purchase your rental machine at any time.

Checks, Credit cards

Computer Software

Egghead Discount Software

Beaverton: 11639 S.W. Beaverton-Hillsdale Hwy ☎ 626–7331
Clackamas: 8864 S.E. Sunnyside Rd. *(Clackamas Promenade)* ☎ 659–4727
Portland: 814 S.W. Broadway ☎ 248–1720
Hours: Generally, Mon–Fri 9–7, Sat 10–6, Sun 12–5

Egghead stores, which make up the largest software chain in the U.S., each carry over 1500 entertainment and business programs. They also have a full range of accessories for IBM and Apple, such as joy sticks, modems, scanners, and mice—all at discounted prices. The house-brand ribbons and disks are quite acceptable, and are cheaper than the name brands. Get your name on their mailing list to find out in advance about sales and special promotions.

Checks, Credit cards

Gemini Shareware
Tigard: 11608 S.W. Pacific Hwy ☎ 620–5096
Hours: Daily, 11–6
This retail store has thousands of programs in just about every category for *IBM, Mac, Amiga, Apple, Commodore*, and *Atari*—all at discount prices. Prices on multiple orders can be as low as $1.25 per program.

Checks, Credit cards

Software Etc.
Portland: 12000 S.E. 82nd Ave. *(Clackamas Town Center)* ☎ 653–9571
Jantzen Beach Center ☎ 289–1556
Ninth & N.E. Halsey *(Lloyd Center)* 249–8672
Tigard: 9585 S.W. Washington Square Rd. *(Washington Square)* ☎ 639–7657
Hours: Generally, Mon–Fri 10–9, Sat 10–6, Sun 12–5
This nationwide chain of discount retailers carries thousands of programs for *IBM, Apple Macintosh*, and *Commodore*, emphasizing such home-use areas as games, budgeting, word processing, and spread sheets. You'll also find computer books and magazines, supplies, and accessories. Almost every month there's a sale on selected items. Get on their mailing list to find out about upcoming sales and promotions.

Checks, Credit cards

Paper Products & Related Supplies

The cost of office and school supplies, as well as party needs, can add up quickly, especially when you run to the drugstore, local card shop, or grocery store every time you need something. You'll really notice big savings when you buy in volume for both home and office from the outlets we've listed.

The large paper retailers—Arvey and Paper Plus, to mention two—are vast cornucopias containing all your office supply needs. Frequent in-store specials make your savings even bigger.

Keep in mind that a number of companies listed in the Office Furniture section, such as Bizmart and Office Club, as well as Costco, also carry paper products, just as some of the businesses listed here stock business machines and furniture.

Arvey Paper & Office Products

Portland: 1005 S.E. Grand ☎ 231–5600
Hours: Mon–Fri 8–5:30, Sat 9–5

This is definitely a one-stop office supplier. You'll find just about every office supply and piece of equipment necessary to equip an office, including paper, envelopes, labels, folders, calculators, typewriters, phones, copiers, Fax machines, and furniture. They also carry janitorial and graphic arts supplies. Their prices are 10% to 50% below the competition. To find out about upcoming sales, get on their mailing list. When you pop into the store, check out their 10- to 15-page flyer that lists the monthly specials and be prepared to save.

Checks, Credit cards

Current Factory Outlet

Beaverton: 2770 S.W. Cedar Hills Blvd. *(Walker Center)* ☎ 646–2822
Clackamas: 11364 S.E. 82nd Ave. *(Clackamas Square)* ☎ 653–4023
Gresham: 900 Eastman Parkway *(Gresham Town Fair)* ☎ 661–5031
Hours: Generally, Mon–Fri 10–7, Sat 10–5, Sun 11–5

This delightful outlet offers a bright, splashy array of creative paper products and gift items. Its aisles are jam packed with low-priced all-occasion and holiday cards, notes, stationery, note pads, labels, gift wrapping, recipe cards, kitchen gadgets, games, toys, calendars, party favors, and gifts (many under $5). There's also a year-round Christmas display of bright, shiny wrap, tags, bows, and cute gift bags and boxes in many sizes. Much of the store's inventory are either discontinued items or seconds from the company's mail-order catalog (located in Colorado) and priced 30% to 50% below catalog prices. Call for a catalog or pick one up at the outlet. Be sure to ask about their frequent-shopper card discount program.

Checks, Credit cards

Laser Resource, Inc.

Portland: 2332 S.E. 122nd ☎ 253–9274
Hours: Mon–Fri 9–5

When your copier or laser printer toner cartridge has run out of toner, don't toss it. Call Laser Resource for the name of the nearest office supply dealer who will take your empty cartridges, send them over to Laser Resource, and have them refilled. Recycling these cartridges will save you about 50% of the price of a new cartridge. Heavy users, such as law and accounting offices, recycle thousands of cartridges and save big bucks in the process. Laser Resource, through its dealer network, services cartridges for over 250 models of printers and copiers. A cartridge can be refilled as many as five times before it must be tossed. Remember, you can't deal directly with Laser Resource, but only through its dealers.

Montavilla Discount Card Shop

8107 S.E. Stark ☎ 252–1575
Hours: Mon–Sat 10–5

Montavilla carries a wide selection of name-brand greeting cards, gift wrap, and stationery at 25% to 30% off retail. Mylar balloons are $2.50 each; you can choose from a large selection and have them make you a bouquet. Their many gift items include Bradley dolls, ceramics, and teddy bears, all at discount prices. Boxed Christmas cards and gift wrap are always good deals.

Checks

Paper Pick-Up

Portland: 5430 N.E. 122nd ☎ 252–4290
Salem: 1880 Commercial ☎ 364–9826
Hours: Mon–Fri 8–5

At Paper Pick-Up, you'll find wholesale prices on a wide variety of paper products for the office (typing paper, envelopes, printing supplies), party needs, janitorial, packaging, restaurant, and fine art needs. The biggest savings are on discontinued merchandise and quantity purchases. For wedding needs, they offer 24 colors in napkins, plates, table covers, balloons, streamers, and plastic cups and bowls; cutlery, trays, and paper wedding bells, too. Be sure to check out the hundreds of invitations they have in stock—it's one of their specialties. Get on their mailing list for advance notice of special price reductions.

Checks, Credit cards

Paper Plus

Portland: 935 S.E. Ankeny ☎ 238–3607
Tigard: 11105 S.W. Greenberg Rd. ☎ 684–1892
Hours: Mon–Fri 7:30–5:30, Sat 9–2

Paper Plus sells a wide variety of office and printing paper and supplies, as well as stationery, shipping boxes and tubes, packing tapes and pellets, and party and school supplies. You'll pick up the biggest savings during their frequent clearance sales. We found several brands of paper, envelopes, and folders marked down 50% to clear them out. In-store specials also pass along good deals. One thousand envelopes, usually priced $14.50, were sale priced at $9.98. "Post-it" notes were 50% off retail. You can also order office furniture, drafting supplies, attache cases, computer accessories, and copiers out of their catalog at a 20% discount.

Checks, Credit cards

Moving Boxes

Moving? Or just putting things out of sight and mind into storage? Save as much as 50% on general-purpose boxes of all sizes by buying them used from the outlets listed here. Inventory constantly changes, so call to make sure they have what you need.

Carton Service
Portland: 2211 N.W. Front Ave. ☎ 227–6428
Hours: Mon–Fri 7–4
> This huge warehouse operation sells used general-purpose boxes for 65 cents to $1.50, and used wardrobe boxes for $5. (New wardrobes run $8.50.) Packing paper runs 50 cents per lb. and packing tape is $1.50 per roll. Buy more than $150 worth of boxes and you'll receive a 10% discount.
>
> Checks

Cheap Moving Boxes
Beaverton: 10022 S.W. Canyon ☎ 297–8292
Hours: Mon–Sat 9–5:30
> At Cheap Moving Boxes, located inside AAA T.V. Service, you'll find a wide selection of new and used boxes with prices that range from 70 cents to $3 per box. Used wardrobe boxes sell for $6 each and move quickly, so best to call about their availability. In addition, they carry packing paper, tape, and bubble wrap at competitive prices.
>
> Checks, Credit cards

Cellular Phones

With the prices of cellular phones coming down, you'll probably be thinking it's time you had one. Whether you buy a hand held, transportable, or bag cellular phone, you'll find many major brands to choose from—and a bunch of dealers competing for your money.

Used phones offer great savings, but it's best to stick with major brand names when buying used. In addition to the sources listed here, be sure to check phone prices at such retailers as Silo and Fred Meyer.

Cellular Networks
Portland: 17227 S.E. Division ☎ 761–4480
1313 W. Burnside ☎ 222–9500
Salem: 1380 12th St. S.E. ☎ 585–2722
Hours: Mon–Fri 8–6, Sat 10–4
> This cellular specialist carries one of Portland's largest selections of name-brand cellular phones (plus accessories) including *Motorola, OKI, NEC, Mitsubishi, Hitachi,* and others at competitive prices. Occasionally, they'll

have used and discontinued phones priced to move quickly. We spotted a used *Motorola* transportable (with partial warranty) marked down about 35%. Call about their frequent in-store specials.

Checks, Credit cards

Communication Enterprises of Oregon
Portland: 2323 N. Williams ☎ 284–2168
Hours: Mon–Fri 8–5:30
Communication Enterprises offers a large selection of *General Electric* cellular phones. You'll find the best prices here on their factory-reconditioned phones, which carry 90-day warranties (parts and labor). In addition, you can save 15% to 20% on selected new phones during the store's annual holiday sale the last week of November through the first two weeks of December.

Checks, Credit cards

City Cellular
Beaverton: 14780 S.W. Osprey Dr. ☎ 644–6006
Hours: Mon–Fri 8–6
City Cellular's small showroom stocks 14 brand names, plus a wide range of accessories. You'll find big savings on their used and discontinued phones (when they're available). We found a used hand held *Diamond Tel* marked down 40% (the customer returned it after one day, opting for an installed model instead).

Checks, Credit cards

Warehouse District Electronics
Portland: 6140 S.W. Macadam ☎ 245–8883
Hours: Mon–Fri 7:30–7, Sat 10–7, Sun 11–6
This low-overhead operation offers some of the lowest prices around on a wide selection of cellular phones from *Motorola, Diamond Tel, General Electric, NovAtel, Mitsubishi, OKI*, and others. We spotted a *Motorola* 8,000 hand held cellular phone everyday priced 25% below that of the nearest competitor's prices. Occasionally, when new stock arrives, they'll sell demo models at an additional 5% to 10% off their everyday low prices.

Checks, Credit cards

Recreation & Hobbies

Sporting Goods & Recreational Clothing

The greater Portland area is fortunate to have a bunch of manufacturers of sporting goods and apparel with numerous factory outlets and discount stores. There is an almost endless array of sports and recreational equipment at discount prices. Incredible savings can be found during the numerous clearance and end-of-season sales, as well as on used and consignment merchandise. Whether it's a ball or a tent, skis or clothing, you're sure to find what you want—and at the price you want—at the outlets we've listed in this section.

Andy and Bax
Portland: 324 S.E. Grand ☎ 234–7538
Hours: Mon–Sat 9–6, Fri 9–9

This sporting goods store is jammed to the rafters with used Army shirts, jackets, trousers, and helmets. There are hats, caps, knives, socks, coats, and tons of other stuff that campers, rafters, and all others who love the outdoors can use. We noted a good selection of wool gloves from $5 to $10; insulated hunting hats at $10.97; new mechanics' overalls at $9.97; and selected boots marked down 20%. In the basement you'll come to white water heaven, where a large stock of rubber rafts awaits both rubber ducky sailors and serious adventurers. Wander over to "bargain corner," where used or repaired white water rafts are priced to move. The sign says "Let's make a deal," so don't be afraid to give it your best shot.

Checks, Credit cards

Bicycle Repair Collective
Portland: 4438 S.E. Belmont ☎ 233–0564
Hours: Mon 10–8, Tues–Sat 10–6

This consumer co-op rents out the space and tools for the do-it-yourself bike-repair person. For an annual membership charge of $30, or hourly fee of $3, you'll get shop work space, tools, and equipment to fix your bike. If you run into problems, shop mechanics can help out for a nominal charge. They also sell parts and accessories, and offer bicycle maintenance classes. Be sure to call for an appointment.

Checks, Credit cards

The Bike Gallery
Beaverton: 2625 S.W. Cedar Hills Blvd. ☎ 641–2580
Portland: 821 S.W. 11th ☎ 222–3821
5329 N.E. Sandy Blvd. ☎ 281–9800
Hours: Beaverton, Mon–Fri 11–8, Sat 10–6, Sun 12–5; S.W. 11th, Mon–Sat 9:30–6; Sandy, Tues–Fri 11–8, Sat 9–6, Sun 12–5

You'll find a wide variety of name-brand bikes and accessories for the entire family here. The best prices are found during their annual spring bike sale, with discounts of 10% to 20% off the prices of the previous year's bikes. The "spring sale," usually held at their large Sandy Blvd. store, starts right after New Year's and lasts until every previous-year's model is sold. All sale bikes are fully assembled and come with a free tune-up and a full guarantee. You can also rent a mountain bike here before buying one. Don't miss the Beaverton store's big October sale of used rental ski equipment.

Checks, Credit cards

By-Wright Golf Company
Beaverton: 8118 S.W. Nimbus Ave. ☎ 641–2279
Hours: Mon–Fri 9–6, Sat 9–5

This local golf club manufacturer offers factory-direct prices, custom fitting, and complete repair services. Custom-tailored sets range from $165 to $289, while good used sets start at around $100.

Checks

Cascadden's
Portland: 1533 N.W. 24th ☎ 224–4746
Hours: Mon–Fri 10–7, Sat 10–5

Cascadden's, around for over 20 years, specializes in name-brand Alpine and Nordic ski equipment and accessories. Choose from a large selection of *Patagonia, CB, Rossignol, Louis Garneau, Scott, Alpina, Look,* and others—all competitively priced. You'll find big savings of up to 70% at their annual winter and spring inventory liquidation sales. Rounding out their inventory are mountain bikes, roller blades, skates, and hiking boots. Be sure to check out the consignment goods, where most things are priced at less than half the original prices.

Checks, Credit cards

Citybikes Workers Cooperative

Portland: 1914 S.E. Ankeny ☎ 239–0553
Hours: Mon–Fri 11–7, Sat 11–5 (closed Wednesdays)

This worker-owned bike co-op repairs and sells used bikes at prices well below the original selling prices. They sell used bicycles that are completely overhauled and reconditioned, including classic English three-speeds, American one-speeds, "commuter bikes," and even antique bikes from the '50s and '60s. When we checked, there were around 30 bikes ready to be sold and about 60 waiting to be worked on in the garage. (Ask for a tour and they'll show you the ones out there.) Citybikes is definitely the place to find a sturdy, non-glamorous, functional bike that works well.

Checks

Courtside Tennis and Apparel

Beaverton: 4907 S.W. 76th ☎ 292–9606
Salem: 1073 Commercial St. S.E. ☎ 399–8681
Hours: Mon–Sat 10–6, Sun 10–4

Courtside's motto is "we're never undersold," so if you find a better price elsewhere they'll match it. Choose your tennis racket from such names as *Prince, Wilson, Head, Wimbledon, Yamaha,* and *Dunlop.* There are always rackets on sale, and we spotted some at 30% to 40% off the original prices. Their unique 30-day demo program lets you borrow different rackets for up to one month without charge, as long as you buy a racket from them. You'll pick up some incredible bargains early in the year when new models arrive and the previous year's models and demos are discounted to move out.

Checks, Credit cards

82nd Avenue Golf Range

Portland: 2806 N.E. 82nd ☎ 253–0902
Hours: Mon–Sat 9–11, Sun 7–11

Beginners on a budget can buy a generic starter set including putter and bag for $150 (a brand-name starter set would cost $250). PGA-qualified pros help you get the right fit and teach lessons on the driving range or putting green. Check out their nice selection of used clubs.

Checks, Credit cards

Herman's World of Sporting Goods

Beaverton: 10108 S.W. Washington Square Rd. (*Washington Square Too*)
☎ 684–8908
Portland: 11211 S.E. 82nd *(Ross Center)* ☎ 659–3815
1880 N. Hayden Island Dr. ☎ 289–8880
Hours: Mon–Fri 10–9, Sat 10–6, Sun 11–5

This large national chain of over 200 stores carries a huge selection of sportswear and sporting goods for team sports, skiing, golf, bowling, racquetball, tennis, camping, and exercise. Watch for their end-of-season sales for some incredible buys. We found kids' winter ski jackets, usually $35 to $40, priced at $15, and adult turtlenecks, regularly $12, priced at $6. You'll also pick up big savings during their seasonal sports sales. The baseball sale, for example, features name-brand gloves, bats, cleats, and team wear from 15% to 35% off retail.

Checks, Credit cards

Las Vegas Discount Golf & Tennis

Beaverton: 2750 S.W. Cedar Hills Blvd. *(Walker Center)* ☎ 646–GOLF
Hours: Mon–Fri 9:30–7, Sat 9–6, Sun 11–5

You'll find the latest styles and models of name-brand gear and equipment for golf, tennis, and racquetball at prices up to 40% off suggested retail. They offer famous-name golf clubs (drivers, putters, wedges, chippers), bags, and balls; tennis rackets by Head, Prince, Dunlop, Yamaha, and others. In addition, there are several lines of tennis shoes and apparel; racquetball racquets by *Head* and *Wilson*; and a wide variety of sports accessories, such as eye guards and jump ropes. Tennis and golf apparel are always 25% off, and several racks of clothing were marked down 40%. A *Wilson* warmup outfit, usually $80, was priced at $64.95, and "Signature" golf shoes, originally $52, were $39.99. Tennis rackets are $5 to $10 off retail, and golf clubs generally carry prices below suggested retail.

Checks, Credit cards

Mountain Bike Factory Outlet

West Linn: 2092 Eighth Ave. *(Willamette Mall)* ☎ 657–4245
Hours: Mon–Fri 11–7, Sat & Sun 10–6 (closed Wed)

Mountain Bike buys in volume and passes along discount prices to its customers. All bikes are priced about 10% to 20% below those of most competitors. Occasionally they'll have factory seconds and the savings can be considerable. We spotted a Mountain Sports Bike (21-speed) with a blemished finish, usually $320, marked down to $259. They also carry a wide range of competitively priced helmets and accessories.

Checks, Credit cards

Nevada Bob's Discount Golf

Beaverton: 10196 S.W. Park Way *(Cedar Hills Shopping Center)*
☎ 297–1808
Portland: 11211 S.E. 82nd *(Ross Center)* ☎ 653–7202
Salem: 831 Lancaster Dr. N.E. *(Lancaster Mall)* ☎ 363–3715
Hours: Mon–Fri 9:30–8, Sat 9–6, Sun 11–5

This large nationwide chain has the most complete line of golf clubs and equipment at discount prices in the Pacific Northwest. Their huge inventory includes woods and irons, men's and women's sportswear, balls, gloves, shoes, bags, and carts—all at prices they claim are the lowest in town. Ask about their "frequent buyer" program club, where members can earn free gift certificates.

Checks, Credit cards

NorthWoods Golf Co.

Portland: 7410 S.W. Macadam ☎ 245–1910
Hours: Mon–Fri 8:30–5:30, Sat 9–4

This custom club manufacturer offers a ready-made beginner set, including three metal woods and eight irons, for under $275. For an additional $100, you can have woods and irons custom tailored. Occasionally you'll find factory seconds here at great prices. Used clubs and demos are not priced, so you'll have to make an offer. Don't miss their annual pre-Christmas sale, where you can shave 15% to 20% off their regular prices.

Checks, Credit cards

Play It Again Sports

Beaverton: 9242 S.W. Beaverton-Hillsdale Hwy. *(Valley Plaza)* ☎ 292–4552
Hours: Tues–Fri 10:30–7, Sat 10:30–5:30, Sun 11–4

At Play It Again you'll find a good selection of new and used sports equipment for golf, archery, bowling, team sports, skiing, tennis, racquetball, and ping pong, as well as performance equipment such as weight benches, rowers, and exercise bikes. Brand names pop up often, and discounts of 10% to 20% on new merchandise and 30% to 60% on used merchandise are typical. A *Wilson* demo glove (never used), usually $90, was priced at $49.95. New baseball bats are priced from $25 to $40, while used bats go for 50% or more off new prices. If you have used equipment you want to sell, give them a call for an estimate. Watch for the opening of their new eastside store.

Checks, Credit cards

Polzel Sporting Goods & Manufacturing, Inc.

Portland: 13580 S.E. Powell Blvd. ☎ 761–0188
Hours: Mon–Fri 9–5, Sat 9–3

This water-sports specialist carries a good selection of boating, rafting, fishing, hunting, and camping supplies and accessories at competitive prices. You'll find the biggest savings at their seasonal sales, where discounts of 20% or more are common. We noted holiday sale prices on dome tents, sleeping bags, rafts, and equipment.

Checks, Credit cards

Pro Golf Discount

Beaverton: 9555 S.W. Cascade Ave. ☎ 646–8673
Portland: 9738 S.E. Washington ☎ 252–8558
Hours: Mon–Fri 10–8, Sat 9–6, Sun 11–5

This 170-store discount chain carries every major brand of golf equipment on the market, including accessories, at prices they guarantee to be the lowest around. Every item in the store is discounted. Men's and women's full sets (eight irons and three woods) start at $199; Gor-Tex raingear and shoes are 15% to 30% off; famous-name sweaters, slacks, shirts, and knickers are 20% to 30% off. Great stocking stuffers at great prices are golf videos, putters, sand wedges, and gloves. Watch for their seasonal sales for even bigger savings on selected items.

Checks, Credit cards

REI (Recreational Equipment, Inc.)

Portland: Jantzen Beach Center ☎ 283–1300
Tualatin: 7410 S.W. Bridgeport Rd. ☎ 624–8600
Hours: Mon–Fri 10–9, Sat 10–6, Sun 11–5

This West Coast chain offers a dazzling array of top-quality recreational equipment for those into climbing, camping, backpacking, skiing, biking, and water sports. By paying a $10 lifetime membership fee, members get a once-a-year dividend (actually a rebate of around 10% on each member's total annual purchases). Members also get 10% off all equipment rentals (i.e., tents, ski equipment, packs, and canoes). They also receive catalogs and flyers informing them in advance of upcoming clearance sales where discounts of at least 10% to 20% are common. Non-members may shop here, but do not get any of the fringes offered to members.

Checks, Credit cards

Style Sport, Inc.

Portland: 7025 S.W. Macadam ☎ 246–8434
Hours: Mon–Fri 9–7, Sat 11–6, Sun 11–3

This warehouse outlet carries a large selection of first-quality, seasonal sportswear, and accessories at bargain prices. When we checked they were loaded with ski clothing, and we found such things as entrant jackets with pants, regularly $280, priced at $129; ski bibs from $25; sunglasses, usually

$14 to $60, from $1 to $10; and ski gloves 50% off retail. You'll save the most at their seasonal sales; call for dates or watch for their ads.

Checks, Credit cards

Tigard Cycle and Ski Shop
Tigard: 12551 S.W. Main ☎ 639–1000
Hours: Mon–Fri 10–6:15, Sat 10–5:15

This shop stocks hundreds of used bikes, downhill skis, and cross-country skis at 40% or more off new prices. We spotted some fully reconditioned three-speeds and cruisers, ranging from $159 to $199 new, priced $89.95 used. There are also over 100 new bikes, fully assembled and ready to go. Several times a year they hold a sale and knock an additional 1% off all new and used bike prices.

Checks, Credit cards

U.S. Outdoor Store
Portland: 219 S.W. Broadway ☎ 223–5937
Hours: Mon–Fri 9–8, Sat 10–6, Sun 12–5

U.S. Outdoor stocks a huge inventory of quality name-brand ski equipment and apparel, backpacking and watersports accessories, and summerwear, including wetsuits, sunglasses, packs, luggage, rollerblades, boots, and more—all at discounted prices. Apparel from *North Face, Columbia,* and *Patagonia* can be found here at everyday low prices 10% to 25% below suggested retail. We spotted a three-man dome tent (priced at $119.95 at a nearby competitor's) everyday-priced at $89.95 here. In early spring they hold their "50% off" sale on all ski equipment and apparel, with plenty of incredible bargains to be found. Wander downstairs and check out their large stock of consignment ski equipment and apparel.

Checks, Credit cards

Cameras and Audio & Video Equipment

A good place to start in your search for the right VCR, CD player, T.V., camera, boom box, camcorder, or other fancy gadget is *Consumer Reports* magazine. It will give you the lowdown on the product you're after, and discuss such things as ease of use, reliability, and value for dollar.

Used and reconditioned cameras (some with warranties) usually deliver discounts of 50% or more off new prices.

To pick up hefty discounts on film, buy it in 10- or 20-roll packs.

Ask about floor-model electronic products. Usually there's a little wear and tear on them—perfect for price dickering.

And it's not a bad idea to scan the classified ads for used electronics. You might find some sellers who are upgrading and disposing of perfectly good "old" stuff at a fraction of the original price.

In addition to the sources we've listed here, you'll also find consistent low pricing on a wide range of consumer electronics at Silo, Costco, Best, George Smith Warehouse Sales, and others listed under Household Appliances.

Camera Connection

Gresham: 1565 N.E. Division ☎ 661–7506
Hours: Mon–Fri 9–8, Sat 9–6

You'll find a nice selection of new and used brand-name cameras to choose from. New "point and shoot" 35mm cameras range from $99 to $300 (depending on features). We spotted several used cameras that looked brand new and carried prices about 40% below the original. Call about their frequent in-store specials. Buy ten rolls of any brand film and save 10%.

Checks, Credit cards

Camera Works

Beaverton: 9214 S.W. Beaverton-Hillsdale Hwy *(Valley Plaza)* ☎ 297–5723
Hours: Mon–Fri 9–6, Sat 9–3

This shop specializes in reconditioned cameras, lenses, accessories, and supplies. All used cameras that the store sells (as opposed to its consignment cameras, which are sold "as-is") come with one-year warranties. Most of their large stock of used cameras ranges from $25 to $300, with used *Nikon, Minolta, Canon,* and *Pentax* starting around $200. Occasionally you'll find a special-of-the-month promotion and save on supplies and accessories.

Checks, Credit cards

Camera World

Portland: 500 S.W. Fifth ☎ 222–0008
Hours: Mon–Thurs 9–6, Fri 9–8, Sat 10–6

Camera World stocks a wide range of camcorders, still cameras, lenses, VCRs, binoculars, accessories, and supplies at probably the lowest prices you'll find anywhere. This low-margin, high-volume retail and mail-order business offers nearly all the big brand-names, including *Sony, Canon, RCA, Hitachi, Minolta, Panasonic, Nikon, Olympus*, and others. While other camera stores may order ten to twenty units, Camera World buys one thousand at a time and passes along big savings. However, it's best to shop at Camera World already knowing what you want—their sales are brisk and the staff often quite busy. Watch for their full-page display ads and special promotions for even bigger savings.

Checks, Credit cards

Citizen's Photo
Hillsboro: 2351 S.E. Tualatin Valley Hwy ☎ 640–6618
Portland: 709 S.E. 7th ☎ 232–8501
Hours: Hillsboro, Mon–Fri 10–7, Sat 10–6; Portland, Mon–Thurs 8–5,
Fri 8–6, Sat 9–2
Since 1955, Citizen's Photo has been offering premiere cameras, accessories, and film supplies to professionals and dedicated amateurs alike. Choose from *Pentax, Olympus, Fuji, Nikon, Hasselblad,* and more at everyday low prices. Quality used cameras sell for around 50% of new prices. You'll pick up a 25% film discount when you buy either ten rolls of Fuji or 20 rolls of Kodak.

Checks, Credit cards

Hollywood Camera Store
Portland: 4039 N.E. Sandy Blvd. ☎ 284–2060
Hours: Mon–Fri 9:30–5, Sat 9:30–4:30
Hollywood Camera specializes in quality used cameras at prices 50% or more below new. Choose from a large selection of major-brand cameras, starting at $65 for used and $100 for new. Most of their used stock comes with warranties.

Checks, Credit cards

Home Video Library
Portland: 16544 S.E. Division ☎ 760–6488
Hours: Mon–Sat 10–9, Sun 11–7
This family owned and operated store offers a large selection of top name-brand electronics including TVs, stereos, camcorders, phones (for car and home), VCRs, laser disks and players, and lots of accessories. By holding down the advertising, they're able to offer prices that are 10% to 20% lower than those of most competitors. They're so confident of their low prices that if you find your purchase cheaper elsewhere within 30 days, they'll refund the difference. The employees are not on commission here, which explains their extraordinary patience and eager willingness to help you make the right choice. In addition to electronics, about half of their business is made up of video rentals.

Checks, Credit cards

The Kida Company
Portland: 127 N.W. Third Ave. ☎ 227–2544
Hours: Mon–Fri 9–5:30, Sat 10–4:30
This small company doesn't try to compete with the enormous volume sales of its large competitors. Instead, it concentrates on offering a small number of top-brand electronics at discounted prices with excellent, friendly service.

Choose among *Sony, Panasonic, Toshiba, Canon,* and *Nikon* for cameras, VCRs, TVs, stereos, radios, and other audio systems. You'll never pay full retail here, and occasionally demos are further reduced to move them out. Kida also has a selection of small appliances (see our listing under Appliances).

Checks, Credit cards

The Shutterbug

Keizer: 4382 River Rd. N. ☎ 390–5088
Portland: 620 S.W. Broadway ☎ 227–5799
　　12000 S.E. 82nd *(Clackamas Town Center)* ☎ 659–5102
Salem: 354 Center N.E. ☎ 363–3432
　　831 Lancaster Dr. N.E. *(Lancaster Mall)* ☎ 585–5088
　　3934 Commercial S.E. ☎ 364–8044
Tigard: 9708 S.W. Washington Square Rd. *(Washington Square)* ☎ 639–5088
Hours: Generally, Mon–Sat 10–9, Sun 10–6

With 16 stores in Oregon, The Shutterbug is the largest photographic chain in the state—competing neck-to-neck with its rival, Camera World. The Shutterbug offers competitive prices on all major brands of cameras, accessories, and supplies. Be sure to check out their large stock of quality used and consignment cameras, where discounts of 50% or more off new prices can be found. Buy ten rolls of any brand film and you'll get a 10% discount.

Checks, Credit cards

Stereo King

Beaverton: 10905 S.W. Canyon Rd. ☎ 646–0664
Gresham: 21855 S.E. Stark ☎ 667–3690
Portland: 12115 S.E. 82nd ☎ 653–8088
Hours: Mon–Fri 10–8, Sat 10–6

Stereo King offers a large stock of name-brand automotive electronics, including car stereos, CD players, radar detectors, alarms, and a small inventory of CBs—all at probably the lowest prices in town. Choose among hundreds of decks from *Sony, Pioneer, Concord, Clarion, Sanyo,* and others. Watch for their ads in the weekly Nickel Ads for even bigger savings on selected new stereo players. For a small charge they'll install your purchase.

Checks, Credit cards

Warehouse District Electronics

Portland: 6140 S.W. Macadam ☎ 245–8883
Hours: Mon–Fri 7:30–7, Sat 10–7, Sun 11–6

This large retailer backs up its claim of being able to deliver the best prices on top name brand stereos, TVs, video equipment, and VCRs by offering a

30-day 130% unconditional price plan. If you find the same item at another store (within 30 days of purchase) at a lower price, Warehouse District will refund you 130% of the difference. They carry a huge selection of all major brand electronics. You'll get a 3% discount for paying by cash or check. From time to time, floor models go on sale and you can pick up even bigger savings.

Checks, Credit cards

Musical Recordings

The best bargains will be found on good used tapes, LPs, and CDs, although selection may be somewhat limited. New recordings may be discounted at time of release, so be sure to ask about promotions or specials. Otherwise, check bargain bins for overstocked and discontinued items.

Most sellers of used recordings also buy—so gather up your old music and sell or trade them. Some used bookstores, second-hand, and thrift shops also sell used musical recordings.

Artichoke Music
Portland: 3522 S.E. Hawthorne Blvd. ☎ 232–8845
Hours: Mon–Fri 10:30–6, Sat 10–6, Sun 12–5
This shop has a small selection of used classical, rock, country, folk, and blues records starting at $1.99. In addition, you'll find a nice inventory of musical instruments such as flutes, guitars, harmonicas, recorders, dulcimers, accordions, and unusual folk instruments. (Be sure to try out the African gourds.) Used instruments are bought and sold here as well. Get on their mailing list for upcoming store specials and community folk events.

Checks, Credit cards

Backbeat Music
Portland: 203 S.W. Ninth ☎ 224–0660
Hours: Mon–Sat 11–6, Sun 12–5
Backbeat music (formerly called Rockport Records) specializes in blues, jazz, and rock LP collectibles from the '50s and '60s. Used cassettes and LPs run around $2 and used CDs, $8 to $10. New CDs are competitively priced starting at $12.99.

Checks, Credit cards

Bird's Suite
Portland: 3736 S.E. Hawthorne Blvd. ☎ 235–6224
Hours: Mon–Fri 10:30–6:30, Sat 10–6, Sun 12–6
This music shop offers thousands of new and used records, tapes, and CDs at low prices. We found used classical records at $2 and an assortment of others priced at two for $1. Used tapes fill several boxes and go for 50 cents

to 99 cents each. Quite a few jazz and pop "cut-outs" (manufacturers' close-outs) to choose from that were priced at $2.99.

Checks, Credit cards

Blue Pacific Records
Oregon City: 514 Seventh ☎ 655–7582
Hours: Mon–Sat 11–7, Sun 11–5
Although tapes and CDs have largely replaced records, Blue Pacific still carries thousands of low-priced records to meet the needs of hard-core record lovers. They also carry lots of quality used cassette tapes and CDs at great prices. Though most of the stock is used, you'll also find some new products, such as hats, T-shirts, and posters. Most of the music here is rock 'n roll (with a smidgen of rap). Owner Ken Basting will gladly help you find whatever you're looking for, however obscure the title.

Checks

Crocodile Records
Portland: 3623 S.E. Hawthorne Blvd. ☎ 238–1957
828 S.W. Park ☎ 222–4773
Hours: Hawthorne, Mon–Sat 11–7, Sun 12–6; Park, Mon–Sat 10–6, Sun 12–5
At Crocodile you'll find a wide selection of quality new and used records, tapes, and CDs covering rock, classical, jazz, new age, opera, folk, and movie soundtracks. (For only $3.99, you can own a copy of "I Was A Teenage Zombie".) We found classical records from Beethoven to Wagner starting at $2.99; rock records featuring just about every rock performer from the Beach Boys to the Youngbloods at $3 and up; tapes from $2.99; used CDs at $5 to $10; and bargain boxes full of 50%-off and 99-cent records. Toward the back of the shop are several incredible bargain boxes, where used records go for 50 cents each, or three for $1.

Checks, Credit cards

Django Records
Portland: 111 S.W. Stark ☎ 227–4381
Hours: Mon–Fri 10–8, Sat 10–7, Sun 11–6
Django's offers about the biggest and most varied selection around of new and used records, tapes, and CDs, all at low prices. Used cassette tapes and records start at $2. You'll find a large stock of in-print and out-of-print records to choose from, as well as 45s, posters, buttons, and cards. Box up your old music and bring it on down to sell—Django's pays cash on the spot.

Checks, Credit cards

Dudley's New & Used Records

Portland: 808 S.W. 10th ☎ 228–3170
Hours: Mon–Fri 10–6:30, Sat 10:30–6:30, Sun 12:30–5:30

Dudley's offers a large inventory of tapes, CDs, and records, as well as rock 'n roll T-shirts ($6.99 each) and posters ($2 each). You'll find low prices not only on used stock but also on selected new tapes, CDs, and vintage 45s.

Checks, Credit cards

2nd Avenue Records

Portland: 418 S.W. Second ☎ 222–3783
Hours: Mon–Sat 10–7, Sun 12–6

This store probably has the best selection and prices anywhere of used imported and independent labels. Check out the nice selection of used CDs priced from $4.99 to $8.49. Used cassettes at $1.99 apiece are jammed into several boxes; you're invited to dig in and search for many a hidden treasure. T-shirts (including some concert shirts) that usually sell elsewhere for around $14 are priced $9.50 here. Patches from most rock groups range from $2.99 to $5.99, and large rock stickers from 75 cents to $1.50.

Checks, Credit cards

Music Millennium

Portland: 3158 E. Burnside ☎ 231–8926
801 N.W. 23rd ☎ 248–0163
Hours: Mon–Sat 10–10, Sun 11–9

Serving Portland for nearly a quarter of a century, Music Millennium proudly boasts of having the largest inventory of CDs, cassette tapes, and records in Oregon. Watch for their weekly Willamette Week ads to save on new releases. Check out the bargain bins for low prices on out-of-prints and "cut-outs" (discontinued titles). Used CDs sell for around $8, used tapes for $3 to $4, and used records for about $3. The N.W. 23rd location is the smaller of their stores.

Checks, Credit cards

Tower

Beaverton: 3175 S.W. Cedar Hills Blvd. *(Beaverton Mall)* ☎ 626–2600
Portland: 4100 S.E. 82nd *(Eastport Plaza)* ☎ 777–8460
Hours: Daily, 9–midnight

This worldwide chain store operation offers a huge stock of CDs, tapes, and music videos in jazz, blues, classical, rock, and country selections. You'll pick up especially good prices during their numerous sales. When we checked they were holding their "music magic sale" and a nice selection of major brand name CDs were priced from $7.99 to $11.99, with cassettes at $2.99 each or four for $10. As you walk down the budget aisles you'll find everyday low-priced CDs from $8.99. Watch for red-tag specials (mixed in with the regular inventory) and pick up some hefty savings.

Checks, Credit cards

Arts, Crafts, & Fabric

Whether you make clothes for the entire family or just able do your own minor alterations, sewing is an excellent way to stretch the family budget. Many fabric stores have expanded their arts and crafts departments, adding all sorts of fabrics—bridal, swimwear, upholstery, and drapery—plus scores of home decorator fabrics and accessories.

Remnants and discounted fabrics continue to be the best buys—often at discounts of 50% or more off regular retail. Sew-it-yourself kits are good values, because they provide all the necessary materials and instructions for you to make your own clothes. Take advantage of free classes, demonstrations, and consultations offered by many fabric outlets. Call the stores, get on mailing lists, and watch newspaper ads for fabric announcements.

Refer to Household Appliances for stores that sell sewing machines and to Paper Products & Related Supplies for arts and crafts supplies.

American Fabric & Foam Outlet
Portland: 308 N.W. 11th ☎ 222–3665
Hours: Mon–Thurs 10–4, Fri (call first)
This small outlet offers a wide selection of fabric for your upholstery, drapery, and marine needs at discount prices. Besides a small inventory of in-store fabrics, you'll have hundreds of books sample from which to choose-and all at prices 20% or more off retail. We found several different upholstery fabrics, usually $30 per yd., priced $15 per yd. They also custom manufacture; take in your measurements and within three weeks you can have a bedspread, drapes, or futon cover. We overheard one customer say that she just drove eight hours from Idaho to shop the great prices here. American Fabric & Foam also sells naugahyde and foam, and makes cushions and futons.

Checks, Credit cards

Best Fabric
Beaverton: 4790 S.W. 76th ☎ 292-4887
Gresham: 2125 E. Burnside ☎ 667–4060
Oregon City: I-205 at McLoughlin ☎ 657–7329
Portland: 10548 S.E. Washington ☎ 253–5710
Tigard: 210 Tigard Shopping Plaza ☎ 639–2434
Vancouver: 5001 N.E. Thurston Way ☎ (206)254–5665
Hours: Mon–Fri 10–9, Sat & Sun 10–6

Patterns by *Simplicity, Butterick, Vogue, New Look,* and *McCall's* are always half off. You'll find a large selection of inexpensive fabrics, especially 100% cotton calico, from *VIP, Wamsutta,* and *Concord.* Craft items and notions are good buys, as are sewing machines, during their periodic sales. Get on their mailing list to find out about upcoming sales and to receive coupons for additional discounts.

Checks, Credit cards

Calico Corners

Portland: 8526 S.W. Terwilliger ☎ 244–6700
Hours: Mon–Sat 10–6, Sun 12–5

Calico Corners offers beautiful decorator upholstery and drapery fabrics at considerable savings. Because they have many unadvertised sales, the smart shopper will get on their mailing list. Do-it-yourselfers can take advantage of the store's custom workrooms to finish windows, sofas, and beds. In-store fabric consultants are available for guidance. Watch for specials that offer savings of 20% or more on custom labor charges when you buy their fabric and let them make your draperies, window treatments, slipcovers, bed-spreads, futon covers, and upholstery.

Checks, Credit cards

Cheryl's Own Design Fabric Outlet

Beaverton: 12675 S.W. Broadway ☎ 641–7271
Hours: Mon–Fri 10–5, Sat 10–3

Sports-oriented seamstresses and tailors go wild over Cheryl's low-priced factory-excess fabrics from such manufacturers as *Nike, Roffe, Duffel, Dehen,* and *Patagonia.* We found a good selection of lycras from $10 to $13.50 per yd. Five dollars worth of *Dehen* rugby excess will make a rugby shirt. At the sale table we found knits at $4 per yd. that originally sold at $7.50, and remnants at 50% off. In addition to an abundance of 100% cotton materials, Cheryl's carries patterns by *Quick Sew, Stretch and Sew,* and *Daisy Kingdom,* as well as their own label. Thread, buttons, bands, collars, and a big supply of ribbing round out the inventory.

Checks, Credit cards

Daisy Kingdom

Portland: 134 N.W. Eighth ☎ 222–9033
12000 S.E. 82nd *(Clackamas Town Center)* ☎ 652–7464
Hours: N.W. Eighth, Mon–Sat 10–6, Sun 1–5; Clackamas, Mon–Fri 10–9, Sat 10–6, Sun 11–6

This remarkable company offers a nearly overwhelming inventory of unique fabrics, gifts, and craft supplies—all attractively displayed in a quaint setting surrounded by antiques. As you wander through their three-story showcase (on N.W. Eighth), you'll find sportswear, bridal fabrics, rubber stamps and accessories, home decorations, decorative buttons, patterns, trims, no-sew appliques, notions, and all sorts of supplies to aid any shopper with creative energies. You'll save up to 50% off their regular prices of ready-made clothing when you purchase sew-it-yourself kits (Clackamas store only) and make you own girls' or women's dresses, pants, blouses, jackets, and coveralls. For your convenience, pick up their free mail-order catalogs and order stylish ski and activewear for the entire family, as well as fabrics and notions for these garments. Watch for their periodic warehouse sales (held across the street from their N.W. Eighth store) for savings up to 80% off retail prices on factory overruns, seconds, and ready-made sample clothing.

Checks, Credit cards

Fabricland

Beaverton: 8540 S.W. Apple Way ☎ 297–6811
Clackamas: 16100 S.E. 82nd ☎ 655–5689
Hillsboro: 2105 S.E. Tualatin Valley Hwy. ☎ 640–5826
Gresham: 320 N.W. Eastman *(Gresham Town Fair)* ☎ 667–9053
Milwaukie: 3601 S.E. Concord Rd. ☎ 659–5715
Oregon City: 1842 Molalla Ave. ☎ 655–2089
Portland: 1928 N.E. 42nd ☎ 281–1033
  2011 N.E. 181st ☎ 661–1595
  2035 N.E. 181st ☎ 666–4511 (*Wholesale Division*)
  335 N.E. 122nd ☎ 252–1885
Salem: 4815 Commercial S.E. ☎ 363–8102
  1570 Lancaster Dr. N.E. ☎ 363–1603
Tigard: 11705 S.W. Pacific Hwy. ☎ 620–8940
Vancouver: 7209 N.E. Highway 99 ☎ (206)694–1141
  5411 E. Mill Plain ☎ (206)696–3391
  4814 N.E. Thurston ☎ (206)254–0777
Hours: Mon–Fri 9:30–9, Sat 9:30–6, Sun 11–6; Wholesale Division, Mon–Fri 8–4:30, Sat 9–2:30
Fabricland's retail outlets have frequent sales and always sell *Vogue, Butterick, McCalls, Simplicity,* and *Burda* patterns at 50% off. Remnants can be found at up to 30% off. Smart shoppers with business cards (their own, of course), such as home-based businesses, retailers, and manufacturers, can shop at Fabricland's warehouse (wholesale division) and pay wholesale prices for fabric, trim, notions, and craft items. There's a $50 minimum purchase from the warehouse, as well as quantity and full-bolt purchase requirements. Ask for a price list when you stop in, then take the warehouse tour and save big.

Checks, Credit cards

Hancock Fabrics
Gresham: 340 N.W. Burnside ☎ 667–9366
Milwaukie: 16074 S.E. McLoughlin Blvd. *(Holly Farm Center)* ☎ 653–9715
Portland: 10335 S.E. 82nd *(Southgate Shopping Center)* ☎ 771–7645
   4500 N.E. 122nd ☎ 252–0253
Salem: 618 Lancaster Dr. N.E. ☎ 363–3551
Tigard: 12244 S.W. Scholls Ferry Rd. *(Greenway Town Center)* ☎ 684–1405
Vancouver: 628 N.E. 81st *(J & M Plaza)* ☎ (206)573–2992
Hours: Mon–Fri 9:30–9, Sat 9:30–6, Sun 12–5
   Whether you want to make an evening gown or a quilt, create a Halloween
   costume, or redo the upholstery—you'll find the fabric to suit your needs at
   Hancock's. Remnants and bolts of discontinued fabric are usually marked
   50% or more off regular prices. Notions, patterns, and arts and crafts supplies
   are good buys. We found *Vogue* patterns at 50% off and *Butterick* patterns
   on sale for $2.22 each. Get on their mailing list to find out about their
   periodic sales.

   Checks, Credit cards

Jantzen Fabric Outlet
Beaverton: 17130 S.W. Shaw ☎ 649–4411
Portland: 2012 N.E. Hoyt ☎ 238–5396
Vancouver: 2421 E. First St. ☎ (206)694–0311
Hours: Generally, Mon–Sat 9:30–5:30, Sun 12–5 (Vancouver store closed
   Sunday)
   Although there are no ready-to-wear clothes sold here, you will find a terrific
   selection of Jantzen fabrics, including Lycra, nylon, and cotton swimwear
   fabrics at wholesale prices. Fabrics by the pound are always good buys.
   During their periodic sales you'll find some incredible bargains. We found
   selected fabrics at 50% off; selected bolts starting at $1.49 per yd.; bulk
   zippers at 5 cents each (10–25 cents regularly); and knit or woven collars
   10 cents each (down from 50 cents).

   Checks, Credit cards

Mill End
Beaverton: 12155 S.W. Broadway ☎ 646–3000
Portland: 8300 S.E. McLoughlin Blvd. ☎ 236–1234
Hours: Mon–Fri 9:30–7:30, Sat 9:30–5:30, Sun 12–5
   Not only does Mill End have the largest selection of fabrics and trims in
   Portland (the McLoughlin store is believed to be the largest single yard-goods
   outlet in the U.S.!), there's also an annex in each store where you'll find
   further mark-downs on dress, upholstery, and drapery fabrics, plus trim. We
   found end-of-the-bolt fabrics (in one- to 16-yard remainders) priced at
   $3.99 per yd. in T-shirt fabrics (regularly $7.99 to $12.99) and lycra for
   $5.99 per yd. (regularly $8 to $12). For savings of 30% or more, check out

the yarn bins for mill-end runs or discontinued colors of wool and synthetic yarns.

Checks, Credit cards

Oregon Craft and Floral Supply Co.
Beaverton: 8620 S.W. Hall Blvd. *(Progress Plaza)* ☎ 646–8385
Gresham: 2101 N.E. Burnside ☎ 661–1469
Oregon City: I-205 at McLouglin *(Oregon City Shopping Center)* ☎ 655–3488
Portland: 4401 N.E. 122nd ☎ 257–0704
Salem: 3842 Center St. ☎ 585–0291
Vancouver: 628 N.E. 81st ☎ (206)573–2420
Hours: Mon–Fri 9–9, Sat 9–7, Sun 10–6
This local chain offers an incredible inventory of art, craft, floral, party, and holiday supplies at prices well below those of most competitors. They're continually running sales and discounting hundreds of specially selected items. Don't miss their holiday sales, such as around St. Patrick's day, when their entire stock of green-colored merchandise is 50% off. Around St. Valentine's Day, you guessed it, all "red" merchandise is 50% off. The Christmas sale boasts "the largest selection of Christmas merchandise ... in captivity." Their parking-lot sales are packed with merchandise that's 40% to 75% off retail. Be sure to watch for their sale coupons on Tuesdays in *The Oregonian* and in *This Week* magazine to pick up those hefty holiday discounts.

Checks, Credit cards

RB Howell's
Portland: 630 N.W. 10th ☎ 227–3125
Hours: Mon–Sat 9–6
Shop Howell's warehouse and you'll save 20% to 30% off list prices for all your craft needs. In addition to basic craft items, you'll find bridal supplies, Christmas decor, fabric and acrylic paints, and jewelry supplies. They claim to have Oregon's best selection of ribbons. Look for clearance items in the back of the second room where wooden items, Christmas decorations, silk flowers, and baskets are marked down an additional 50% from their already low prices. If you have a business license and can meet their first-time minimum order of $100, you'll pay 25% less on future purchases.

Checks, Credit cards

Super Yarn Mart
Milwaukie: 16074 S.E. McLoughlin *(Holly Farm Mall)* ☎ 659–9276
Portland: 10592 S.E. Washington *(Plaza 205)* ☎ 257–9276
Hours: Mon–Fri 10–8, Sat 10–5:30, Sun 11–5
These chain discount yarn shops buy mill ends in volume and have yarn

specially made for them, and they pass the savings along to you. Most of their yarn is orlon, acrylic, or blends, with a small stock of pure wool in primary colors. Mill ends, usually acrylic, sell for 22 cents per oz.; available colors vary. We found 25 acrylic balls of yarn in gold and a rainbow of other such close-outs. A 3-oz. skein of 100% Dupont acrylic four-ply was $1.19— probably the best price anywhere.

Checks, Credit cards

Used Books, Magazines & Comics

Used bookstores abound in the greater Portland area! For those who enjoy reading, shopping at used bookstores (and using the library, of course) can ease the strain on the family's recreation budget. The selection of used paperbacks and hardcovers is wide and varied. Some shops carry a good stock of old, rare, and collectible books—a real treasure trove of literary gems.

In addition to lots of recently used comics, you'll find several sources with rare and vintage comics, as well as old old magazines, that make great birthday and anniversary gifts.

Check before you haul in your books and comics to trade or sell; most stores have special hours for these transactions. Also, be on the alert for good used books while shopping at secondhand stores and estate and garage sales.

Autumn Leaves Bookstore
Portland: 2512 S.E. 122nd ☎ 760–5607
Hours: Mon–Fri 10–7, Sat 10–6, Sun 12–5
  With over 100,000 volumes to choose from, Autumn Leaves has a good selection of topics on science, history, psychology, medicine, literature, and a hundred other categories. In addition to used paperbacks and hardcovers, they carry used comics. The store accepts books in trade and credits one-quarter of the original cover prices of books that are brought in toward purchases of other books or comics.

Checks, Credit cards

Beaver Book Store
Portland: 3747 S.E. Hawthorne Blvd. ☎ 238–1668
Hours: Mon–Sat 10–6, Sun 12–4
  With over 50,000 titles to choose from here you'll find a wide variety of new and used books—all classified, alphabetized, and in good condition. New books are publisher remainders and sell for 60% or less of the cover price. Included in their large stock are books on art, photography, technical topics, fiction, and nonfiction—some old, rare, and collectible.

Checks, Credit cards

Cal's Books & Wares

Portland: 732 S.W. First ☎ 222–5454
Hours: Mon–Fri 10:30–5:30, Sat 11–4

The 5,000 or so hardcover volumes are mostly upstairs in this antique-collectibles store. They carry mostly nonfiction books on topics of general interest, as well as vintage magazines. The owner buys and sells.

Checks, Credit cards

Cameron's Books & Magazines

Portland: 336 S.W. Third ☎ 228–2391
Hours: Mon–Sat 10–6, Sun 12–4

Spend a few hours browsing through Portland's oldest used bookstore with over 40,000 books, magazines, and comics. You'll find a wide selection of fine books on such topics as psychology, history, biography, fiction, World War II, the Civil War, travel, and classics—with savings of 50% or more off the original prices. We found lots of hardbound books on Abraham Lincoln from $3 to $5 each, and hundreds of paperback Harlequins priced at five for $1 (used) and 80 cents each for those in mint condition. Generally, paperbacks start at 25 cents, vintage magazines from 65 cents, and back issues of contemporary magazines sell for 50 cents to 85 cents. They have a large stock of sports car magazines that sells for 65 cents each. An interesting gift idea: Give a magazine published on the same day or week that a birthday celebrant was born. Call the store and they'll check in back to find the issue you're looking for.

Checks, Credit cards

East End Books

Lake Oswego: 335 S.W. Second Ave. ☎ 636–3499
Hours: Mon–Fri 11–6, Sat 11–5

East End carries over 20,000 used hardcover and paperback books, including lots of best sellers and current titles. Many are in mint condition and are priced at one half or less of the original cover prices. You'll find a good general selection in stock, as well as a comfortable, cozy ambience complete with plants, oriental rugs, antiques, and classical music. The owner only takes paperbacks on trades.

Checks, Credit cards

Excalibur Books & Comics

Portland: 2444 S.E. Hawthorne Blvd. ☎ 231–7351
Hours: Mon–Sat 11–6, Sun 12–6

Portland's largest comic book seller (over 20,000 on the sales floor) offers new and used comics, rare and vintage comics, paperback and hardcover books of general interest, a large stock of science fiction and horror, and a smattering of other paper collectibles. Comics buyers frequently head over to the racks where comics are 25 cents apiece. Except for those on the quarter rack, comics are individually bagged in plastic and neatly displayed.

Checks, Credit cards

Friends of the Multnomah County Library

Portland: 216 N.E. Knott St. ☎ 294–0537

Hours: Annual sale

Cancel all of your out-of-town trips for the first week in October! Thousands of donated books from private collections, covering hundreds of subjects, become available each year at the Friends of the Library's annual book sale. Most hardcovers go for $1 to $2, paperbacks for 50 cents to $1, and the literary gems are priced from $5 to $7. Help out the library (proceeds benefit the library) while helping yourself to some incredible book buys.

Checks

Future Dreams

Portland: 1800 E. Burnside ☎ 231–8311

10508 N.E. Halsey ☎ 255–5245

Hours: Mon–Fri 10–7, Sat & Sun 10–6

You'll find thousands of moderately priced used comics here. Value-packs go for $1 each and hold four to five comic books. Reader racks are jammed with comics that sell five for $1, or 25 cents each. Future Dreams also carries thousands of used paperbacks and hardcovers specializing in science fiction and fantasy themes at prices at least one-third off original cover. The store buys, sells, and trades.

Checks, Credit cards

Goodwill Book Attic

Portland: 1925 S.E. Sixth ☎ 238–6165

Hours: Mon–Sat 9–6

Upstairs in the main Goodwill store you'll find the Attic, where thousands of used hardcover and paperbacks, covering most categories, go for around one-third the original cover prices. Regular-size paperbacks are priced from 69 cents to $1.50, and comics at 50 cents apiece. Several times a year the Attic holds big sales where all books are marked down an additional 50%. Call the store to find out when they take place.

Checks, Credit cards

Great Northwest Book Store

Portland: 1234 S.W. Stark ☎ 223–8098

Hours: Mon–Fri 9–7, Sat 11–7, Sun 12–5

With over 100,000 hardcovers and paperbacks in stock (including rare books) this store boasts the largest selection of "only used" books in Portland. Paperbacks are priced at 50% or less of original, and hardcovers usually less than that. The store buys, sells, and trades. Ask about their liberal trade-in and cash purchase policy.

Checks, Credit cards

The Happy Ending
Portland: 8021 S.E. Stark ☎ 256–5386
Hours: Mon–Sat 10–6

Among the 30,000 titles, you'll find many with "happy endings"! There are science, nonfiction, literature, metaphysics, art, westerns, history, biography, and more. Books are shelved by subject matter and priced at 50% to 75% or more off the original price for both paperbacks and hardcovers. You'll also find a rack of used postcards to sift through. The owner buys, sells, and trades. (Ask about their liberal trade allowance.)

Checks

Hawthorne Blvd. Books
Portland: 3129 S.W. Hawthorne Blvd. ☎ 236–3211
Hours: Tues–Sat 11–7, Sun 11–5

Hawthorne Blvd. Books carries over 20,000 used hardcover books on all subjects, with an emphasis on Americana, literature, and history (we counted about 400 books on World War II alone). The store buys used hardcover books.

Checks, Credit cards

Holland's Books
Portland: 527 S.W. 12th Ave. ☎ 224–4242
Hours: Mon–Sat 11–6

Holland's carries a general selection of reasonably priced used books (mostly hardbound and more of the "academic"-type books), including history, art, fiction, literature, and science fiction. Hardbacks and paperbacks are 50% or more off list. From 15,000 to 20,000 titles can be found here.

Checks

House of Fantasy
Gresham: 2005 N.E. Burnside ☎ 661–1815
Hours: Mon, Tues, Thurs, Fri 12–7; Wed & Sat 12–5

This store specializes in current and vintage comics and carries a small stock of books dealing with Dungeon and Dragon games. Comic buyers always check out the racks out front, where prices are 20 cents per issue. You can save 20% off comic cover prices by subscribing to comics and picking the issues up at the store (the owner orders your comics and stores them in your own "mail" box at the store). Depending on what the store's comic buyer is looking for, you may be able to sell or trade your old comics.

Checks, Credit cards

Longfellow's Books & Magazines
Portland: 6231 S.W. Milwaukie Ave. ☎ 239–5222
Hours: Mon–Sat 12–5:30
Longfellow's may have short hours, but the inventory of 60,000 used paperbacks and hardcovers is long on selection and quality. You'll find lots of books in most categories, as well as vintage magazines (such as every issue of Life magazine from 1936 onwards) and used sheet music, too. The owner buys, sells, and trades.

Checks, Credit cards

Murder By The Book
Portland: 7828 S.W. Capitol Hwy ☎ 293–6507
3210 S.E. Hawthorne Blvd. ☎ 232–9995
Hours: Mon–Sat 10:30–6:30, Sun 12–5
When we checked there were no corpses or cobwebs here—just a great selection of new and used mystery, spy, and horror novels. The 10,000 or more suspense volumes rest in well-defined, cleverly named cubbyholes. Titles are divided into such types as women detectives, science fiction detective stories, gothic novels, and police procedurals. You'll also find games, T-shirts, and gift baskets.

Checks

Old Oregon Bookstore
Portland: 1128 S.W. Alder ☎ 227–2742
Hours: Mon–Sat 11–5
History buffs love to browse (and buy!) in this store where the specialty is used hardcover history books. With about 100,000 titles in stock, there's also a good selection of general interest books, scholarly works, Northwest, and old and rare books. The owner buys, sells, and trades.

Checks

Paper Moon
Portland: 3729 S.E. Hawthorne Blvd. ☎ 236–5195
Hours: Mon–Sat 10–8, Sun 12–5
Paper Moon specializes in quality used books on literature and fine arts, including art, photography, philosophy, Eastern religions, and children's and illustrated works. Choose among 30,000 hardcover and paperbacks, and don't forget to bring in your own used books because the owner buys. You'll also find a small section of back issues of old magazines—all types.

Checks, Credit cards

Periodicals Paradise

Portland: 3415 S.E. Belmont ☎ 236–8370
3437 S.E. Belmont ☎ 232–2818
Hours: Mon–Sat 10–7, Sun 11–4

As their name suggests, periodicals are their specialty. The shop at 3415 S.E. Belmont carries about 20,000 current-issue magazines (issues not older than 12 months). The other location has over 50,000 older and vintage magazines, including used paperbacks at 50 cents apiece and new Western paperbacks at 50% to 75% off original cover prices. They buy tons of used magazines, and what they can't resell, goes to the recycler. Stock includes general interest magazines, as well as obscure professional and trade journals and subscription-only publications—many that are vintage and in mint condition.

Checks

Pilgrim Discount Book & Bible Supply

Portland: 322 S.E. 82nd ☎ 255–7620
Hours: Tues–Thurs 10–6, Fri 10–8, Sat 10–5

This store offers thousands of Christian books, both new and used, hardcovers and paperbacks, as well as Bible studies, communion ware, and gift cards. Most of their new hardcover books are discounted 20%; new paperbacks are 15% off; new English Bibles are 20% off; and gift cards are generally 10% off. They also offer imprinting services for those wishing to have a Bible inscribed with a name.

Checks

Powell's Books

Beaverton: 8775 S.W. Cascade Ave. *(Cascade Plaza)* ☎ 643–3131
Portland: 3739 S.E. Hawthorne Blvd. ☎ 235–3802
1005 W. Burnside ☎ 228–4651
Hours: Beaverton, daily 9–9; Hawthorne, Mon–Sat 9:30–7, Sun 11–5; Burnside, Mon–Sat 9–11, Sun 9–9

Powell's is far too well known for any description to add or detract from its impressive operation. Suffice it to say that this Portland landmark offers over a million new and used titles (about two thirds of which are in the mammoth store on Burnside) on theology, history, literature, cooking, science fiction, business, women's studies, travel, and just about any other field you care to enter. New and used hardcovers and paperbacks are placed side by side, and you'll find the main store's color-coded rooms and anterooms a mind's delight to wander in. As you enter the main store, head over to the right to sell your used books—you'll be pleased with their liberal pay-out policy; then grab a map, head out, and load up. The Hawthorne store primarily sells books to cooks.

Checks, Credit cards

Second Hand Prose
Vancouver: 713 Grand Ave. ☎ (206)693–9344
Hours: Mon–Sat 10:15–5
> The inventory consists of about 25,000 used paperbacks and hardcover books covering all categories. The owner buys, sells, and trades.
>
> Checks

Second Story Books
Portland: 3530 S.E. Hawthorne Blvd. ☎ 234–0343
Hours: Tues–Sat 12–5
> Second Story Books (located upstairs, of course) carries used hardcovers and some paperbacks on what is probably Portland's finest collection on the Beat writers (as in "beatniks"), American Indians, natural history, contemporary fiction, and feminist topics. There are some new books at discounted prices scattered throughout the shop's four rooms of books.
>
> Checks, Credit cards

Skidmore Village Childrens Books
Gresham: 79 N.W. Miller ☎ 661–5887
Portland: 50 S.W. Third ☎ 222–5076
Hours: Gresham, Mon–Sat 10–5; Portland, Mon–Sat 10–5:30
> In addition to their wonderful selection of new children's books, this store carries fine used kids' books (mostly paperbacks) at 50% or more off original cover prices—many as low as 50 cents apiece. The used books are off in a section of their own. Due to limited space, some used books may be in the back room or hiding elsewhere, so be sure to ask at the store for any other used books. Don't be afraid to ask the staff for help—they love what they do and are always cheerful and helpful.
>
> Checks, Credit cards

Spencer's Bookstore
Vancouver: 10411 N.E. Fourth Plain ☎ (206)892–9862
Hours: Mon–Fri 10–5, Sat 10–4
> This store has about 30,000 used titles (27,000 are paperbacks and 3,000 are hardcover) that sell for about one-half the original cover. The books cover areas of general interest and there's a comic book department with comics priced at 50 cents to $1 each. The owner also selectively buys hardcover books
>
> Checks

The Title Wave
Portland: 216 N.E. Knott St. ☎ 294–3243
Hours: Mon–Sat 10–3
> Over 20,000 hardcovers and paperbacks, magazines, art prints, and records

can be found neatly arranged here. At least 75% of their items are priced at $1 or less. Many books go for as little as 50 cents. There are many children's books, general and Northwest references, scholarly works, fine classics, and encyclopedia sets scattered around the store. All the books come from the Multnomah County Library system, having been withdrawn to make room for newer books. The bookstore itself is housed in a cozy old building that makes one think of a childhood spent hanging out in libraries. On top of the great prices, the store holds periodic sales—usually with another 25% off all book prices.

Checks, Credit cards

U.S.A. Book Company

Portland: 13611 N.W. Cornell Rd. ☎ 626–4743
Hours: Mon–Thurs 10–6, Fri 10–7, Sat 10–5

This store offers over 40,000 titles (mostly used) covering all categories (with an emphasis on Northwest history and first-edition rare books). The stock is pretty evenly divided between hardcovers and paperbacks. Paperbacks are 50% off the original cover prices, while hardcover art and cookbooks are 50% to 75% off the original. About a quarter of their stock is new, some of which is sold at discount. A small but growing collection of used magazines can also be found.

Checks, Credit cards

U.S. Government Printing Office Bookstore

Portland: 1305 S.W. First Ave. ☎ 221–6217
Hours: Mon–Fri 9–5

Whatever your interest—agriculture, astronomy, nutrition, science, business, space, transportation, law, military history, weaponry, education, or gardening—you'll find it in any number of books put out by U.S. government agencies at prices from expensive to as little as $1.25. If you're thinking of starting a new business or expanding an existing business into an unknown area, here is a good place to begin. For a couple of dollars you'll find such books as *Starting A Small Business From Your Home*, *Doing Business With the Federal Government*, *The Code and Federal Regulations Concerning Patents*; and many more. Stop by and pick up their free catalog that describes hundreds of books (from virtually every government agency) available for sale at the U.S. Government Bookstore.

Checks, Credit cards

Vintage Books

Vancouver: 6613 E. Mill Plain ☎ (206)694–9519
Hours: Mon–Fri 10–8, Sat 10–6, Sun 12–5

Vintage carries a large general selection of used hardcover and paperback books, including a small collection of vintage magazines. Comics can be found in the 25-, 40-, and 75-cent boxes. Saturday mornings the comics buyer is available to buy your comic treasures. Besides books of general interest, the store specializes in automotive, literature, and Northwest topics.

Checks, Credit cards

Webfoot Bookman

Portland: 8235 S.E. 13th ☎ 239–5233
Hours: Tues–Sun 10–5
Webfoot specializes in quality hardcover books on hunting, fishing, the Northwest, and the West. They also carry old prints and collectibles, many quite old and rare, as well as a wide selection of titles on other topics. The owner buys and sells.

Checks

Wrigley Cross Books

Portland: 8001 S.E. Powell Blvd. *(Powell Street Station)* ☎ 775–4943
Hours: Mon–Sat 10–7, Fri 10–9, Sun 12–5
This store carries a wide selection of general subject used hardcovers and paperbacks. Books are priced at 50% or more off original cover prices. They also carry a fine stock of collectibles, chiefly of the science fiction, horror, and mystery genres—some with the author's signature. The owner buys, sells, and trades.

Checks, Credit cards

Coupon Books & Discount Cards

You can save hundreds of dollars each year by buying coupon books and discount cards. Discounts can be found on dining, traveling, entertainment, tourist attractions, merchandise, sports activities, and much more. Many businesses listed in the books and cards offer two-for-one specials—so the savings can add up quickly for frequent users. After only a few uses, your book or card will have paid for itself! They also make great gifts—especially for those on tight entertainment budgets.

Coupon books and discount cards are usually sold by nonprofit organizations as fund-raisers. Not only will you get more for your dollar, you'll be helping a good cause when you buy the books or cards.

Arts Card

Portland: 418 S.W. Washington, Room. 202 ☎ 224–1412
Hours: Mon–Fri 8:30–5:30
Students in grades K through 12 can pick up an Arts Card for $2 and save 50% off the admission prices of many arts events. The card allows the student to buy two half-price admission tickets for theater, musical, and opera

events, as well as to receive discounts on admissions to art galleries and arts and crafts programs. Arts Cards are also honored on Tri-Met's buses and MAX. For a free ride home from the event for two people, just show the card and ticket stubs from that day's Arts Card event. The Arts Card is a wonderful way to encourage young people to experience quality arts events first hand. Arts Card registration forms are available at U.S. Bank branches, local libraries, and by phone.

Entertainment Publications, Inc.

Beaverton: 8196 S.W. Hall Blvd. suite 100 ☎ 646–8201
Hours: Mon–Fri 8:30–5

These books are $40 apiece and are chock full of money-saving discounts. Listings include fine dining, fast foods, theater and special events, tourist attractions, travel offers, sports, auto and truck rentals, and fine hotels and motels where you'll save 50% off the regular prices. Use the book (you'll get a membership card) just once or twice and it will have paid for itself. The company puts out similar books for about 100 other cities (including Canadian and foreign); if you buy one book, you qualify to buy up to three other books at 50% off.

Gift Checks/ Wardco, Inc.

☎ (800)548–2831
Hours: Mon–Fri 9–5

These coupon books, which cost $5 for 50 "checks," are sold by many organizations as fund-raisers. The coupons, which look like real checks, get you one-half off at popular restaurants, merchants, and family entertainment centers. Kids will especially love using these "checkbook-size" coupons at video stores, bowling alleys, roller skating rinks, fast-food establishments, and other recreational spots. Local coupon books are available for Portland, Vancouver, and Salem.

Gold C Saving Spree

Beaverton: 8196 S.W. Hall Blvd. suite 100 ☎ 646–8201
Hours: 8:30–5

Many school, community, youth, charitable and religious groups sell these coupon books as fund-raisers. For $9 you'll get a coupon book the whole family can enjoy. The two-for-one coupons can be used for fast foods, as well as for restaurant dining, theaters, tourist attractions, sports activities (those you can play and those you can watch), merchandise and services; an entire section is devoted to youthful family members. These books are put out by Entertainment Publications and are available for 28 other cities.

PDX TIX

Portland: 921 S.W. Morrison *(Galleria)* ☎ 241–4903

Hours: Thurs–Sat 12–6, Sun 12–5

The nonprofit Portland Area Theatre Alliance sells day-of-the-show tickets for performances at most Portland theatrical events at half-price (plus a handling fee of $1.50 per ticket). You'll find tickets for such local theaters as New Rose, Portland Repertory, Oregon Shakespeare Festival/Portland, and about 25 others. Validated parking at the Galleria garage or a one-way Tri-Met pass is free with a purchase of $10 or more.

Museums, Performing Arts & Movies

Museums

Portland offers a limited but fascinating array of museums that will delight people of all ages. Take advantage of the days and hours that these museums admit patrons for free. At other times, junior and senior discounts are available, as well as hefty group-rate savings.

American Advertising Museum

Portland: 9 N.W. Second Ave. ☎ 226–0000

Hours: Wed–Fri 11–5, Sat & Sun 12–5

This wonderful display of the history of advertising features many colorful exhibits highlighting printed and broadcast advertisements. The museum, as well as a reference library and an auditorium, are housed in the Erickson Saloon building, and it has no equal anywhere else in the U.S. Adult admissions are $3; seniors and kids ages six to 12 pay $1.50; kids under six are admitted free. Special group-tour rates for six or more are available at $1.50 per person, and include a guided tour of the museum.

Children's Museum

Portland: 3037 S.W. Second Ave. ☎ 823–2227

Hours: Mon 9–1, Tues–Sat 9–5, Sun 11–5

Kids love this place because they get to put their little hands on most things here. There's a grocery store, an African Village, a clayshop, and changing exhibits that allow for hands-on learning opportunities, as well as just plain having fun. A playground and infant playspace are available. Adults $3; kids $2.50. Admission is free on Mondays. For groups of seven kids or more, the charge is only $1 per child.

Oregon Historical Society Museum

Portland: 1230 S.W. Park ☎ 222–1741

Hours: Mon–Sat 10–5, Sun 12–5

This delightful museum holds exhibits that chronicle Oregon history from prehistoric times to the present. You'll also find changing exhibits, a research library, and a bookstore crammed full of historical and unique books and cards. Admission is free.

Oregon Maritime Museum

Portland: 113 S.W. Front ☎ 224–7724

Hours: Fri–Sun 11–4 (Summer, Wed–Sun 11–4)

This place is a ship-lover's delight! This small museum, a short walk from the Willamette River, houses collections of ship models and navigation instruments, as well as a fascinating array of nautical hardware, photos, paintings, and artifacts. Adults pay $2; those over age 62 and kids 8–18, $1.25. There's a special family rate of $4.50.

Portland Museum of Art

Portland: 1219 S.W. Park ☎ 226–2811

Hours: Tues–Sat 11–5, Sun 1–5

The Museum contains European sculptures and paintings from the past five centuries, as well as American art of the 19th and 20th centuries. You'll also find changing exhibits of Pacific Rim and Northwest art and periodic lectures and films. Adults pay $3; students, $1.50; kids ages six to 12, 50 cents; and those under six, no charge. Every Thursday, seniors (62 or older) are admitted free. The general public is admitted without charge on the first Thursday of each month from 4–9 P.M..

Portland Police Historical Museum

Portland: 1111 S.W. Second Ave. ☎ 796–3010

Hours: Tues–Fri 10–3

Located on the 16th floor of the Justice Center, this sparkling gem of a museum features a fascinating look at local police history. Exhibits include uniforms, badges, handcuffs, guns, photos, and other police memorabilia. Kids (and adults, too!) can climb on a police motorcycle or wander into old jail cells. Admission is free.

Washington Park Zoo

Portland: 4000 S.W. Canyon Rd. ☎ 226–1561

Hours: Call for hours

Major exhibits, such as the Asian elephants, penguins, big cats, polar bears and monkeys, are popular attractions. Enjoy a meal in the cafeteria while viewing the adjoining African bird aviary. Or take the zoo train on a four-mile journey through the hills and forests of the park past the International Rose Test Gardens, Japanese Garden, and breathtaking city views. Adults $4.50; Seniors $3; ages 3–11, $2.50; those under age 2 are free. After 3 P.M. on the second Tuesday afternoon of each month, the gates are opened for free admission. There is a separate charge for the train ride.

Performing Arts

The greater Portland area hosts a nice selection of theater, concert, and sports events that can be enjoyed without straining one's budget. Free concerts abound, as do junior, senior, and group discounts. You can save a whopping 65% off regular theater ticket prices when you show up an hour before performances and purchase "rush tickets."

Old Church Concerts

Portland: 1422 S.W. 11th ☎ 222–2031

In this historical building (it's no longer used as a church), you'll find free concerts every Wednesday throughout the year that start at noon and last for 45 minutes. The auditorium holds 300 and you're invited to bring your lunch (coffee is provided free). There is a wonderful variety of music with harps, flutes, an antique pipe organ, and a chorus. Pick up a free schedule of concert events.

Oregon Shakespeare Festival/Portland

Portland: 1111 S.W. Broadway ☎ 248–6309

Shakespeare and modern plays are presented at matinee and evening performances during the season, which runs from November to April. While regular tickets are priced from $21 to $25 each there are several ways to save. "Rush tickets" are available one hour before any performance that's not sold out and cost $8 each. Your best bet on these rush tickets is to come during the week and at the beginning of a show run. Students and seniors pay $8 per ticket during matinees; tickets for "slip seats" (side seats on the first balcony) are $8 at all performances. Groups of 15 or more get 15% shaved off the regular ticket price.

Pioneer Courthouse Square Concerts

Portland: S.W. Sixth & Yamhill ☎ 223–1613

The Peanut Butter and Jam series (so-named to remind people to bring their sack lunches) presents free concerts each Tuesday and Thursday from mid-June through mid-August from noon to 1 P.M. at Pioneer Square. It's an eclectic series that can offer a duo on Tuesday, a large group on Thursday, followed by bluegrass, jazz, and classical on succeeding days. You'll certainly enjoy the performances (and, it is hoped, your lunch) at this popular city center square.

Portland Beavers Baseball

Portland: 1844 S.W. Morrison *(Civic Stadium)* ☎ 2BE–AVER

You'll find real "big-league" action with the Portland Beavers, a farm team for the Minnesota Twins, at Civic Stadium. It's about the best baseball in Oregon, and the intimate, usually uncrowded Civic Stadium allows fans to be closeup on all the action. General admission is $4.50; kids 14 and under pay $2. A book of ten tickets costs $38. Watch the ads for their free nights and "can nights" when admission is free (pick up your tickets at no charge at one of the sponsoring retailers or banks) or just bring in a can of food. If you have a group of 25 or more you can negotiate in advance for a special group price.

Portland State University "Brown Bag" Concerts

Portland: 1625 S.W. Park. *(Lincoln Hall)* ☎ 725–4452

Every Tuesday and Thursday from noon to 1 P.M. (when school is in session) PSU presents a variety of free concerts in room 75 of Lincoln Hall. The musical fare includes classical, light classical, folk, and jazz, performed by music students on Tuesdays and by faculty and outside guests on Thursdays. Bring your "brown bags" and enjoy.

Tom McCall Waterfront Park

Portland: S.W. Front Ave. on Salmon

Throughout the summer at Waterfront Park, you'll find a wonderful variety of free concerts and festivals with music and entertainment from jazz and blues to pops and classics. In August, the renowned Oregon Symphony holds four free concerts here. Check the Friday Arts and Entertainment section in *The Oregonian* for details, or call the Portland Visitors Association at 222–2223 for a free calendar of events.

Movie Theaters

Many movie theaters offer discounts for selected showings. Attend during these "economy times" and you'll pay 40% to 50% less than at other times. Student and senior citizen discounts often range from 25% to 60% off. Ask at your favorite theater about purchasing booklets of discounted tickets.

Also, be sure to refer to Coupon Books & Discount Cards for discounts at theaters, movie houses, and other attractions.

Act III Theatres

Beaverton *(Westgate)* 3950 S.W. Cedar Hills Blvd. ☎ 248–6979
Gresham: *(Gresham Cinema)* 221st & S.E. Burnside ☎ 248–6976
Hillsboro: *(Town Theatre)* 253 E. Main ☎ 248–6989
  (*Tanabourne*) N.W. 185 & Sunset Hwy. ☎ 248–1604

Portland: *(Broadway Metroplex)* 1000 S.W. Broadway ☎ 248–6960
(*Clackamas Town Center*) 12000 S.E. 82nd ☎ 248–6985
(*Eastgate*) 2025 S.E. 82nd ☎ 248–6975
(*Guild Theatre*) Ninth & S.W. Taylor ☎ 248–6964
(*Jantzen Beach Center*) ☎ 248–6984
(*Koin Center*) 222 S.W. Columbia ☎ 243–3515
(*Lloyd Center*) 1510 N.E. Multnomah ☎ 248–6938
(*Mall 205*) 101st & S.E. Washington ☎ 248–6978
(*Movie House*) 1220 S.W. Taylor ☎ 222–4595
(*Southgate*) Hwy 224 at 99E ☎ 248–6982
Tigard: *(Tigard Cinemas)* Hwy. 99 ☎ 248–6973
(*Washington Square*) Washington Square Center ☎ 248–6980
Vancouver: *(Cascade Park)* I-205 at Mill Plain ☎ (206)892–6940
(*Hazel Dell*) 7631 Hwy. 99 ☎ (206)693–4785
Usually the first three shows each day are economy times (unless movies are very long) and you pay $3—which is 50% of their regular prices. You have to be in your seat generally before 5–5:30 P.M. for economy rates. Special engagements are not discounted. Economy rates also apply to Monday night shows, so in effect, all day Monday, seats are $3. You'll get one-third off the regular prices for large groups. (Call 221–0213 for more information.)

Act III Theaters

Beaverton: *(Valley Cinema)* 9300 S.W. Beaverton-Hillsdale Hwy
☎ 248–6981
Portland: *(Hollywood Cinema)* 42nd & N.E. Sandy ☎ 248–6977
The price for all seats, shows, and times (seven days a week) is only $1.50.

Cinema 21

Portland: 616 N.W. 21st ☎ 223–4515
General admission is $5, but students with student I.D. cards pay $4 and seniors pay just $2.

Cineplex Odeon Theaters

Portland: 9600 S.E. 82nd ☎ 774–7731
Adults pay $6; juniors from age 12 to 15 pay $5; kids under 12 pay $3.50; and seniors pay $4. Seven days a week all shows before 6 P.M. are bargain matinees with all seats at $3.50.

Lake Twin Cinema

Lake Oswego: 106 N. State ☎ 635–5956
Every Monday and Thursday, all seats in both auditoriums are $1 all day.

Laurelhurst Theatre

Portland: 2735 E. Burnside ☎ 232–5511

All seats for all shows and for all ages are $1.49 except on Monday nights when the price falls to just $1. There are four separate auditoriums here.

Family Theaters

Aloha: 18295 S.W. Tualatin Valley Hwy. ☎ 642–9000
Milwaukie: 11011 S.E. Main ☎ 653–2222
Portland: 1323 S.E. Tacoma ☎ 234–2000
Tigard: 11959 S.W. Pacific Hwy. ☎ 639–1482
Tualatin: 8345 S.W. Nyberg Rd. ☎ 692–5000

General admission is $3; children age 12 and under and seniors age 62 and above pay $2. On Mondays all seats are just $1. Generally, all box offices open at 7 P.M.

Mt. Hood Theater

Gresham: 403 E. Powell ☎ 665–0604

General admission is $3; kids age 11 and under and seniors age 62 and above pay $2.

Forest Theater

Forest Grove: 1911 Pacific ☎ 357–5107

Wednesday and Thursday nights are economy nights, with all seats priced $1.75. All seats for Saturday and Sunday matinee shows are $2.50.

M Entertainment

Portland: *(Rose Moyer)* 16501 S.E. Division ☎ 778–8065
Vancouver: *(Vancouver Mall)* 5001 N.E. Thurston Way ☎ 254–0000
Wilsonville: *(Grand Parkway)* I-5 at Stafford exit ☎ 778–8066

Matinee prices of $3.50 apply to any movie before 5:30 P.M. Tuesdays are known as "tightwad Tuesdays," and all seats (except for special engagements) are also $3.50. Wednesday nights are "Fred Meyer Nights"; with one sales receipt from Fred Meyer stores, you pay $3 for any seat (except special engagements). Advance tickets in quantities of ten or more (good for one year) are $5 each and available for purchase at Moyer Theaters Corporation, 1953 N.W. Kearny (call the corporate office at 226–2735 for further information).

Toys, Party Supplies, & Newsprint

Toys & Party Supplies

Toy prices and Roman candles have this much in common—both tend to rocket into space rather quickly. Bargain shoppers know that consignment and thrift shops can be great sources for quality, barely used toys and games. Clearance aisles at many toy retailers contain close-outs and overstock that can be very price appealing. Watch the ads for clearance sales, too.

Party supplies and favors need not break the budget when you shop the sources we've listed here. You'll find several outlets that are chock full of inexpensive items just perfect for any festive occasion.

Kay-Bee Toys & Hobby Shop
Portland: 12000 S.E. 82nd *(Clackamas Town Center)* ☎ 652–1472
Jantzen Beach Center ☎ 286–2774
Ninth & N.E. Halsey *(Lloyd Center)* ☎ 284–2997
9900 S.E. Washington *(Mall 205)* ☎ 253–7092
Tigard: 9975 S.W. Washington Square Rd. *(Washington Square)* ☎ 639–4900
Vancouver: 5001 N.E. Thurston Way ☎ (206)254–4809
Hours: Generally, Mon–Fri 10–9, Sat 10–6, Sun 11–6
Kay-Bee doesn't go in for the large items such as swing sets and bikes, but they do carry a good selection of smaller games and toys at good prices. Some close-outs bring discounts of 40% to 70% off suggested retail. Generally, you'll find the biggest savings on the merchandise they stock at the front of the store (to entice the customer into entering and looking around, of course!). Call about their close-outs—they'll gladly tell you what they have and the prices.

Checks, Credit cards

Learning Palace Liquidation Center
Portland: 4455 S.E. 52nd ☎ 775–6097
Hours: Fri–Sun 11–6
Learning Palace Liquidation Center carries a good selection of new toys, games, puzzles, books, and learning aids that are overstock, factory close-outs, out-of-prints, or discontinued models. You'll find items from *Trend, Fisher Price, Playskool, Milton Bradley,* and others—all at prices from 10% to 50% off retail.

Checks

The Lippman Co.
Portland: 2727 S.E. Grand ☎ 239–7007
Hours: Mon–Fri 8:30–5, Sat 8:30–12

You'll have a blast exploring this place! Lippman's stocks a huge and colorful inventory of party favors, carnival supplies, and decorations for all occasions. At 60 cents per doz., it's easy to load up on whistles, rings, bugs, eye patches, and fingernails. You'll find all your balloon needs here at great prices. Plush animals are priced from $2 to $5, except for the life-size tiger that goes for $64.50. Some exceptional buys: Table covers (54"x84" and 54"x108") starting at $2.50; cocktail napkins (available in 14 colors) in the 200 count for $5.50. If it's noisemakers, horns, squawkers, clown suits, paper streamers, bibs, trophies, fake noses, hats, and bracelets you're looking for—this is the place.

Checks, Credit cards

Pacific Party & Video
Portland: 3570 S.E. Division ☎ 234–3858
Hours: Mon–Fri 10–9, Sat 10–10, Sun 12–9
In a large building that once housed several neighborhood taverns, you'll find a party-accessory wonderland that's packed with colorful mylar balloons, banners, party favors, invitations, loot bags, plates, flatware, and more. Just about anything you'll need for any child's (or adult's) party can be found here. If you own a business or represent a charitable organization, you can get a discount card and save 20% off retail prices.

Checks, Credit cards

Party Distributors
Portland: 606 S.E. Grant ☎ 239–8439
Hours: Mon–Fri 8:30–5:30, Sat 9–4
You and the children will love browsing at this place. You'll find inexpensive party favors, crepe paper, napkins, decorations, pinatas, balloons, and much more. Some super deals: Paper placemats at 5 cents apiece; mylar helium balloons, $2 if filled, $1 empty; gift wrap, usually $5.95 elsewhere, $1.99 here; a complete gorilla outfit, $69 (down from $92)—now that's something not to be passed by! *Paper Art* napkins, cups, and plates in wedding patterns are always 10% off. Party Distributors also rents helium tanks.

Checks, Credit cards

Toys "R" Us
Clackamas: 12535 S.E. 82nd ☎ 659–5163
Portland: 1800 Jantzen Beach Center Dr. ☎ 289–4691
Salem: 1200 Lancaster Dr. N.E. ☎ 363–4328
Tigard: 10065 S.W. Cascade ☎ 620–9779
Hours: Generally, Mon–Sat 9:30–9:30, Sun 10–6
The "world's biggest toy store" boasts over one million toys in stock with the widest selection available of the hottest (and not-so-hot-anymore) toys and games at super everyday low prices. Each store is stacked to the rafters with

merchandise—everything from diapers to nursery furniture. Clothing goes up to 6X. They also carry bikes, hot wheels, play furniture, and gym sets. Give them 24 hours and $8 and they'll assemble any of these products for you. They are continually running advertisements, so it's easy to price-shop. While shopping, we sure to check out the clearance aisles for toys, games, and stuffed animals—all marked 50% off.

Checks, Credit cards

Newsprint

Newsprint (from newspapers) is great for artwork, tablecloths, murals, box packing, gift wrapping, and more. We've included those sources that practically give the stuff away. Newsprint comes on rolls that are usually two to three feet wide. It's best to call ahead as to availability, price, and where to pick up.

The Columbian
Vancouver: 701 W. Eighth St. ☎ (206)694–3391
Hours: Mon–Fri 8–5
The Columbian does not sell roll ends but does hand them out (limit two per person) at no charge if you ask at the front office. Roll widths vary, as does the amount of paper left on each roll.

Enterprise Courier
Oregon City: 10th & Main ☎ 656–1911
Hours: Mon–Fri 8–5
You can buy as many roll ends as are available at $4 per roll. The rolls are about 27" wide, with from two to three inches of paper remaining on each roll. Although they usually have roll ends, it's best to call in advance to check on availability. Their big rushes on roll ends occur in summer and around Christmas.

Gresham Outlook
Gresham: 1190 N.E. Division ☎ 665–2181
Hours: Mon–Fri 8–5
Roll ends are sold here by the pound. In addition to white paper, they sometimes have yellow. When we checked, they had yellow roll ends in $2\frac{1}{2}$-ft. and white in 3-ft. widths at 35 cents per lb. The Outlook charges a maximum of $5 per roll. Because these rolls weighed over 20 pounds apiece, the effective price dropped to less than 25 cents per lb. They also have short one-foot-wide rolls and infrequently have a glossy, heavy book-paper stock on roll ends for which they charge 75 cents per lb. The best times to call regarding availability are right after printing runs on Mondays and Thursdays.

Nickel Ads

Portland: 7818 S.E. Stark ☎ 251–7526
Hours: Mon–Fri 8–5

They do their printing on Wednesday nights so you'll find the biggest stock of roll ends available on Thursday mornings. Their rolls come in 27" and 30" widths and sell for 20 cents per lb. The rolls range from 2 to 7 lbs. in weight, and besides the standard off-white, can occasionally be found in yellow. If you can't make it in on Thursday mornings, it would be best to call regarding availability.

The Oregonian

Portland: 1629 S.W. Taylor ☎ 221–4309
Hours: Mon–Fri 8–5

There's no charge if you just need several roll ends. Call the press room in advance and they'll leave them at the security desk. Common sizes are 30", 45", and 55". There's anywhere from $\frac{1}{8}$" to $\frac{1}{2}$" of paper left on the rolls, which is about 150 feet each.

Pry Publishing

Portland: 600 N.W. 14th ☎ 226–8335
Hours: Mon–Fri 8:30–5

Pry charges 35 cents per lb. for roll ends that come in widths ranging from 18 to 36 in. On average, the rolls weigh around 8 lbs. and have one or more inches (thickness) of the off-white newsprint remaining. Stop by any time to pick up the paper without having to call in advance.

Statesman-Journal Newspaper

Salem: 280 Church N.E. ☎ 399–6611
Hours: Mon–Fri 8–5

End rolls are available in three widths and at three prices. The 21" rolls sell for $1.50; the 41" for $2.50; the 60" for $3.50. You'll find at least 250 feet of paper per roll. Occasionally you can buy brown paper (like shopping bags) on these rolls, besides the basic off-white newsprint. Call in advance regarding the availability of these rolls in the sizes and color you want.

Tualatin-Yamhill Press

Hillsboro: 250 S.E. Washington ☎ 648–5171
Hours: Mon–Fri 8–5

Their usual practice is to give one roll end for free and charge 22 cents per lb. on subsequent rolls. However, if you're going to be using the paper for a church event or activity or in a preschool setting (or for any other "good cause"), you can have four or five roll ends at no charge. Best to call a day in advance to arrange for your pick-up. Roll ends come in either 29- or 35-in. widths.

Luggage & Travel Accessories

Low-cost luggage and travel accessories are nice complements to your bargain travel plans. In addition to the sources we've listed below, refer to Mass Merchandise Discounters for additional outlets of luggage at discount prices.

AAA Travel Store

Beaverton: 8555 S.W. Apple Way ☎ 243–6444
Portland: 600 S.W. Market ☎ AAA–6734
Salem: 2909 Ryan Dr. S.E. ☎ 581–1608
Hours: Mon–Fri 8–5

Club members will be delighted by the low luggage prices available to them when they shop the AAA Travel Store located in major AAA offices. We found *Samsonite* Profile II 28-inch suitcases (with wheels) with a regular retail price of $175 priced here at $104; *Samsonite* carry-ons were $145 (down from $200); and *Samsonite* attache cases were 40% off retail. *Oleg Cassini* boarding bags and 26- and 29-inch Pullman bags (with wheels) were all priced 50% below regular retail. Also great prices on luggage carriers and garment bags here. Non-members pay 25% over members' discount prices.

Checks, Credit cards

Caye's Luggage

Portland: 833 S.W. Second Ave. ☎ 227–4322
Hours: Mon–Fri 9:30–5, Sat 11–3

At Caye's Luggage you'll find a wide selection of luggage, attache cases, and traveler's accessories, including converter kits (when you want to plug your shaver into a foreign electrical outlet), money belts, and shoe-shine kits. Watch for their frequent sales. Ask about their commercial discounts on luggage and cases for business travelers, and courtesy discounts for the rest of us. Their in-store service department frequently makes same-day luggage and case repairs.

Automotive

New Automobiles

Buying a new car can be both exciting and frightening. We wind up spending a lot of money in an activity that we don't do enough of to get really good at. Often, we go eyeball-to-eyeball with professional car sellers, then one of us blinks, and we walk away with the car (or in some cases, just walk away).

By doing his or her homework before the shopping process begins, the bargain shopper can save hundreds, if not thousands, of dollars in the purchase of an automobile.

Shoppers who decide first on the make, model, options, and how much they want to spend, are not likely to be "traded-up"—that is, sold a car that's "loaded" and thereby more costly. Call as many dealers as you can within an hour's drive of your home for the best price. If a dealer who's located far from your home offers the lowest price, call some local dealers to see if they'll match it.

Typically, a dealer's cost runs 80% to 90% of the car's sticker price. Negotiate up from the dealer's cost (ask to see his factory invoice on your chosen car) rather than down from the sticker price. Ask the dealer for the minimum dollar profit he has to make on that car.

Often you'll get a much better price on a car that's been on the lot a long time. (Factory invoice should indicate when a car came in.) The longer a car sits, the more interest a dealer has to pay on it. You can also save big by buying your new car in September or October, when dealers are getting rid of cars to make room for "new" cars.

Because most car salespeople are on a monthly quota system, you'll be in a good position to further wheel and deal if you buy at the end of the month. They're likely to try anything to sell one more car—it could make the difference between their receiving a bonus or keeping their sales job.

If you have a used car you're thinking of trading in—don't! Dealers tend to price used trade-ins quite low. Try to sell it yourself; you're more likely to get top dollar for it from a private buyer than if it's part of your new car purchase. However, if you intend to trade in your used car, don't mention this to the dealer until you have a firm new-car price in writing. This way, you'll get the best new-car price first; then you can haggle over the used-car value.

For those looking for an easier way around high car prices than by going through all this research and price-haggling, we've included several sources that offer the lowest possible new-car prices. These auto-buying and referral services can save both money and time. Bargain shoppers can then decide which way they want to go when in the market for a new car.

Car/Puter International
Hollywood, Fl: ☎ (800)221–4001
Hours: Mon–Fri 8–10, Sat 8:30–7

For 20 years, Car/Puter has been helping bargain shoppers save hundreds off new-car prices. Here's how it works. Give them a call with the make and model of the automobile you're interested in. For $20 plus $2 shipping, they'll send you a detailed computer printout listing that car's factory invoice price plus the manufacturer's cost on all available options. You select the options and return a "price adjustment form" to Car/Puter. They will then find out which auto dealer in the nation can sell you the car of your choice (and deliver it locally, if necessary) at the lowest price. With Car/Puter, your new-car price haggling is over.

Checks, Credit cards

Auto Insider
Van Nuys, CA: ☎ (800)446–7433
Hours: Mon–Fri 8:30–5:30

If you belong to a credit union or an organization such as Costco, you'll have access to super-low auto and truck prices. Many of these institutions have contracted with the Auto Insider and vehicle dealers to provide special pre-arranged prices on new vehicles (usually the lowest prices dealers can offer). Go to your credit union or Costco customer service representative and ask for a list of Auto Insider vehicle dealers. You'll deal with an Auto Insider representative at the dealer of your choice—who'll make you an offer you may not want to refuse.

Used Automobiles

A used car that's been carefully selected can be the bargain-shopper's best automotive value. Used cars cost much less than new, are cheaper to insure, and depreciate at a much lower rate than new cars.

As with purchasing a new car, a shopper must decide what kind of car will match his or her life style and budget. Typically, one starts either by looking through a newspaper's classified ads and buys from a private seller, or one heads to used-car-lot row to see what dealers have on their lots.

Used-car lots usually charge more for cars than do private sellers—but dealers often offer some sort of guarantee. Shop the used-car dealers that have been around a long time and who have no complaints lodged against them with the Better Business Bureau. Check before you buy!

When you've found a car that catches your eye, give it a good inspection. Bring a friend (preferably one who's mechanically inclined) and check out the car both when it's parked and when it's zipping down the highway. A final inspection by a reliable mechanic or diagnostic service is your best bet before buying.

If you're planning to buy a newer used car, a good place to start is at a car rental agency. They buy cheap and sell often. You'll find a large stock of fairly new fleet cars—in any number of sizes, makes, and models. While many of these cars have been driven long and hard, some have "low" mileage and even warranties still in effect. Also, most of these cars have been regularly maintained and repaired—a definite plus for any used car you're thinking of buying!

Government auto auctions can be good sources of low-cost used vehicles— although you won't know much about the background of the vehicles. You'll be getting a car "as-is"; it could have been a stolen car, repossession, government surplus, or confiscation. But, if you know cars (as to condition and worth), you're apt to drive off with a real steal.

Rental Sales

Agency Rent-A-Car

Beaverton: 9955 S.W. Beaverton-Hillsdale Hwy. ☎ 643–1123
Milwaukie: 16111 S.E. McLouglin Blvd. ☎ 659–1273
Portland: 1313 W. Burnside ☎ 224–2009
    8383 N.E. Sandy Blvd. ☎ 259–0873
Salem: 315 Mission St. ☎ 362–2616
Hours: Mon–Fri 8–5:30, Sat 9–12

> Each Agency location has up to five rental cars for sale—and all are four-door, mid-size automatics. Available cars include Toyota Corollas and Camrys, Dodge Aries and Spirits, Chevy Cavaliers, and Olds Cutlasses. All are under two years old and have no more than 40,000 miles apiece. The number of available cars is small, so it's best to call before heading over.

Bee Rent-A-Car

Beaverton: 9500 S.W. Canyon *(in Bickmore Dodge)* ☎ 292–3545
Gresham: 243 S.E. Powell Blvd. *(in Gresham Ford)* ☎ 252–7368
Hours: Mon–Sat 8:30–9, Sun 8:30–8

> This rental agency sells its Dodge (Shadows, Spirits, and Dynastys) and Ford (Escorts, Tauruses, and Tempos) rentals out of the respective auto dealers above. Cars are usually sold after 5,000 miles, at discounts of up to 30% off

new sticker prices. All are well maintained, with financing available to qualified buyers.

Hertz Car Sales

Portland: Portland International Airport ☎ 249–5722
Hours: Mon–Sat 9–7, Sun 11–5

You'll have over 100 cars to choose from (many of them loaded!), including Ford Escorts, Thunderbirds, Tempos, and Tauruses, and Pontiac Sunbirds and 6000s, as well as other fine rental cars—all at up to 30% to 40% off new-car prices. These cars are exceptionally well-maintained (oil changes every eight weeks) and look like new, even though most have around 20,000 miles on them. Each comes with its own maintenance records and many have remaining warranties.

Snappy Car Rental

Beaverton: 10550 S.W. Allen Blvd. ☎ 626–3032
Portland: 6130 N.E. 78th Ct. ☎ 254–2225
Salem: 3338 Market St. N.E. ☎ 581–9797
Hours: Mon–Fri 7:30–5:30, Sat 9–1

All their rental cars are for sale, including Dodge Shadows, Spirits, and Monacos, Jeep Eagle Premiers, Toyota Corollas, Plymouth Acclaims, and Sundances. These cars typically have 15,000 to 20,000 miles apiece, have been on the lot under a year, and are priced at 25% or more off new-car prices.

Government Vehicle Auctions

City of Portland Vehicle Auction

Portland: Various city-wide locations ☎ 823–1800

Twice a year the city holds a "hot deals on city wheels" auction, selling off around 50 older, city-owned cars, pickups, vans, and trucks. Watch for their ads or call for more information. Get on the mailing list to receive flyers listing the details on the vehicles that will be available.

General Services Administration (Federal) Vehicle Auctions

Vancouver: 9226 N.E. Highway 99 ☎ (206)931–7562

Every two months, this mammoth federal property management agency auctions off from 100 to 150 used government vehicles at its fleet management center in Vancouver, Washington. You won't find any splashy makes or models—just a reliable fleet of well-used American cars. General Services also sells surplus property from many other federal agencies through a sealed-bid process. Find out more about this by getting on their mailing list.

Call for more information and watch for their ads about a week or so in advance of each vehicle auction.

Multnomah County Surplus Vehicle Auctions
Gresham: 1620 S.E. 190th ☎ 248–3424

Twice a year, usually in fall and spring, Multnomah County auctions off used county-owned vehicles at its fleet facility in Gresham. The auctions start at noon and last until all 25 to 50 cars are gone (a couple of hours). You can get there as early as 10 A.M. to inspect the cars prior to bidding. These vehicles are up to ten years old each, and condition varies. Get on their mailing list for more information or call the number above. They also advertise a few weeks in advance of each auction.

Washington County Vehicle Auction
Hillsboro: 2470 S.E. River Rd. *(County Fleet Center)* ☎ 648–8737

From noon to around 2 P.M. for one day only in late April, Washington County holds its annual car auction, where about 30 to 40 cars are moved out. Some vehicles are county surplus and others are confiscated or forfeitures. Some are in pretty good shape and others might have to be towed off the lot. The auction opens an hour early to allow the public to inspect the cars. Usually a few hundred bidders turn up and the action can get fast and furious. Because inventory changes up to the last minute, there's no property list available in advance. Watch the papers in early spring or call to find out about the auction.

Batteries

In addition to those outlets carrying new batteries exclusively, we've included a few sources that also handle used, reconditioned, and rebuilt batteries. Some will check your old battery and install a new one without service charges. For a complete listing of Portland-area battery outlets, refer to the Yellow Pages.

AMP Factory
Gresham: 17309 S.E. Division ☎ 760–7078
Portland: 6735 S.E. 82nd ☎ 771–2663
Hours: Mon–Fri 9–6, Sat 9–5, Sun 11–3

Checks, Credit cards

Battery Specialists
Portland: 11207 S.E. Powell Blvd. ☎ 761–2370
11257 N.E. Sandy Blvd. ☎ 255–7423
Hours: Powell, Mon–Fri 8–6, Sat 9–5, Sun 10–4; Sandy Mon–Fri 8:30–6, Sat 9–5

Checks, Credit cards

Battery X-Change
Beaverton: 12990 S.W. Canyon Rd. ☎ 644–3425
Hillsboro: 311 Baseline Rd. ☎ 640–3793
Oregon City: 7th & Washington ☎ 656–7407
Portland: 2003 S.E. Belmont ☎ 232–6584
    2930 S.E. 82nd ☎ 774–3131
    3007 N.E. M.L. King Blvd. (*Union*) ☎ 249–0101
Salem: 1676 Center N.E. ☎ 371–8211
Hours: Mon–Fri 8:30–5:30, Sat 9–4, some locations open Sun

Checks, Credit cards

Standard Batteries
3750 S.E. Belmont ☎ 234–7251
Hours: Mon–Fri 7–5:30, Sat 9–2

Checks, Credit cards

Tires

Most people tend to sell their cars before it's time to buy replacement tires. However, for those in need of tires, we've included outlets that sell new tires, and some that sell used tires.

For most of us, it's very difficult to tell the difference between one tire and another. To help consumers compare tires, the Auto Safety Hotline (1–800–424–9393) provides tire mileage and safety ratings. Call and ask for their free Tire Quality Grading Report as well as for other free highway safety information.

New

You'll find few consumer products as competitively priced as tires. Never pay list price—in fact, you should routinely find discounts of one-third or more off suggested list price. When comparing tire prices, be sure to ask about any extra costs for balancing, mounting, and valve stems. Also, compare warranties—they vary from manufacturer to manufacturer.

Costco
Aloha: 15901 S.W. Jenkins Rd. ☎ 626–3200
Milwaukie: 13350 S.E. Johnson Rd. ☎ 653–0413
Portland: 4849 N.E. 138th ☎ 252–1045
Tigard: 18120 S.W. Lower Boones Ferry Rd. ☎ 620–4556
Hours: Mon–Fri 10:30–8, Sat 9:30–6, Sun 10–5

Discount Tire Centers
Beaverton: 12620 S.W. Canyon Rd. ☎ 644–8088
Milwaukie: 18101 S.E. McLoughlin Blvd. ☎ 654–5454

Oregon City: 1677 Molalla Ave. ☎ 657–4704
Portland: 5811 N.E. Sandy Blvd. ☎ 281–7788
   5960 S.E. Division ☎ 775–1892
   6050 S.W. Macadam Ave ☎ 246–9783
Tigard: 13707 Pacific Hwy ☎ 624–7970
Tualatin: 17705 S.W. Boones Ferry Rd. ☎ 636–0927
Hours: Mon–Fri 8–6, Thurs 8–8, Sat 8–5, some locations open Sun
Checks, Credit cards

W/D Tire Liquidators
Rainier: 75936 Rockcrest St. ☎ 556–6308
Salem: 4795 Portland Rd. N.E. ☎ 393–8007
Hours: Mon–Thurs 8–6, Fri 8–8, Sat 8–5, Sun 12–5
Checks, Credit cards

Used

A sure way to save up to 50% on the price of new tires is to buy retreaded tires. Retreads are actually used tire "shells" that have had brand-new treads attached through a heated curing process. But don't buy poor-quality retreads—whatever the bargain price; they can come apart under certain conditions. The National Tire Dealers and Retreaders Association (NTDRA) rates the retread plants that rebuild tires. An "A" or "B" grade is acceptable, but tires rated "C" through "F" should be avoided. When buying a retread, find out what the manufacturer's NTDRA rating is.

A-1 Used Tires
Portland: 5619 S.E. Johnson Creek ☎ 775–0093
Hours: Mon–Fri 10–6, Sat 10–7
Checks

Big O
Beaverton: 11020 S.W. Canyon Rd. ☎ 646–9113
Gresham: 2001 E. Powell ☎ 665–3154
Hillsboro: 943 S.W. Baseline ☎ 640–8847
Oregon City: 875 Molalla Ave. ☎ 657–9554
Portland: 4215 S.E. 82nd ☎ 771–0121
   2002 S.E. Stark ☎ 235–3118
   7911 N. Lombard ☎ 286–9449
Salem: 437 Lancaster Dr. N.E. ☎ 371–2440
Vancouver: 3400 E. Fourth Plain ☎ (206)695–2471
   705 S.E. Crest Ave. ☎ (206)254–2526
Hours: Generally, Mon–Fri 8–5:30, Sat 8:30–5
Checks, Credit cards

Bob Brown Tire Center
Portland: 12030 N.E. Sandy Blvd. ☎ 255–8710
Hours: Mon–Fri 8–6, Sat 8–5

Checks, Credit cards

Carothers Tire
Hillsboro: 166 S.W. Freeman ☎ 648–7099
Hours: Mon–Fri 9–5:30, Sat 9–5

Checks, Credit cards

Ed's Hi-Treads
Portland: 4535 N. Lombard ☎ 286–4520
Hours: Mon–Fri 9:30–5:30, Sat 9–3

Checks, Credit cards

Flatt Tire Supply
Portland: 7921 N.E. M.L. King Blvd. *(Union)* ☎ 285–5470
Hours: Mon–Fri 9–6, Sat 9–4

Checks, Credit cards

Gateway Tire & Wheel Co.
Portland: 9111 N.E. Halsey ☎ 256–3001
Hours: Mon–Fri 8–6, Sat 8–5

Checks, Credit cards

Good Used Tire Center
Portland: 4510 S.E. 52nd ☎ 777–6549
Hours: Mon–Fri 9–6, Sat 9–4

Checks

Jack Engle Tire Center
17650 S.E. Division ☎ 761–7600
Hours: Mon–Fri 8–6, Sat 9–4

Checks, Credit cards

McCann Tire Inc.
Hillsboro: Jackson Quarry Rd. ☎ 647–2607
Hours: Mon–Fri 8–6, Sat 8–4

Checks, Credit cards

McCollum Tire & Auto Center
Portland: 7510 S.E. Foster Rd. ☎ 777–6005
Hours: Mon–Fri 8–5:30, Sat 8–2

Checks, Credit cards

Molalla Discount Tires
Molalla: 14377 S. Macksburg Rd. ☎ 632–7252
Hours: Mon–Fri 8–6, Sat 8–3

Checks, Credit cards

Norene Tire & Battery
Portland: 1616 S.E. M.L. King Blvd. *(Union)* ☎ 232–2622
Hours: Mon–Fri 8–5:30, Sat 8–12

Checks, Credit cards

Tire Factory
Beaverton: 301 N.W. Murray Rd. ☎ 643–6767
Gladstone: 19210 S.E. McLouglin Blvd. ☎ 657–9600
Hillsboro: 4th & Baseline ☎ 648–0546
Portland: 1706 E. Burnside ☎ 233–5979
    11614 S.E. Stark ☎ 257–9181
    10431 N.E. Sandy Blvd. ☎ 252–0229
    902 N. Lombard ☎ 283–3102
    435 N.W. Tenth ☎ 223–6193
    8228 S.E. Division ☎ 775–1334
Tigard: 11596 S.W. Pacific Hwy ☎ 639–1106
Hours: Generally, Mon–Fri 8–5:30, Sat 8–3

Checks, Credit cards

Woody Froom Tire Center
Portland: 18120-A N.E. Wilkes Rd. ☎ 667–7098
Hours: Mon–Fri 7–5:30, Sat 7:30–12

Checks, Credit cards

Road Services

By joining an auto club, you'll receive free towing (up to a certain number of miles), emergency lodging reimbursement, battery services, bail-bond services, trip planning, and much more. In addition to the two "local" auto clubs we've listed, you can get membership and benefit information on the established clubs by calling their toll-free numbers.

American Automobile Association (AAA)
Beaverton: 8555 S.W. Apple Way ☎ 243–6444
Portland: 600 S.W. Market ☎ AAA–6734
Salem: 2909 Ryan Rd. S.E. ☎ 581–1608
Hours: Mon–Fri 8–5
    Over 30 million Americans belong to the "Auto Club." New members pay $43 the first year, $38 thereafter. Associate membership at $17 is available

to spouses and unmarried dependent children (under age 23) of members. Auto club members receive what is probably the most complete travel and emergency road service available. These services include towing (whether on account of accident or because your car just dies on you), battery service, mechanical first aid (i.e., minor adjustments to get your car moving again), tire changing, fuel delivery, lockout service (to get you back into your car), emergency check cashing, notary service, travel agency services, car rental and hotel discounts, personalized auto travel services (including "Triptiks," tour books, travel guides, and maps), discount passport photos, legal fee reimbursement (up to $1,000), bail bond protection, no-fee travelers' checks, and away-from-home accident expenses. Call for a membership packet, which describes their services in detail.

Amway Motoring Plan

Amway offers a motoring plan similar in scope and cost to the AAA plan. The plan includes various reimbursements for towing, locksmith service, ambulance charges, attorney and bail bond services, and emergency travel expenses regarding any car, truck, motorhome, or motorcycle you're driving. Another feature of this plan enables members to purchase cars at fleet prices. Amway will send you the names of local participating auto dealers who will sell at $150 above dealer cost. Discount parts, service, and auto repairs are also available with this motoring plan. Contact an Amway distributor (under Amway in the white pages of your phone directory) for information and application packet or call toll-free: 800–992–6929.

Allstate Motor Club
800–323–6282

Amoco Motor Club
800–334–3300

Cross Country Motor Club
800–225–1575

Montgomery Ward Motor Club
800–621–5151

U.S. Auto Club
800–348–5058

Senior Citizen Discounts

By virtue of age, senior citizens are automatically eligible for a wide range of discounts on the full spectrum of goods and services in the marketplace. And by joining the senior and retirement organizations we've included, seniors are often able to pick up even bigger price-breaks.

Wherever seniors shop, they should ask for senior discounts. No sense in missing out on a discount because it isn't asked for.

Travel & Transportation

Airlines

When it comes to air travel, seniors over 62 have a lot going their way! Virtually every airline offers seniors a 10% discount (and usually passes along that same discount to a companion traveler who need not be a senior) on all domestic travel.

Probably the best travel deal for seniors is the airlines' senior coupon books. These books are available from travel agents and airlines alike. They come in four-coupon books (around $475) or eight-coupon books (around $750). Each coupon is good for a one-way trip anywhere in the U.S—and the savings off regular advance-purchase tickets can be dramatic! For example, the coupons would shave nearly 50% off the cost of an advance-purchase ticket for round trip travel from Portland to the East Coast! Now, that's a deal!

Coupon-book prices and travel restrictions vary from airline to airline. However, we found that Delta Airlines (1–800–221–1212) has about the best prices and fewest restrictions of all the carriers we surveyed.

Continental Airlines (1–800–248–8996) offers seniors either Domestic Passports for unlimited U.S. travel or Global Passports for unlimited world travel—each at a price that will save the traveler thousands of dollars a year. Companion Passports (for those under 62 who travel with a senior) are available at the same prices charged seniors.

For a list of airlines (and phone numbers) flying out of Portland International Airport, see the section on Airline Travel.

Trains & Buses

After locking up great prices for air travel, it's time for seniors to concentrate on getting the best deals on ground transportation.

For those 65 or older, Amtrak (1–800–USA–RAIL) offers a 25% discount on all regular, full-fare tickets. However, before you take them up on their offer, don't overlook other discounts available to Amtrak travelers that might be better deals than the senior discount.

Greyhound/Trailways Bus Line (243–2323) offers seniors 65 or older a standard 15% discount on all regular travel. However, as with Amtrak, seniors should inquire about any current specials or fares that might be lower than the senior-discounted fare.

Tri-Met offers special "Honored Citizen" rates to seniors 65 or older (including disabled persons and medicare card holders). For only 40 cents the Honored Citizen may purchase a daily ticket good for travel during all hours and in all zones. For $8.25, he or she may pick up a monthly pass valid for unlimited trips during all hours and in all zones. These specials represent discounts of 65% to 80% off regular fares. Call Tri-Met (233–3511) for the nearest location of these special tickets and passes.

Cabs

In order to pick up additional savings on ground transportation, seniors need only call any of the local cab companies we've listed here.

Broadway Cab
Portland: ☎ 227–1234

In business for over 50 years, Broadway Cab offers seniors 60 or older a 10% discount on all cab rides. Seniors are asked to inform the dispatcher of a requested senior discount when calling in for a cab. Seniors who wish to pay cab fare with script instead of cash may purchase script books (in $50, $20, $10, or $5 amounts) at a 10% discount. However, seniors may not use script to pay for a discounted cab fare.

Checks, Credit cards

Pioneer Cab Company
Gladstone: ☎ 657–TAXI

Pioneer services Gladstone, Oregon City, and Milwaukie. Seniors 60 or older may request and receive a 10% discount on cab fare. Ask for the discount when calling for a cab.

Checks

Radio Cab
Portland: ☎ 227–1212

Seniors 55 or older may purchase script in $20, $10, or $5 amounts and receive a 10% discount. For example, order a $20 script books and pay only $18. Script can be used for cab fare in lieu of paying cash. There are no other senior discounts available.

Checks, Credit cards

Recreation, Entertainment, & Education

Lifelong learning, as well as lifelong fun and play, need not end when we become senior citizens. Portland-area seniors will find a wide range of offerings that provide intellectual stimulation, recreation, and physical adventure—at prices bargain shoppers are sure to love!

Many private health clubs, resorts, and sports centers don't advertise—but do offer—discounts to seniors. Area YMCAs, for example, offer senior membership discounts of 20% or more. Whether you're skiing or bowling, taking in a museum or going back to school, always ask about senior discounts!

Recreation & Entertainment

The following golf courses, operated by the Bureau of Parks & Recreation, provide quality playing experiences for golfers of all levels. Seniors 65 and older can save up to 40% on greens fees at these courses with possession of a Senior Golf Identification Card. This card costs $5 (one-time fee) and is available from the Bureau of Parks & Recreation at 426 N.E. 12th in Portland. More information can be obtained by calling 248–4328.

Eastmoreland Golf Course and Driving Range
Portland: 2425 S.E. Bybee Blvd. ☎ 775–2900

Heron Lakes Golf Course
Portland: 3500 N. Victory Blvd. ☎ 289–1818

Progress Downs Golf Course and Driving Range
Beaverton: 8200 S.W. Scholls Ferry Rd. ☎ 646–5166

Rose City Golf Course
Portland: 2200 N.E. 71st ☎ 253–4744

The Grotto
Portland: N.E. 85th Ave. & Sandy Blvd. ☎ 254–7371
Hours: Daily, 9:30–5
> This 58-acre park and religious shrine is an oasis of tranquility and a place of reflection for people of all faiths. A large cave in a 10-story cliff serves as

a cathedral. At the cliff top you'll find a monastery, gardens, and breathtaking views of the Columbia River. Seniors pay $1 for the elevator fee, a 50% discount off the regular rate.

Japanese Gardens

Portland: In Washington Park on S.W. Kingston ☎ 223–4070
Hours: Generally, daily 10–5
The city of Portland and distant mountains form a beautiful backdrop to the five traditional styles of Japanese gardens. Regular adult charges are $3.50 each; Seniors 62 or older pay only $2.

National Senior Sports Association

Fairfax, VA: 10560 Main St., suite 205 (22030)
Members of this senior citizens' organization receive discounts at many facilities offering tennis, bowling, and golf, as well as at numerous resorts and sports centers. Members must be 50 or older. Write for a brochure and membership information.

Oregon Maritime Center & Museum

Portland: 113 S.W. Front Ave. ☎ 224–7724
Hours: Fri–Sun 11–4 (Summer, Wed–Sun 11–4)
Seniors save 40% off the regular $2 admission. See Museums for a description of this attraction.

Oregon Museum of Science & Industry (OMSI)

Portland: 4015 S.W. Canyon Rd. *(across from Washington Park Zoo)*
☎ 222–2828
Hours: Daily, 9–5 (Summer, 9–7)
Most displays in this impressive museum are hands-on or walk-in exhibits. The computer center and hurricane and tornado simulators are not to be missed! Planetarium and laser shows are also given. Seniors pay $4.25, a $1 discount off the regular admission price.

Pittock Mansion

Portland: 3229 N.W. Pittock Dr. ☎ 248–4469
Hours: Daily, 1–5
This restored French Renaissance mansion, built around the turn of the century, offers a commanding view of Portland and distant mountains. Furnishings include many early American and European antiques. Seniors receive a 15% discount off regular admission fees of $3.50.

Portland Museum of Art

Portland: 1219 S.W. Park ☎ 226–2811
Hours: Tues–Sat 11–5, Sun 1–5

Regular admission is $3, but seniors are admitted free of charge every Thursday. See Museums for a description of this attraction.

Washington Park Zoo

Portland: 4000 S.W. Canyon Rd. ☎ 226–1561
Hours: Daily, 9:30–dusk
Seniors 65 or older receive one-third off the regular $4.50 admission charge. See Museums for a description of this attraction.

World Forestry Center

Portland: 4033 S.W. Canyon Rd. ☎ 228–1368
Hours: Daily, 10–5
The Forestry Center contains many interesting exhibits on forestry, as well as a multi-media forest presentation. You're not losing your mind! There really is a 70-foot "talking tree" that will strike up a conversation with passersby. Seniors 65 or older pay a $2 admission charge (regular adult admission is $3).

Education

Oregon Elderhostel

Monmouth, OR: Western Oregon State College, Administration #305(97361)
☎ 838–8435
Oregon Elderhostel offers seniors 60 or older a multitude of educational programs combined with hosteling—guaranteed to satisfy anyone's spirit of adventure. This combination of education and travel is so popular that programs are now offered at hundreds of U.S. colleges and conference centers for thousands of seniors. The low-cost fees include everything but transportation: Classes, meals, accommodations, even entertainment. Another nice thing—no homework, tests, or grades. Write or call the state office above for both the Oregon and U.S. class schedule.

Oasis

Portland: 621 S.W. Fifth *(10th floor of Meier & Frank)* ☎ 241–3059
OASIS (Older Adult Services and Information System) is a nonprofit educational organization (sponsored by Meier & Frank and Good Samaritan Hospital & Medical Center) that offers educational, informational, cultural and health programs to seniors. Membership is free and entitles the senior to participate in all special events, classes, and programs. Call for more information and class schedules.

Portland Community College

Portland: 12000 S.W. 49th ☎ 244–6111 x2485

Seniors 62 or older who are residents of the Portland Community College (PCC) district may take PCC courses at one-half the tuition rates charged other students. Seniors who are unable to afford the reduced tuition may apply for scholarships.

Portland State University

Portland: 632 S.W. Hall St., #113A *(Senior Registration Office)* ☎ 725–4739
Seniors 65 or older may audit classes at Portland State University without paying tuition as long as space is available. Seniors may use any of the University's facilities, including the library and gym. Call for registration hours, a class schedule, or more information.

Senior Leisure Services

Portland: 426 N.E. 12th ☎ 823–4328
Portland's Bureau of Parks and Recreation, through its Senior Leisure Services, offers seniors a wide range of classes and special events for low-cost fees. For those unable to pay, alternate financial arrangements may be made. Call for a complete class and event schedule and registration information.

Shopping

Bargain shopping is especially important for seniors on fixed incomes. Seniors can pick up big savings by practicing wise consumer habits: Shopping sales; selecting house or generic brands instead of highly advertised name brands; comparison shopping for best deals; following a shopping list to minimize impulse buying; and shopping large wholesale and warehouse outlets.

Don't be shy about asking if a quoted price includes a senior discount. The more you ask for discounts, the easier it will get for you. Your persistence will pay off and you will routinely find savings of 10% to 20% or more.

The following stores are just a few of those that give senior discounts. The Portland area has many more that will do so. All you have to do is ask. Requesting a discount is a great habit to get into wherever you shop!

Beaverton Mall

Beaverton: 3205 S.W. Cedar Hills Blvd. ☎ 643–6563
Hours: Generally, Mon–Fri 10–9, Sat 10–6, Sun 11–6
Every Tuesday, seniors 60 or older receive a 15% discount at many of this mall's 40 retail shops. Discounts are available on apparel, shoes, beauty services, cards, gifts, toys, books, jewelry, photo services, home entertainment, and more. Call the Beaverton Mall office for more details.

The Daily Grind

Portland: 4026 S.E. Hawthorne Blvd. ☎ 233–5521
Hours: Mon–Thurs 9–9, Fri 9–3, Sun 10–7

One day each month, this large health food store and bakery offers seniors a 10% discount on every item in the store—including sale items. The senior discount day is the Wednesday immediately following the fourth of each month. Call for more details.

Deseret Industries
10330 S.E. 82nd ☎ 777–3895
Hours: Mon & Sat 10–6, Tues–Fri 10–8
This large thrift store offers a 10% discount on all used items to seniors 60 or older. There's an abundance of quality clothes, furniture, and household goods for seniors to rummage through.

Emporium
Beaverton: 3255 Cedar Hills Blvd. *(Beaverton Mall)* ☎ 643–9482
Gresham: 40 N.W. Eastman Parkway ☎ 667–6371
Oregon City: I-205 at McLoughlin *(Oregon City Shopping Center)*
☎ 656–1331
Portland: 10106 S.E. Washington *(Mall 205)* ☎ 252–0281
Hours: Generally, Mon–Fri 10–9, Sat 10–6, Sun 11–6
Seniors 60 or older qualify for membership in the Emporium Senior Saver Club and a 10% discount on all merchandise purchased Sunday at any Emporium. Members are given additional days of savings during December. Call for specific dates.

Franz Bakeries
Refer to Bakery Goods for locations and hours
Franz Bakeries offers seniors 62 or older a discount of 10% on all baked goods with their Franz discount card. Call the Franz bakery nearest you for details.

Goodwill
Refer to Thrift Shops for locations and hours
Seniors 55 or older are entitled to a discount of 10% on any of the thousands of items Goodwill stocks. Purchases must be made on Wednesdays to qualify for the discount.

Lamonts
Clackamas: 8658 S.E. Sunnyside Rd. *(Clackamas Promenade)* ☎ 653–9770
Hillsboro: 2175 S.E. Tualatin Valley Hwy *(Sunset Esplanade)* ☎ 693–1345
Portland: 14th & N.E. Halsey *(Lloyd Center)* ☎ 284–5311
Jantzen Beach Center ☎ 289–8044
Tigard: 9009 S.W. Hall Blvd. ☎ 624–0702
Vancouver: 7809-B N.E. Vancouver Plaza Dr. *(Vancouver Plaza)*
☎ (206)256–9443

Hours: Mon–Fri 10–9, Sat 10–6, Sun 11–6

Lamonts' department stores offer seniors 65 or older a 10% discount on all regular and sale merchandise purchased on Sundays. Call for information on how to receive a senior discount card.

Orowheat Bakery Outlets

Refer to Bakery Goods for locations and hours

Every day of the week, seniors 60 or older can receive a 10% discount on all Orowheat baked good. By showing proof of age with a driver's license, a senior can pick up a discount card and start saving immediately.

St. Vincent DePaul

Refer to Thrift Shops for locations and hours

Seniors 62 or older can receive discounts of 10% to 15% by shopping this thrift any day of the week.

Williams Bakery Thrift Stores

Refer to Bakery Goods for locations and hours

Every Wednesday, seniors 60 or older receive a 10% discount on all baked goods.

Restaurants

If you're a senior with a penchant for dining out, be sure to ask at each restaurant you patronize for discounts. Sometimes an eating establishment will note special prices on the menu—or they may not. The best time to ask for discounts is before you place your order. You might even be handed a special seniors-only menu with discounted prices.

While the elegant, expensive restaurants tend not to give senior discounts, family-style restaurants often do.

We've included a small sampling of Portland-area eateries that provide discounts to seniors. Many others in the area give similar discounts and may—or may not—advertise that they do so. Bargain shoppers, however, should have no trouble finding those discounts. All they need do is ask!

Country Bill's

Portland: 4415 S.E. Woodstock ☎ 774–4198

By purchasing a Senior Dining Card for $5 (one-time fee only), seniors 55 or older are entitled to several benefits. These include: 10% off menu prices; 10% off gift certificates; special discounts on selected holidays and promotions; and coupons good for two-for-one specials. Get on the mailing list to find out about special events and promotions with discounted meals.

Grandma's Table

Beaverton: 12255 S.W. Denny Rd. ☎ 644–2372

Seniors 60 or older may purchase a Senior Citizens' Club Card for $1 (valid for one year) that entitles the bearer to a discount of $2.25 off any complete adult dinner or Sunday Brunch. Grandma's Table is a member of the American Heart Association's "Dine To Your Heart's Content" club.

JJ North's Grand Buffet

Portland: 10520 N.E. Halsey ☎ 254–5555

Seniors 60 or older can "fill up" at this all-you-can-eat buffet and receive a 10% discount off the regular dinner price at the same time.

Kings Table Buffet

Portland: 8233 N. Syracuse ☎ 286–5482

4006 S.E. 82nd ☎ 777–2870

Tigard: 11419 S.W. Pacific Hwy. ☎ 246–6126

Vancouver: 616 N.E. 81st St. ☎ (206)574–3455

Seniors 55 or older can pick up a free Club 55 discount card that entitles the bearer to a 10% discount on all lunch and dinner buffet items.

Lyon's

Portland: 1215 M.L. King Blvd. *(Union)* ☎ 233–5008

302 N.E. 122nd Ave. ☎ 257–9686

Lyon's has created a senior menu with smaller portions and lower prices. Seniors 60 or older may pick up a Senior Discount Card and receive a 10% discount off all menu prices, including the low-cost senior menu.

Pietro's Pizza

Gresham: 345 N.W. Burnside ☎ 667–7851

Beaverton: 11485 S.W. Scholls Ferry Rd. ☎ 641–5172

Pietro's offers senior discounts of 10% or 20%, depending upon the time of day the meal is eaten. Each location has its own discount policy, so best to call beforehand.

Pioneer Pies Restaurant

Tigard: 11960 S.W. Pacific Hwy. ☎ 684–0662

The Senior Citizen Bonus at Pioneer Pies includes a 10% discount on all menu items any time of the day.

Saylor's Old Country Kitchen

Beaverton: 4655 S.W. Griffith Dr. ☎ 644–1492

Portland: 105th at S.E. Stark ☎ 252–4171

This famous steak house offers a special seniors' menu that ranges from

$7.50–$10.95 for complete dinners—about a 25% discount off regular menu prices. The senior discount is valid every day.

Shenanigans
Swan Island: 4575 N. Channel ☎ 289–0966

This elegant eatery serves fresh seafood and broiled steaks, with an unsurpassed view of Portland and the Willamette River as backdrops. Shenanigans offers seniors a 20% discount on the Champagne Sunday brunch from 10 A.M.–3 P.M.

Sylvia's
Portland: 5115 N.E. Sandy Blvd. ☎ 288–6828

Sylvia's serves full-course authentic Italian dinners. On Monday through Wednesday (until 6pm), seniors are offered special menu prices that are over 40% off regular prices.

Our Daily Bread Family Restaurant
Portland: 3330 S.E. 82nd ☎ 775–7379

8680 N. Ivanhoe ☎ 286–9087

Seniors 59 or older are offered the "seniors only" menu. Portions are smaller than those of the regular menu, and prices are lower, too.

Banking

Seniors should inquire at their banks or savings and loans about all the specific services and discounts offered to senior citizens. Shopping for the best financial services should be done as carefully as shopping for other consumer products or services.

Because of stiff competition, many financial institutions offer a wide range of senior specials, including: Free checking services, free travelers' checks, free safe deposit boxes, free photocopying, and free financial advice.

We've included a sampling of Portland-area financial institutions and focused on senior checking account services. When calling your local banker, find out about all the other services offered to seniors.

Bank of America
Refer to Yellow Pages for nearest branch

Seniors qualify for the "Service 55" plan. There's no monthly charge for a checking account and no minimum balance required. Two hundred free checks are provided, and there are no service charges on travelers' or cashiers' checks.

Far West Federal Bank
Refer to Yellow Pages for nearest branch

With a minimum balance of $100, seniors qualify for the "55 & Better" checking package. It offers checking with interest; 600 free checks each year; no checking service charges; $100,000 in accidental death insurance; valuable travel and entertainment discount coupons; and a dozen more benefits.

Key Bank
Refer to Yellow Pages for nearest branch

Those 60 or older qualify for the "Senior Account" with no monthly service charge and no minimum balance requirement.

Pacific First Bank
Refer to yellow pages for nearest branch

Their senior "Golden American" checking account for those 55 or older provides for free checks, interest, and no monthly service charges as long as the senior has a $5,000 savings account or certificate of deposit with the bank.

Security Pacific Bank
Refer to Yellow Pages for nearest branch

There are two senior plans here. The regular checking plan for those 62 or older does not require a minimum balance or monthly service charge. The "Masters Package" requires a $5,000 deposit in any account and provides for free checking; no service charges; free safe deposit box; interest on checking; and several other benefits.

U.S. Bank
Refer to Yellow Pages for nearest branch

For seniors 62 or older there is no monthly service charge and no minimum balance required for a regular checking account.

Washington Federal Savings
Refer to yellow pages for nearest branch

This savings and loan offers seniors $59\frac{1}{2}$ or older a basic checking plan without a service charge or minimum balance requirement.

West One Bank
Refer to yellow pages for nearest branch

Those 50 or older are offered a checking plan with several features: No monthly service charge; free checks and unlimited check writing; and no minimum balance. In addition, there's no service charge on the purchase of travelers' or cashiers' checks. Free notary service.

Medical

Seniors can cut down on their medical bills by learning as much as possible about their Medicare benefits. The local Social Security Administration Office is the place to start for information.

A senior covered by Medicare can cut down on out-of-pocket medical expenses by finding doctors who accept the Medicare payment in combination with the senior's 20% co-payment as payment in full. Many doctors who participate in Medicare will even handle all the paperwork for seniors. There are many other features of Medicare to learn about—and the savings are substantial.

We've included several sources that specifically provide medical services to seniors at reduced prices.

For additional sources of low-cost medical care and products, refer to Health-Related Services, Dental Services, Optical Services, and Drugs & Sundries.

American Association of Retired Persons (AARP)
Portland: 921 S.W. Morrison, 5th floor *(The Galleria)* ☎ 227–5268
Hours: Mon–Fri 10–2:30
> This nationwide nonprofit organization offers its 30 million members low-cost supplemental health insurance, publications on health topics, and wholesale prices on prescription drugs, over-the-counter medications, and a wide range of medical equipment and supplies. AARP is open to persons 50 or older, retired or not, for a nominal annual membership of $5. In addition to discounts on medical products, AARP offers members participation in the AARP Federal Credit Union and the AARP Motoring Plan. A number of other valuable benefits are available to members. More information can be obtained by calling the local office or writing the AARP National Office at 1909 K St. N.W., Washington,D.C. 20049.

AARP Pharmacy Service Hearing Center
Beaverton: 9800 S.W. Nimbus Ave. ☎ 646–3500
Hours: Mon–Fri 8:30–5
> The Center provides AARP members with free electronic hearing tests and consultations. AARP members receive discounts on the sales and service of a wide variety of hearing aids. Appointments required.

Portland Community College Dental Clinic
Portland: 12000 S.W. 49th ☎ 244–6111 x4909
Hours: Mon–Fri 9–3
> The PCC Dental Clinic offers seniors a variety of low-cost dental services, such as cleanings, fillings, X-rays, and other routine work. Refer to Dental Services for more information on this clinic.

Senior Smile Dental Service

Portland: ☎ 223–4731

The Senior Smile Dental Service, sponsored by the Multnomah Dental Society and Oregon Dental Service, provides seniors with low-cost dental services. Specifically, the program is for seniors 60 or older who are on a limited income, have no dental insurance, are not receiving welfare benefits, and reside in Multnomah County. Nearly 100 dentists participate in offering a full range of dental care and services at 50% off regular rates. For more information and an application form, call the above number.

Something for Everyone

Factory Outlet Malls

Area bargain shoppers are fortunate to have two factory outlet malls within a 90-minute drive of Portland and one just 20 minutes away! Each of these malls has dozens of stores owned and operated by manufacturers.

Although merchandise varies from store to store, most shops seem to carry clothing and related items. Shoppers can expect to find most merchandise first-quality, current stock; the rest will be prior-season goods, irregulars, and seconds, or items specially made for the outlet.

Most outlet stores boast of prices 25% to 75% below retail. Of course, many department stores frequently make the same claim. However, if you look for terrific deals at the outlet malls, especially on the sale racks, you won't be disappointed.

Centralia Factory Outlet Center
Centralia: I-5, 82 miles north of Portland, Exit 82 ☎ (206)736–6406
Hours: Mon–Fri 9–8, Sat 9–6, Sun 11–6
> You'll find over 30 factory stores at this Northwest shopping adventure (about 1½ hours north of Portland) featuring men's and women's clothing, shoes, socks, toys, kitchenware, and more. When you're done here, pick up a map from any of the outlet stores and head into downtown Centralia (about two miles away) to visit the antique mall housing a collection of over 80 antique dealers and specialty shops.

Columbia Gorge Factory Stores
Troutdale: 450 N.W. 257th Ave. *(Exit 17 off I-84)* ☎ 669–8060
Hours: Mon–Sat 9–8, Sun 10–6
> While other factory outlet centers are several hours drive from population centers, Columbia Gorge Factory Stores is only about 20 miles from

downtown Portland on a major freeway and near an intersection that provides easy access. There are over 30 brand-name manufacturers here offering big discounts on factory-direct goods, including overruns, returns, and quality seconds. After a day of sizzling-hot discount shopping, take a short drive to Multnomah Falls and cool off in the spray of one of the highest waterfalls in America.

Quality Factory Village
Lincoln City: On Highway 101 ☎ 996–5000
Hours: Mon–Sat 9:30–8, Sun 9:30–6
Their slogan is "take a vacation from retail prices," and you'll do just that at over 45 factory outlet stores here. You'll find brand-name merchandise in contemporary men's and women's fashions, shoes, sportswear, accessories, and fragrances—all at 20% to 70% off retail. While some stores sell only first-quality items, you'll find the best deals on seconds and irregulars that many stores offer. These "imperfections" are usually cosmetic only and are so slight you'll need a magnifying glass to find them.

Here's a list of stores in the Factory Outlet malls as we went to press: Centralia's Factory Outlet Center (F), Columbia Gorge Factory Stores (C), and Lincoln City's Quality Factory Village(Q).

Adolpho II
Famous-maker apparel for women. (Q)

Accessorize
Fashion jewelry, watches, and accessories. (Q)

Aileen's
Moderately priced ladies sportswear. (F,C,Q)

American Tourister
Luggage, business cases, and sports and travel bags. (F,Q)

Bannister Shoes
Forty famous brands of men's, women's, and athletic shoes. (F,C,Q)

Bass Shoe Outlet
Classic casual and dressy shoes for men and women. (F,C)

Book Warehouse
Books, computer software, and cassettes. (C,Q)

Brindar
Women's sweats and T-shirts. (C)

Campus Factory Outlet
Casual and traditional sportswear for men and boys, plus Tall and Large sizes. (F,Q)

Cape Isle Knitter
Sweaters in 100% cotton and knits for men and women. (F,C,Q)

Capezio Factory Outlet
Current fashions from *Evan Picone, Bandolino, Liz Claiborne, Capezio* and more. (Q)

Churchill Gloves
Leather and semi-dress gloves for men and women. (F)

Converse Factory Outlet
Athletic shoes and clothing for the entire family. (Q)

Corning/Revere Factory Store
Cookware, ovenware, and dinnerware in sets and open stock. (F,Q)

CYA (Cover Your Assets)
Junior activewear. (C)

Duffel/In-Sport
Quality traditional-style women's and men's sportswear and exercise wear. (F,Q)

Designer Brands Accessories
Costume jewelry and sunglasses. (C)

Eddie Bauer
Quality men's and women's outerwear, sportswear, and footwear. (Q)

Famous Brand Housewares
Variety of housewares and kitchen gadgets. (C)

Famous Footwear
Active footwear for the entire family. (C)

Fashion Flair-Gant
Traditional men's, women's, and children's apparel from *Izod* and *Ship 'n Shore*. (F)

Fragrance World
Name-brand cosmetics and perfumes. (Q)

Full Size Fashions
Quality sportswear and foundations for women wearing size 16 or larger. (Q)

Gitano
Trendy clothing for men, women, and children, plus accessories. (F,C,Q)

Hanes Activewear
Activewear for men and women. (F,Q)

Hang Ten
Sportswear for children and women. (C)

Harve Bernard
Designer women's apparel and accessories and men's furnishings. (F)

Hathaway
Men's and women's apparel. (C)

Ideas Apparel
Sportswear for girls, juniors, and women. (F)

Izod
Men's sportswear. (C)

John Henry & Friends
Fashionable men's and women's apparel from *Perry Ellis, Thomson*, and more. (Q)

Jordache
Streetwear, accessories, and shoes for men, women, and children. (F,C)

Kitchen Collection
Proctor-Silex appliances, *Wear-Ever* cookware, and *Anchor Hocking* glassware. (F,C,Q)

Leather Loft Factory Outlet

Luxury leather handbags, luggage, briefcases, jackets, and designer accessories. (F,C,Q)

L'Eggs/Hanes/Bali Factory Outlet

Lingerie and hosiery. (F,C,Q)

London Fog

Men's and women's rainwear, jackets, outerwear, wools, shirts, sweaters, and accessories. (F,Q)

Maidenform

Complete selection of lingerie and undergarments. (Q)

Manhattan Jewelry Manufacturers

Diamonds (loose and mounted), 14K and 18K gold jewelry, gemstones, pearls, watches, etc. (F)

McKenzie Outfitters

Quality outdoor clothing and equipment. (Q)

Mikasa China

Place settings, glassware, giftware, cookware, fine crystal, and china. (Q)

Mushroom Shoes

Dress, casual, and athletic shoes for women. (F)

Old Mill

Women's fashions by *Country Miss*. (F,Q)

Olga

Women's nightgowns, robes, slips, bras, and panties. (C)

Oneida

Flatware by *Rogers, Buffalo*, and *Oneida*. (F,Q)

Oshkosh B'Gosh, Inc.

Sportswear for the entire family. (Q)

Polly Flinders

Dresses, sportswear, and accessories for girls. (Q)

The Paper Factory
Paper products, including gift wrap, party supplies, and home and office supplies. (Q)

Pfaltzgraff
Dinnerware, giftware, and tabletop accessories. (Q)

Prestige Fragrance
Men's and women's fragrances and cosmetics. (F,C)

The Ribbon Outlet
Three thousand varieties of ribbon and trim, craft supplies, bridal and party accessories, gifts, and wrapping paper. (F,C,Q)

Royal Doulton
China, figurines, crystal, and giftware. (Q)

Sam & Libby Shoes
Men's and women's shoes. (C)

Socks Galore
Over 60,000 pairs of socks. (F,C)

Sierra Shirts
Casual sportswear for the entire family. (Q)

Sunglass World
Sunglasses by *Ray Ban, Serengeti, Jones,* and *Vuarnet.* (Q)

Totes
Umbrellas, raincoats, rain hats, luggage, bags, and travel accessories. (Q)

Toy Liquidators
Mattel, Hasbro, Fisher-Price, Playskool, and other brand-name toys. (F,C,Q)

Van Heusen
Fashion apparel for men and women. (F,C,Q)

Wallet Works
Men's and women's leather wallets, luggage, handbags, and briefcases. (Q)

Welcome Home
Country-style home furnishings. (F,C,Q)

Wemco
Thousands of neckties. (Q)

Westport Limited
Women's dresses and separates. (C,Q)

Wicker Factory
Silk plants, wicker home furnishings, and decorative accessories. (F,Q)

Mass Merchandise Discounters

These stores do exactly as their name implies—consistently discount an incredible array of merchandise. Often, big chains and supermarkets go head to head with the mass merchandisers by offering rock-bottom prices on advertised specials. The bargain shopper should comparison-shop and reap the benefits of such "economic warfare" between the giants.

In addition to the sources we've listed below, general merchandisers such as Fred Meyer, Target, K-Mart, and Pay Less can be relied on to deliver big savings on a wide selection of products.

Best Products
Beaverton: 10500 S.W. Beaverton-Hillsdale Hwy. ☎ 643–6771
Gresham: 2095 S.E. Burnside ☎ 667–5500
Milwaukie: 16250 S.E. McLoughlin Blvd. ☎ 653–2500
Salem: 3105 Lancaster Dr. N.E. ☎ 585–0880
Hours: Mon–Fri 10–6, Sat 10–9, Sun 10–6
This giant retailer (around 200 showrooms in 27 states) offers a wide selection and everyday low prices on small appliances, housewares, sports equipment, electronics, baby furniture, jewelry, toys, and games. Watch for their periodic sales for even bigger savings. When we checked there was an un-announced sale in progress, with a flyer describing such selected items as jewelry, baby furniture, tables, lamps, and chairs at reduced prices. Check out the clearance tables and shelves for great buys on returns or flawed merchandise. Pick up one of their catalogs—it's great for price comparing.
Checks, Credit cards

Costco Wholesale Club
Aloha: 15901 S.W. Jenkins Rd. ☎ 626–3200
Milwaukie: 13350 S.E. Johnson Rd. ☎ 653–0413
Portland: 4849 N.E. 138th ☎ 252–1045
Tigard: 18120 S.W. Lower Boones Ferry Rd. ☎ 620–4556
Hours: Mon–Fri 11–8:30, Sat 9:30–6, Sun 10–5 (Business members only, Mon–Fri 10–11)

Costco offers its members self-service warehouse shopping with big savings on a wide range of brand-name food and general merchandise. Each store is about 125,000 sq. ft. in size and carries nearly 4,000 different items— hardware, food, clothing, jewelry, automotive (including tires), electronics, home furnishings, tools, and office supplies, to name a few. Their fresh food section offers produce, baked goods, deli items, and quality cuts of meat. Although you should compare prices when buying big-ticket items, we found that Costco's "warehouse shopping at wholesale prices" concept offered bona fide lowest prices on thousands of items on a consistent basis.

Checks

Kida Company

Portland: 127 N.W. Third ☎ 227–2544
Hours: Mon–Fri 9–5:30, Sat 10–4:30

This family-operated store offers small name-brand appliances, cameras, and electronics at super prices. Many items are everyday sale-priced, and even bigger savings can be found on the in-store specials. We spotted: Six-piece *Corning Ware* starter sets for $20.90; *Farberware* fry pans marked down from $24.99 to $9.95; *Hamilton Beach* food processors, usually $79.95, priced at $38.95; and a store full of items at least 25% off retail. Trophies were 50% off and all *Seiko* watches 30% off. All goods are top quality and the service is both friendly and helpful.

Checks, Credit cards

Sears Outlet Store

Portland: 10542 S.E. Washington (*Plaza 205*) ☎ 257–6144
Hours: Mon–Sat 9–9, Sun 9–6

Items purchased through the Sears catalog but later returned are shipped over to the outlet store and sold at 20% to 70% below original prices. In addition to customer returns, you'll find discontinued items, freight-dam-aged goods, surplus, and irregulars—most of which are new and priced at a fraction of original prices. Inventory includes such big-ticket items as refrigerators, sofas, washers and dryers, dinette sets, recliners, sectionals, sleepers, electronics, and housewares, clothing, linens, sporting goods, games, toys, and automotive supplies. Every Thursday they run an ad in *The Oregonian* with selected items further reduced.

Checks

Surplus & Liquidators

One thing you can be certain of—surplus and liquidation outlets always have plenty of special bargains! You'll find incredibly low prices on a wide range of consumer goods such as housewares, tools, sporting goods, apparel, beauty products, furniture, supplies, and some of the most unusual bric-a-brac you could imagine.

Most of the merchandise you'll encounter is either close-outs, overstocks, manufacturers' samples, or first-quality, brand-name goods. Besides great savings, half the fun of shopping these outlets is in not knowing what you'll find. Inventory changes continually, so visit often, and grab the good stuff before someone else beats you to it!

City Liquidators
Portland: 823 S.E. Third ☎ 238–4477
Vancouver: 902 Main St. ☎ (206)694–9663
Hours: Mon–Sat 9–6, Sun 10–5

> This place is a browser's delight! It's filled to the rafters with general merchandise of all sorts, at bargain prices. City Liquidators stocks a wide range of items, including housewares, small tools, paper goods, watches, toys, carpet samples, planters, and work gloves. Several aisles of "dollarama" merchandise (low-priced goods marked $1 to $2) offer such things as pet supplies, kitchen gadgets, and housewares. Quality office furniture and equipment (including folding tables and office supplies) are sold at prices well below regular retail. Its Portland furniture warehouse (on the second level) displays a huge selection of chairs at great prices, including wing-back chairs, formal dining chairs, upholstered parsons' chairs, video chairs, and rattan swivel rockers. Also upstairs we found excellent bargains on couches, dining and bedroom sets, futons, framed art works, and much more. Big bucks can be saved at their periodic "scratch 'n dent sale" on desks, entertainment centers, bookcases, and stereo cabinets. Both locations offer clean, clearly marked, and neatly displayed merchandise. (The Vancouver store is smaller but still carries a large range of goods.)
>
> Checks, Credit cards

The Liquidator
Beaverton: 11950 S.W. Broadway ☎ 641–0093
Hours: Tues–Sat 10–5

> You'll find quite a collection here of close-outs, overstock, and samples. There's a continually changing inventory of sporting goods and wear, camping and fishing gear, tools, and hardware at 30% to 50% off regular retail. Brand names pop up frequently. We found a *Gore-Tex* running suit for $25; *Lita* ski pants and jacket for under $45; and a *Coleman* waterproof floating sport light for $3.60. Athletic shorts for $1 apiece and carpet samples

(great for door mats!) at 80 cents each were good buys, as were three-person inflatable rafts for under $40. They also rent tents, packs, and other camping gear.

Checks, Credit cards

National Liquidation Center

Portland: 1001 S.E. Water ☎ 239–7023
Hours: Mon–Sat 10–5

Located on the second floor of the Portland Liquidation Center Building, the National Liquidation Center carries a wide variety of new name-brand merchandise for the whole family. You'll find clothing, kitchenware, sporting goods, beauty products, party supplies, work gloves, tools, and small rugs, all neatly displayed and at prices well below retail. We found some terrific buys on sports shoes (as low as $10), athletic shirts (from $1 to $3), cotton flannel nightgowns (two for $17), cotton hooded sweatshirts (two for $15), a variety of housewares, and *Foster Grant* sunglasses. The day we were in, a coach was sorting through stacks of shorts and shirts assembling uniforms for his team and beaming all the while on how low the prices were.

Checks, Credit cards

99 Cents Or Less

Aloha: 18105 S.W. Tualatin Valley Hwy ☎ 591–1222
Tigard: 11945 S.W. Pacific Hwy ☎ 684–7830
Hours: Mon–Sat 10–6, Sun 1–5

As its name implies, this store is a great place to find inexpensive items: Kitchen and bath accessories, picture frames, note pads, wallets, party favors, prizes, and many other novelty items. All the merchandise is neatly displayed and clearly marked either 99 cents or two for 99 cents. Kids can find address books, large squeeze bottles, and slap bracelets at 99 cents apiece (these same slap bracelets were priced $1.50 or more in the mall stores). Ambassador cards and envelopes (with an assortment of cute teddy bear motifs), usually $2.19, were 99 cents. There are lots of close-outs, so merchandise is always changing.

Checks

99 Cent Stores & Party Center

Gresham: 2345 E. Powell ☎ 666–7552
Portland: 8001 S.E. Powell *(Powell St. Station)* ☎ 777–8647
Camas: 3rd St. *(Las Camas Center)* ☎ (206)835–7919
Hours: Gresham & Camas, daily 10–7; Portland, daily 10–9

You'll find lots and lots of stock here priced under $1. Party favors, stationery, note pads, files, kitchen gadgets, novelties, and much more fill up the store. Their beauty-aid inventory includes three brands of cosmetics, nail polish, and lipstick, each priced at $1.99. About one-fifth of their stock includes such larger items as skateboards, pictures, tools, video tapes, cassette headphones, VCR head cleaners, and more—all at about 50% off the regular retail prices found in variety stores.

Checks, Credit cards

The Price Is Right
Portland: 1125 S.E. Division ☎ 233–0349
Hours: Mon–Fri 9–6, Sat 9–3

This liquidator carries a large selection of close-outs, overstock, and samples of automotive supplies, kitchenware, health and beauty items, tools, shirts, pants, and other merchandise. The store is neat and tidy, with all items nicely displayed. We found imprinted T-shirts at three for $10; sweatshirts with Playboy bunny or U.S. Marine Corps prints for $5.99 each; handsaws for $14.99 (priced elsewhere for around $30); 20 sizes of tarps (including the big one, that can cover 30x60 ft.); ladders; hoses; greeting cards (including jumbo-size greeting cards of 2 ft. x 1$\frac{1}{2}$ ft.); tool handles; videotapes; and much, much more.

Checks, Credit cards

R & G International Marketing
Portland: 4218 N.E. Sandy Blvd. ☎ 249–1985
Vancouver: 76th & 117th *(Orchards)* ☎ (206)896–7193
Hazel Dell Ave. & 99th ☎ (206)574–7704
Hours: Mon–Sat 10–6

You'll find a wide assortment of merchandise here all neatly arranged on banquet tables—actually, row after row after row of display tables. Discounts generally run at least 30% to 50% off retail, with tons of items priced at $1 or less. Greeting cards were 50% off; stationery, seen elsewhere at from $3 to $4, was marked 99 cents; bags of wildflower seed mix, priced at $13.99 at one major retailer, was $4.99 here. We also found great prices on a wide variety of kitchenware, toiletries, pet supplies, garden and painting supplies, small tools, party favors, and more. All stock is new and first quality and is identical to what's sold in the retail chain stores. The Portland store is the largest.

Checks, Credit cards

R. Brown 99 Cents Store
Portland: 3511 S.E. 82nd ☎ 788–0689
Hours: Mon–Sat 10–8, Sun 10–6

Thousands of items priced 99 cents each are neatly crammed in this tidy bargain shop. This store literally has a little bit of everything; you're sure to find something you need as you wander up and down the neatly displayed aisles. Some 99 cent bargains include: Hardware and electrical items, pet supplies, hair and nail products, party supplies, kitchen gadgets, posters, baskets, shelf liners, and wrapping paper. You'll even find things under 99 cents, such as glassware, keychains, tapered candles (three for 99 cents), novelty pencils (two for 99 cents), and sample-size health and beauty aids.

Checks

Wacky Willy's Surplus

Portland: 417 S.E. 11th ☎ 234–6864
Hours: Mon–Sat 9–6:30
You'll find quite a collection of close-outs and overstock at this surplus store—auto supplies, electronics, scientific equipment, hardware, motors, fans, cables, ropes and belts, and writing equipment—all at fantastic prices. If you don't mind esoteric transfers, you can pick up T-shirts for $2 each, as well as painters' caps at 35 cents each. There were tubs and tubs of colored pencils, pens, and pen sets at wholesale prices or less. *Sno-Treds* (traction devices) were going for $10 a set; previously owned U.S. Army jackets sold for around $15 each. One satisfied customer was overheard telling the cashier that the electronic gadget that he was paying just a few dollars for would've cost $20 anywhere else. This place is pure fun to wander through, and if you're not careful, you'll wind up buying a lot of things you weren't even looking for.

Checks, Credit cards

Government Property Auctions

Government auctions are not only places to pick up some good buys—they're also a lot of fun to shop. The range of available merchandise is unlike anything you'll find in any retail outlet. Auctioned merchandise can be surplus, confiscated, or even unclaimed stolen goods! Expect to see lots of bicycles, tools, electronics, jewelry, furniture, and much more. Some of the more interesting items come from school districts and police and fire departments.

While some of the property may be in very good condition, a lot has definitely seen better days. Because everything is sold "as-is," be sure to inspect the merchandise carefully, establish its value, then—go for it!

City of Beaverton Auctions

Beaverton: Fifth and Hall *(Fire Station)* ☎ 526–2229
Hours: Periodic sales
Each October and June, Beaverton holds an all-day Saturday auction (9 A.M. to 4 P.M.) of surplus city, fire, and police department property—including unclaimed stolen property. Merchandise to be auctioned can include: Bikes (lots of them, going from $5 to $180 each), stereos, CD players, hedge trimmers, casserole dishes, tires, twin beds, mattresses, lockers, oxygen tanks, typewriters, and just about anything else that may have been stolen.

Come an hour before auction time to check everything out. Watch for their ads or call for more information.

City of Portland Confiscated Surplus Property Auction

Portland: 2100 N.E. Pacific *(Property Warehouse)* ☎ 823–4395

Hours: Periodic sales

About every six weeks (Thursdays, from 7:30 A.M. to noon), the city holds a giant garage sale auction offering surplus city-owned property, as well as confiscated and unclaimed stolen property. You'll find bicycles, radios, hand tools, camping equipment, backpacks, desks, cabinets, and other office equipment. Watch for their ads or call to get more information.

Clackamas County Auction

Oregon City: 902 Abernethy Rd. ☎ 655–3348

Hours: Annual sale

Clackamas County's once-a-year fall auction features a wide variety of county surplus goods, as well as unclaimed stolen property. While some of the items are in good condition, you'll also find a lot of stuff in extremely worn shape, such as typewriters with several keys missing. Come before the auction starts and separate the wheat from the chaff; you'll be sure to get some good buys. Merchandise may include: jewelry, tires, camping equipment, desks, chairs, computers, and other items that once belonged to the fire or police departments, community college, or other county agencies. Call or watch for their ads for specific information.

Multnomah County Confiscated Property Auction

Portland: 4415 N.E. 158th *(Warehouse)* ☎ 251–2500

Hours: Periodic sales

Every two or three months, several police agencies in the county auction about 75 seized cars (from junkers to Porsches) and other confiscated property, such as television sets, VCRs, camcorders, furniture, and about 50 to 60 bikes. Auctions are advertised a week in advance and are usually held on Saturday from 11 A.M. to 2 P.M. All the property can be previewed the day before each auction. Call in advance to get on their mailing list and receive a flyer with a detailed property listing.

Multnomah County Surplus Property Auction

Portland: 2060 N. Marine Dr. *(Expo Center)* ☎ 248–5111

Hours: Annual sale

Their annual auction of surplus Multnomah County property includes desks, chairs, cabinets, and other office equipment, as well as "a little of everything else." You'll also find a collection of unclaimed stolen property and selected confiscated items. The auction is held in December at the Expo

Center, and is usually advertised well in advance. For more information call
the county purchasing office at the number above.

State of Oregon General Store

Salem: 1655 Salem Industrial Dr. N.E. ☎ 378–4714
Hours: Fri 9–2, some Sat

At Oregon's only retail outlet for state surplus property, you'll find a wide
variety of used merchandise, including office equipment, furniture, electronics, cars, motors, tires, and items from such state institutions as
hospitals, food services, printing, and education. Prices are low and many
incredible bargains can be found. Every week they add "new" inventory,
and every two months they hold a "special Saturday Sale" where prices are
further reduced. More cars, as well as vans, pickup trucks, and heavy
equipment are available at their annex located at the corner of Airport Road
and State Street in Salem.

Washington County General Surplus Auctions

Hillsboro: 872 N.E. 28th *(Washington County Fairgrounds)* ☎ 648–8737
Hours: Annual sale

You'll never know what can turn up at these giant annual "garage-sale"
auctions held each April for one day only from 9:30 A.M. to 5 P.M. Washington County pools property from school districts, special districts, cities,
and ten different agencies (all in Washington County) for the auction.
Property is usually county surplus, confiscated goods, or stolen and unclaimed,
and can include: School desks, tables, typewriters, playground and gymnas-
tic equipment, picnic tables, jewelry, cameras, clothes—even knives and
bows and arrows. And especially bicycles—tons of them, from $10 to $200
apiece. Call or watch for ads for specific auction information. Food and
drinks are available.

General Merchandise Thrift Stores

In the chapter on clothing, we covered those thrifts that specialized in used
apparel. In this section, we've listed several thrift stores that carry a wide range
of goods, including housewares, furniture, appliances, books, and knickknacks
of all kinds. Inventory is constantly changing, with the best stuff being snapped
up quickly. Prices and quality of merchandise vary widely—but you can always
pick up many a good steal! For a complete listing of Portland-area thrifts by
location, check the Yellow Pages under "Thrift Shops."

Deseret Industries

Portland: 10330 S.E. 82nd ☎ 777–3895
Hours: Mon–Sat 10–6, Tues & Fri 10–8

Deseret Industries has thousands of quality used items—from large reconditioned appliances to kitchenware, and from mattresses to books. They sell new sofas, couches, dressers, and other bedding manufactured in their Utah factory. Call about their special sales and mailing list.

Checks, Credit cards

Goodwill
Beaverton: 4700 S.W. Griffith Dr. ☎ 643–6099
Gresham: 2231 E. Burnside ☎ 661–1614
McMinnville: 526 N. 99 West ☎ 472–3230
Portland: 1925 S.E. Sixth ☎ 238–6165
Salem: 2655 Portland Rd. N.E. ☎ 585–4684
Vancouver: 6425 N.E. Fourth Plain ☎ (206)695–4669
Hours: Generally, Mon–Sat 9–6, some locations open Sun
Goodwill stores have a huge offering, mostly donated, of everything from soup to nuts. The Portland store (on Sixth) is their largest store. It carries books and clothing on the upper level; furniture and appliances on the main level; and an entire department of such notions as lace curtains, tablecloths, and placemats. Call about their free decorating workshops—and learn how to decorate your home at a cost that won't strain your budget. Also ask about their seasonal sales.

Checks, Credit cards

St. Vincent de Paul
Milwaukie: S.E. 32nd & S.E. Harrison ☎ 654–5220
Gresham: 21939 S.E. Stark ☎ 665–3310
Hillsboro: 646 S.W. Oak ☎ 648–5097
Oregon City: 700 Molalla ☎ 655–6927
Portland: 2740 S.E. Powell Blvd. ☎ 234–0598
740 N. Killingsworth ☎ 233–5588
Tigard: 12230 S.W. Main ☎ 639–9898
Hours: Generally, Mon–Sat 10–6, some locations open Sun
St. Vincent de Paul stores carry clothing, appliances, furniture, sporting goods, lamps, electronics, glassware, books, and kitchenware. The Portland store (on S.E. Powell) is their largest. It offers a great antique boutique and vintage clothes collection on the main level. Above is their well-stocked book loft; below, you'll find a large selection of clothing and reconditioned appliances and furniture. Wander around back to the dock and you'll see lots of bikes and assorted pieces of furniture. Call about their store-wide special sales.

Checks, Credit cards

Value Village Thrift Store
Milwaukie: 18625 S.E. McLoughlin ☎ 653–7333
Portland: 3534 S.E. 52nd ☎ 771–5472

Tigard: 12060 S.W. Main ☎ 684–1982
Hours: Mon–Fri 9–9, Sat 9–6, Sun 10–6

Value Village stores (the Tigard one's the biggest) take in thousands of items each day—and prices are cut to move them out so they don't sit around too long. They carry mostly used merchandise, including furniture, appliances, household items, apparel, luggage, and a ton of general merchandise. On Sundays, their huge stock of used merchandise is marked down 20%. Also, clothing and selected merchandise go for 50% less on major holidays. Call about specifics and special sales.

Checks, Credit cards

Estate Sales

Estate Sales are conducted by professionals hired to appraise and sell the contents of a household or estate. There's usually plenty of quality merchandise available—at prices higher than at garage sales, but lower than at antique stores or retail outlets.

Look for especially good buys on such "hard goods," such as jewelry, antiques, and furniture. Once you get into estate sale shopping, you'll be hooked. Take note of which companies put on the best sales, so that when you see their ads, you can follow them around the local circuit.

We've included a small sampling of area estate sales professionals. For a complete listing, check the Yellow Pages under "Estates". Also watch for their ads in the Friday and Saturday issues of *The Oregonian* under "Garage Sales."

Anita Sedig Estate Sales
Portland: ☎ 652–0343

Diane Roluffs Sales
Portland: ☎ 659–2372

Eleanor Stoddard Estate & Moving Sales
Portland: ☎ 222–7190

Joy M. Olson
Portland: ☎ 244–2245

Harriett Anderson/ Attic To Cellar
Portland: ☎ 248–9184

Sandy's Peddlers Two
Portland: ☎ 289–3822

Flea Markets

Flea Markets (also called swap meets or outside bazaars) offer bargain shoppers an almost overwhelming variety of merchandise at great low prices. Row after row of vendors rent tables and spread out their merchandise. This can include glassware, appliances, jewelry, furnishings, clothing, tools, books—just about anything imaginable.

Although the good stuff may get snatched up early, the end of the day can bring its own rewards. Most sellers have to pack up their goods and cart them home. Because they'd really rather sell than pack, they are ripe for aggressive bargaining. Watch the prices drop drastically in front of your eyes!

You can find out about upcoming flea markets from the classified ads. Here are a few in the Portland area. Call if you need specific information.

Banner Flea Market
Hillsboro: 4871 S.E. Tualatin Valley Hwy. ☎ 640–6755
Hours: Fri–Sun 12–5:30

#1 Flea Market
Portland: 17420 S.E. Division ☎ 761–4646
Hours: Sat & Sun 9–5

Salvage Sally's
Portland: 8725 N.E. Sandy Blvd. ☎ 256–2844
Hours: Sat & Sun 8–5

Sandy Barr's Flea Market
Portland: 1225 N. Marine Dr. *(Interstate Pavilion)* ☎ 283–6993
8725 N. Chautauqua ☎ 283–9565
Hours: Marine Dr., Sat & Sun 8–3; Chautauqua, Sun 8–3

INDEX

T

About the Authors:

Carolyn Gabbe has been an avid bargain shopper nearly her whole life. Along the way, she earned a degree in marketing from San Diego State University and spent several years working in advertising. The former co-owner (with her husband) of two retail gift stores in California and Oregon, Carolyn knows how to ferret out a bargain on just about anything.

David Gabbe, a former investigator with the IRS and U.S. Labor Dept., is the author of a just published book on U.S. Wage and Hour Law. He has also been a contributor of newspaper and magazine articles on a wide range of issues, including taxation, labor laws, nutrition and political satire.